THE
LEISURE
ECONOMY

THE LEISURE ECONOMY

How Changing Demographics, Economics, and Generational Attitudes Will Reshape Our Lives and Our Industries

LINDA NAZARETH

BICENTENNIAL
1807
WILEY
2007
BICENTENNIAL

John Wiley & Sons Canada, Ltd.

National Library of Canada Cataloguing in Publication Data

Nazareth, Linda, 1963-
    The leisure economy : how changing demographics, economics, and generational attitudes will reshape our lives our and our industries / Linda Nazareth.

Includes index.

ISBN 978-0-470-84034-4

    1. Leisure–Economic aspects–Canada. 2. Leisure–Economic aspects–United States. 3. Leisure industry–Canada–Forecasting. 4. Leisure industry–United States–Forecasting. 5. Economic forecasting–Canada. 6. Canada–Economic conditions–1991-. 7. Economic forecasting–United States. 8. United States–Economic conditions–2001-. I. Title.

HC95.N39 2007   330.971'00112   C2007-902557-9

Production Credits
Cover and interior design: Adrian So
Typesetter: Thomson Digital
Cover photos: Getty Images
Wiley Bicentennial Logo: Richard J. Pacifico
Printer: Tri-Graphic Printing Ltd.

John Wiley & Sons Canada, Ltd.
6045 Freemont Blvd.
Mississauga, Ontario
L5R 4J3

Printed in Canada

This book is printed with biodegradable vegetable-based inks. Text pages are printed on 60lb. 100% PCW using TG ECO100 by Tri-Graphic Printing, Ltd., an FSC certified printer.

Recycled
Supporting responsible use
of forest resources
www.fsc.org Cert no. SW-COC-1352
FSC © 1996 Forest Stewardship Council

1 2 3 4 5 TRI 11 10 09 08 07

For Madeline

CONTENTS

# ACKNOWLEDGMENTS

The idea of a "leisure economy" started to take shape for me over the course of the past few years as I made business presentations to audiences planning their industries' futures. Frequently I found that their observations and questions taught me a great deal and helped me to formulate what eventually became this book. So sincere thanks goes to all of those—too numerous to list—to whom I have had the privilege to speak. Huge thanks also to the National Speakers Bureau, with whom I have had the pleasure to work over the past six years, and in particular to Perry Goldsmith, Theresa Beenken, Jennifer Clarkson and Jeanne-Marie Robillard.

Many, many people have shared their observations and insights for this book. As well as the experts whose names appear in the text, my special gratitude goes to all those who shared their stories of work and leisure and life that appear throughout the text. You gave up your precious—very precious—time to tell me your tales, and I am incredibly grateful.

I'd also like to thank my agent, Rick Broadhead of Rick Broadhead and Associates, without whom this project would not have gone forward. I'm so happy, too, to have had the chance to work with the talented staff of John Wiley & Sons. Special thanks to my editor Karen Milner, who "got" the idea of the leisure economy right away and let me run with it.

Finally, thanks to my husband, Lou Schizas. I know I turned down your offer to be my celebrity co-author (only because you weren't actually willing to do any writing) but your support, encouragement, and unflagging faith, as well as your willingness to eat out frequently, have made this book possible. Thanks to you too, Maddie—especially for your help with the book. Since you've been born you've totally blasted away my concepts of what work and leisure are, but you make our lives a joy.

INTRODUCTION:
A EUROPEAN LIFE

"It's kind of embarrassing to talk about," says Kerry, sipping her latte and looking surreptitiously around the exclusive women's club where she and her guest are practically the only people in sight at 11:30 in the morning. "It's not something I think people will understand." A forty-something second-wave boomer with a husband and three kids, she gives the impression that she is about to confess to secret alcoholism or perhaps an affair with her son's soccer coach. As it happens, her secret is one that is discussed much less than is adultery in the soccer-mom set. "I have a lot of leisure," she whispers. "I started this wanting something I thought of as a 'European Life' even though I wasn't really clear on what that meant, and unbelievably, I got it. I have a great career and I have time too. I'm not time-crunched the way I used to be."

"This" refers to her decision to leave corporate life for self-employment: there's nothing embarrassing about that. Kerry can be forgiven, though, for thinking that people would be shocked by the rest of her story. In a world where being time-crunched is a status symbol, admitting that your obligations take up less than every working hour of your day is not something that you want to reveal without knowing your audience. The time crunch is what makes our lives,

1

and our economy for that matter, go round. Opting out is going to be viewed as pretty suspect.

Kerry remembers the switch away from the time-crunch economy as being almost violent in its difference from her former life. Armed with an MBA and a couple of decades of working in corporate finance, she made the leap to management consulting when it seemed that her teenage children needed her to be around more than her executive position at a bank allowed her to be. The first thing that shocked her was that life went on outside of the office. "I'd sit and look out the window," she says, remembering how different it felt to be in her own neighborhood rather than in a glass-and-steel tower. "It felt so weird to not be tied down to having to be in a certain place between 9:00 and 5:00, or more like 8:00 and 6:00." Eventually, her consulting clientele grew enough that she brings in roughly as much money as she did in her prior career. But if she has matched her previous income, she has not gone back to her old working hours or her old time crunch. "I love this," she says. "It's hard to describe. I would never, ever go back to the kind of work I had before ... well, okay maybe if my family was starving or something. But this is such a strong feeling, and it is something I absolutely cannot talk about with friends who are still in the corporate world."

For years we have been living in a time-crunch economy. You can see evidence of it wherever you look. Commuters start their treks before sunrise, toting special coffee cups that fit right into the cupholders provided by auto manufacturers. Workers use their breaks to arrange rides for their kids to get to their soccer games, and arrange to pick up other kids on the days that they are in charge of the car pool. Dentists offer appointments at 7:00 in the morning, or 7:00 at night. Fast food, frozen food, restaurant food or simply skipping meals has replaced cooking. For every person who makes it to the gym on a regular basis, there is another who uses the elliptical machine they bought in January as a handy place to hang laundry. "I'm so busy you would not believe it," is the sincere lament of millions. But it's said with a mix of exasperation and pride.

Some of the hallmarks of the time-crunch economy are negative, but not all. In fact, many are positive. For decades now, we have had a huge majority of the population working—and working ever longer hours. In many ways, that has been great for the North American economy. The time-crunch economy moves a lot of merchandise too, from the cupholders to the three-hour spa passes that fit the consumers' need for de-stressing (from all the other activity) and the efficient use of time (forget getting away for a full day). As for whether it is better to eat at home or eat out, that's a value judgment, but plenty of people would agree that spending less time in the kitchen can only be a good thing.

But what if, no matter which is better or worse, more people chose to be like Kerry? What if a lot of people suddenly had a lot more time? What if a lot of people wanted a lot more time? What if they started making decisions not on the basis of speed—choosing things that can be consumed or done fast, or which let them do things faster—but on other values? The results would be radical. These consumers would give us a "leisure economy," and it would affect everyone from workers to investors to businesses to governments.

In fact, the leisure economy is already in progress, and over the next couple of decades it will only gain steam. If you want to be ahead of the curve, you have to understand why it is happening and what the possible fallout from it will be. Concentrate too much on the time-crunch economy and you may be missing the biggest economic shift to hit North America in decades.

The premise for this book came out of a series of presentations I did for clients, many of whom work in the leisure industries. Preparing a keynote address for a group of large golf course operators, I found that one of their main problems was that people were too time-crunched to play golf; consequently, many were choosing nine holes over 18. Accordingly, the golf course operators had shifted their resources to accommodate them. I looked at who was playing the most golf—the industry calls them "core" golfers—and realized that they were heavily skewed towards those in their 50s and older. Using some demographic projections and doing some straightforward calculations, I realized that their problem in a few years might be accommodating all those who want to not just play 18 holes, but maybe linger a while after their games. Continuing to serve the time-crunch economy would not serve the golf operators well.

But the leisure economy is not just about demographics, which we already know is effecting big changes in North America. People in general want more time, and not necessarily to play golf. In many instances, that means time away from the workplace. Workers want to telecommute to avoid the pile-ups on the highways. Working parents want flexible work arrangements so they can spend more time with their children. Workers of all ages want six months off, not two weeks, so they can trek through Asia rather than spend a couple of weeks at the cottage. Many are willing to sacrifice a chunk of income to get it.

As I realized that the leisure economy was already taking shape, I also saw that it had a strong generational dimension to it. Baby boomers are creating the leisure economy because they are being forced into it. Although many plan to work forever, many are also seeing the day when they will leave their nine-to-whatever existences and have to craft different kinds of lives. Even for those who have embraced life after work, many are going to experience the same trauma of not being time-crunched that Kerry described. As a generation, they are going to have more time.

What the post-boom generations want most seems to be "not to be like the baby boomers." That was especially true for the tail end of Generation X and for Generation Y—basically those from their teens to 30s—who are determined to have lives that incorporate a menu of interests, from work to family to volunteerism to hobbies. After all, they have been brought up being encouraged to try out soccer and ballet and art appreciation camp and dozens of other activities. Many do not want to be pigeonholed into the baby-boom model of what they see as workaholism at the expense of everything else. Now, it is certainly true that it could be the naiveté of youth that is coloring their views, and that the need to pay off student loans and get started on their mortgages may soon beat the desire out of them to keep snowboarding. But unlike other generations, theirs is going to have a unique opportunity to wield some economic power. Baby-boom retirements, after all, are going to give them some power in the labor market. What if they use some of that power to get time off, rather than just more money?

Based on what I learned from listening to people, I boiled my observations down into two questions that I posed to myself for every client I spoke to: first, what if people had more time? Second, what if people wanted more time? I asked these key questions when I spoke to operators of private clubs, who had been suffering much the way that golf course operators had during the time-crunch years. I looked at the demographics of the aging population, but also asked what would happen if Generation X and Y decided that they wanted to carve out more family time. Could the clubs find a way to lure them in? I asked these questions when I spoke to a group of accountants from a government agency that was planning its workforce strategies for the next decade. They knew well that their workforce was aging and that they needed a plan to deal with it. But what they had not thought of was the different ways that the younger generations view their leisure time. If Generation X was more family-oriented, would it work to offer them more money to take the positions the boomers were vacating? Gen X parents want time, not money, and are likely to go to the organizations that provide it. I asked it too when I spoke with retailers. To a group of drugstore operators I asked, "What if people had time to hang around for longer than it takes to fill a prescription? Are you offering services that would make people linger?"

The questions are simple, but radical, too. After all, we have spent decades accepting that we have less and less time, and our economy has grown around that. That the leisure economy is just around the corner is a hard concept to grasp, but it's an important one. You need to understand the leisure economy if you run a business. If you have been serving a market that wants instant everything and speed over quality, then you need to start thinking about what consumers who are *not* time-starved want. If you are an investor, you need to understand this. Your portfolio needs to be diversified to include more than stocks and bonds and money market instruments: it needs to include companies that understand the leisure economy as well as the time-crunch economy. You need to understand it if you are a manager. It may have never occurred to you to ask, "What if people want more time?" Or if you have, you might have answered, "Who cares, anyway?" If that's the case, chances are you're a baby boomer; you need to understand what the next generation of workers want now and are likely to want as they ascend in the labor force. If you are a worker and a consumer, you need to understand the leisure economy and your part in it. Some things will change for you in the coming decades—making the most of those changes will put you ahead of the curve.

There are some important caveats to keep in mind when we talk about the leisure economy. The first is that not everyone is going to be part of it. After all, not everyone has been part of the time-crunch economy. There have always been retired people who have time on their hands, as well as those who can afford not to work or can afford to buy so many services that they are leisure-rich even with demanding jobs. But the time-crunch economy is different. Since the 1970s so many baby boomers have become part of it that it has exerted a huge economic influence. It will be the same with the leisure economy that will emerge as the baby boomers retire. The leisure economy's power may not even lie in the percentage of the population that is part of it, but rather in its growth through the number of people who shift towards it.

The second caveat is that the leisure economy may be inequitable, when it comes to income distribution, and that is going to create problems in itself. There are huge income disparities within North America at present, and they have been growing larger over the past decade. There are also huge wealth disparities within our population, and more specifically within the baby-boom population. Some boomers will be able to retire when they want—whether early or late. Their leisure economy will be a glittering place if they want it to be, complete with treks to Nepal or spending thousands of dollars to acquire the right piece for a newly acquired model train hobby. They'll work a little if they want to, and not work at all if they do not. Other boomers will have to work far more and longer than they ever planned. Their leisure economies, when they finally get them, will be much more modest in scope.

The income and wealth disparities will also touch the post-boom generations. Generation Y may want very much to try self-employment, or to take chunks of time out of the labor force as they raise their families. Many are saddled with student debt, or simply find themselves with the wrong skills to make big economic strides in any kind of a hurry. The idea of getting a piece of the leisure economy may seem like a joke to them too. For others who have had parents foot some of their school bills, or who make fortunate career choices, the desire to "not be like the boomers" may well be fulfilled. All in all, it may make for some inter-generational envy, and some cross-generational envy too. Even as we move to the leisure economy, plenty of people are going to feel as time-crunched as ever. Of course, that will be true for those who are still in the throes of the time-crunch economy—families with two working parents and a gaggle of activities to taxi the kids to—but also for others who seem to have exited the time-crunch economy. Plenty of retirees will tell you they don't know how they ever fit in working, given that their post-work lives seem to fill up all of their available time. Picking up stamps takes longer if you make it into a separate errand, rather than one of 15 other things you have to do on your way home from work.

But perhaps most important is the fact that our time-crunched habits are going to die hard. The baby boomers, in particular, are used to having a dearth of time and may be tempted to schedule all available hours with consulting work or book clubs or fencing lessons or creating their new blogs. Many will say that they are as time-crunched as ever. But the point of the leisure economy is that these same boomers will indeed be branching out into all of those things, maybe even including waiting in line at the post office. We may even have the leisure economy concurrently with a version of the time-crunch economy—but it will be a very different version. Don't rule out, either, that once the baby boomers discover the joy of leisure, they will make it their next big thing, just as they have done with rock music, bell bottoms—and workaholism. Then too, many in the post-boom generations want to be done with the time-crunch economy, and in many ways, they will be the ones in the driver's seat. If they succeed even a little in shifting away from the time crunch, the results will be dramatic.

You'll recall Kerry, who was happily living "The European Life" but was embarrassed to reveal that she was less time-crunched than she used to be for fear of being judged as a slacker. In fact, Kerry is ahead of the curve. A decade from now, anyone who talks about how over-the-top-scheduled they are might be thought to be a behind-the-curve loser. That's a heady change about to take place, and as it takes shape, everything in its midst will change too.

THE COLOR-CODED REFRIGERATOR

Finally, the perfect calendar to help parents control the chaos! This superbly designed wall calendar provides ample room to record all the school activities, music lessons...carpooling schedules, team practices, and vacations of even the busiest family...the spacious daily blocks are divided into morning, afternoon, and evening....

> — *Amazon.com description of The Thinkbin Family Wall Calendar 2004/2005: The Perfect Organizer for Busy Families, Large Deluxe Edition*

"Three kids, three activities each, every week. That means soccer and T-Ball on Monday and swimming and music on Saturday—those are the double days. The other days are only single activity days. And we both work full time, of course. Theoretically we both get home in time for dinner at 6:30, but at least a couple of times a week one of us leaves the office late, and at least a couple of times a week one of us gets caught in traffic. I volunteer for a ton of activities at the kids' schools—I guess it's partly out of guilt, because I can't be the one to take them to school every day. And I help out at the Sunday School too—we decided we wanted to take them to church, but if we were going to do that, we had to be involved." Thirty-nine-year-old Allie,[1] a technical sales executive and the mother of three boys, barely pauses for breath as she rattles off her description of a typical week. "Leisure time? None. Absolutely none, not for us, or for me anyway. We are filled up, and over-scheduled and over-stressed every single waking minute of every day."

As she speaks, Allie gestures to the calendar stuck on her refrigerator amidst the hodgepodge of photos, kids' artwork, school permission forms and take-out menus. It's not the kind an earlier generation got free from the local savings bank, with a neat square for each day of the week and just enough space to note the day that the milkman needed to get paid. Allie's calendar is a serious study in organization, as indeed befits her advanced degree in computer science. The full-page photo that graced her mother's calendars is gone, freeing up two pages' worth of date blocks for each month. Each of those are divided into morning and afternoon sections, and within each of those segments are five separate rectangles—one for each member of the family. To further differentiate everyone's activities, Allie uses different colors of ink, too. Red is for doctor's appointments, blue is for school activities, green is for sports and black is for social events. Still, without looking carefully, it is hard to distinguish any particular hue. The calendar is a literal kaleidoscope, illustrative of the kaleidoscope of activities that is family life today.

Allie's refrigerator is not an anomaly. Calendars with names like "Mom's Family Organizer" or the "15-Month Super Family Organizational System" are everywhere, all with lots of squares (some even include stickers, with pictures of planes to denote trips, or soccer balls to mark "game days"). They are in kitchens across North America, with the appropriate scrawls across them. Stationery stores do a brisk business. Indeed, for households like Allie's, picking up a calendar around New Years is more important than stocking up on hats and

---

1. All names have been changed.

noisemakers. In a time-crunched society, navigating tools like fancy calendars are a necessity.

And a time-crunched society is what we are. The numbers actually tell a jumbled story, some actually suggesting that North Americans are awash in more leisure time than they have ever had. But the numbers lie: the proof is in the economy. From the growth in packages of pre-cut apple slices to the advent of online bill paying to the surge in home cleaning services, business initiatives that save people time have been the success story of the past two decades. If not everyone in North America is time-crunched, a big enough chunk of key consumers certainly are, and the economy has effectively been reconstructed to fit their needs. The lack of time is, in a sense, an important economic driver, one that has shaped the North American economy as much as population or income growth.

Despite the evidence, a debate still occasionally erupts as to whether we are actually time-crunched or if it's just fashionable to pretend we are. In fact, both are true. We are time-crunched, and, oddly, many of those who are time-crunched see it as a status symbol. The time crunch is mostly a problem for the affluent, which is why it has created so many business opportunities to serve the needs of a world where leisure time is the scarcest resource.

MEASURING LEISURE TIME

By definition, being time-crunched suggests that we have a lack of leisure time in our economy. Like Allie, we have so many things scheduled that we have no time left over to do things that are relaxing. But the issue is muddied by the fact that part of what is crowding the calendar is a plethora of leisure activities. So coming to terms with exactly how time-crunched we are should perhaps start with a definition of exactly what we mean by "leisure." Strangely enough, although there is a society-wide perception that we do not have much of it, there is no single accepted definition of what leisure actually is.

The strictest economist's definition of leisure pegs it as being the opposite of labor market work: basically all non-labor market activities in which one's labor services are not exchanged for money.

In economic analysis, the decision of whether to take a job is often described as making a decision between work and leisure. By this measure, an individual who chooses to stay out of the labor market is said to have chosen leisure, no matter whether he is spending his time watching television or studying medicine.

And indeed, much of the dearth of leisure that we feel comes from the fact that we devote such a large part of our lives to our jobs. In North America, as in most industrialized countries, the percentage of the population that works at paying jobs has been increasing since the end of the Second World War. As of 2006, about 66 percent of all Americans and 67 percent of all Canadians—up from 59 and 54 percent respectively in 1960—were in the labor market. Family households are also much more likely to have both parents working—by no means a bad thing, but stressful for many. Still, although there are more people working, there is some evidence that they are working fewer hours than they used to. By most conventional measures, the average workweek has not increased over the past several decades. According to the U.S. Bureau of Labor Statistics, in 1970, the average worker was putting in about 37 hours a week. In 2006, that had dropped to 33.9 hours.[2]

But the government statistics may not accurately gauge work and leisure hours. For example, a contrasting view of work versus leisure comes from economist Juliet B. Schor, whose thoughtful book, *The Overworked American,* was first published in 1992. In the midst of a devastating recession and with consumer and business confidence flagging, Schor put forth the thesis that Americans were more overworked than they had been since the 1960s. One of her assertions hit a national nerve: she suggested that Americans were putting in an extra month of work every year compared to how much they had worked a couple of decades earlier. According to her calculations, in 1969 workers worked an average of 39.8 hours a week. By 1987 (the last year of data she had available) she calculated that the average workweek had risen to 40.7 hours. Schor also asserted that workers were putting in whole weeks more of work per year, too. She detailed 47.1 workweeks

---

2. U.S. Bureau of Labor Statistics, average weekly hours of production workers derived from the Survey of Employment, Hours and Earnings.

in 1987 compared to 43.9 in 1969. Putting the two trends together, gives you the extra month of work.

Schor's work continues to be the subject of some debate. Rather than using conventional datasets available from government sources, she created her own model, using some government data as inputs and then making various statistical adjustments to the figures.[3] As she noted at the time, her figures were at odds with the data from the establishment survey of employment, which showed that over the period, weekly hours actually fell and paid time off rose. However, she suggested that the official figures did not take into account the fact that moonlighters were on the rise, nor the fact that the number of weeks worked per year was also increasing. Since her original publication, the Economic Policy Institute in Washington has continued to update her model. Their data show that by 2000, American workers were putting in about 1,878 hours a year, or about five weeks of work more than they did in 1973.[4]

Still another way to check for a leisure shortage is to look at holidays. It is indisputable that North American workers get scandalously little vacation time. According to a survey by Expedia.com, U.S. workers get an average of 14 days off a year, compared to 26 for German workers and a stunning 36 days for the French. Only Canada, where workers get an average of 18 days off, comes close to the meager U.S. vacation allowance. Perhaps the most shocking thing is the number of North American employees who do not get around to using the few days they are allowed off per year. About one-third of employed U.S. adults usually do not take off all of the vacation days they receive each year. As of 2007, 23 percent of Americans admit to checking email or voicemail when they are on vacation, up from just 16 percent in 2005.[5]

---

3. Schor used data from the National Income and Product Accounts of the United States to calculate total hours. She then divided the total population aged over 16 to come up with per capita figures. These estimates were then deflated by the total labor force less self-employment, to bring them to a labor force basis.

4. See Schor, Juliet. "The Ever More Overworked American" in *Take Back Your Time: Fighting Overwork and Time Poverty in America*. John de Graaf (Editor), San Francisco, Berrett-Koehler Publishers Inc., 2003, p. 7.

5. Expedia Vacation Deprivation Survey 2007, http://media.expedia.com/media/content/expus/graphics/promos/vacations/Expedia_International_Vacation_Deprivation_Survey_Resutls_2007.pdf

Despite the fact that work is a huge factor behind the time crunch, defining leisure as the opposite of working for a paying wage is not particularly accurate. By that definition, leisure could refer to staying home with small children or going to university full time, rather than whiling away the days lying on a chaise longue and sipping a drink with a little umbrella. That's why the strictest economists' definition does not really capture why leisure is in such short supply. A better definition of leisure may be the one that comes from the online encyclopedia, Wikipedia:

> Leisure time is time not spent on compulsory activities like employment, education, running a business and household chores. The distinction is not strict, since necessity can be larger or smaller, and things may be done for pleasure as well as for longer term usefulness.

Indeed, that definition captures the somewhat murky nature of the demands on our time, and our leisure, as they now exist. Wikipedia also tells us that the word *leisure* "descends from the Latin word *licere*, meaning "to be permitted" or "to be free." The Old French *leisir* first appeared in the early 14th century and the "u" first appeared in the early 16th century, probably by analogy with words such as *pleasure*.

Much of the leisure bust of recent years is a result of scheduling compulsory activities into time that once would have been "free." That's probably most evident in the case of parents, both stay-at-home and working, who now spend their lives shuttling from one activity to another. "I see them all the time," says Kelly, the owner of a children's consignment store in a particularly leafy, upscale suburb. "Stay-at-home mothers who are never home. They feel they have to justify giving up work, so they spend all day in their vans, playing chauffeur to their kids. They come in here with stacks of clothes they have sorted out of their kids' cupboards, because they are determined to keep their homes ultra-organized. I told one the other day that she had to give herself a break before she had a meltdown."

Activities seem to have crowded into everyone's life to the extent that even the smallest children have calendars that are packed to bursting. The 1990s saw what child psychiatrist Dr. Alvin Rosenfeld calls "hyper-parenting" kick into high gear. Rosenfield, in his book *The Overscheduled Child*, maintains that parents are trying so hard to give their children a taste of everything that both parents and children become overwhelmed.

Where it might once have been acceptable for a stay-at-home mom to confine her toddler to the playpen while enjoying a coffee with a friend, by today's standards that would practically be considered neglect. Typically, the best that today's mothers of children under a year old can count on is sitting around in organized "Babies, Music and Creative Play" classes. As their kids get older, the activities multiply far beyond circle time. From soccer to cooking to ballet to art appreciation, classes and activities for children abound, and it is up to parents to get their kids to them. This, of course, is positive in many ways for the children who are learning how to swim or skate or play musical instruments. It does, however, seem to be leading to a surfeit of family stress as parents shuttle their offspring from activity to activity. Whether in or out of the labor force, parents are worn down by the activity cycle. "It's crazy," says Julie, a working mom of a five-year-old and a three-year-old. "I finally cut down on the kids activities...I told Sophie that if she was taking jazz dancing she couldn't take ballet. It's impossible to get them to everything." Julie's motives are the same well-meaning ones that affect many parents in her social and income group—mainly highly paid professionals who live in comfortable homes that afford them many luxuries, albeit not enough time. She wants to keep her children physically active, mentally stimulated and happy, and she wants them to experience lots of activities when they are young so they can perhaps pare things down to a few choices later on. Although she agrees that there is "practically a law" that her kids take both swimming and soccer, conforming to the social norm has relatively little to do with it. Her feeling is that to be a good parent involves a certain amount of sacrifice, and what tends to get sacrificed is time.

As good as Julie's motives may be, they also have a flipside. The negative consequences of overscheduled families are serious enough that they have caught the attention of the National Mental Health Association. On their website, the association posts a list of ways for parents to lighten their load, warning that children in overscheduled families are more prone to stress, depression and lower self-esteem. "Resolve to eat dinner together as a family at least three to five times a week, even if this is sandwiches before you head out to a game or lesson," they warn. Of course, from a business perspective, the rush means an opportunity to serve families who may not get around to having that dinner at home.

Whoever you ask, there is widespread agreement that the time crunch is an issue in our society. Leisure time, that is, time that can be used in any way you wish, is in short supply. In this category are big blocks of free time—basically days and weeks when no labor force work is scheduled and vacations can be planned (although childcare and other chores still have to be done on these days off, of course). Daily and weekly hours of "free" time are even scarcer. Interestingly enough, although there is a virtually universal agreement that there is not enough time, the numbers simply do not tell the same story.

BY THE NUMBERS: A GLUT OF LEISURE TIME

Although anecdotally the time crunch can be heard loud and clear, the numbers actually tell a different and somewhat puzzling story. According to the data, North Americans actually have a large amount of leisure time, and indeed, that time has been growing at a nice clip over the past couple of decades.

The most comprehensive data on leisure time comes from the American Time Use Survey (ATUS), a project of the U.S. Bureau of Labor Statistics administered through the University of Maryland. Since 1965, a representative sample of households have been asked to keep "time diaries" recording their activities. Participants are asked to track exactly what they did over a given day in 15-minute increments—working, commuting, shopping, preparing dinner and participating in leisure activities. For purposes of the use-of-time project, leisure activities are defined as being comprised of socializing and communicating, watching television, participating in sports, exercise and recreation. As in life, leisure, for the purpose of the survey, is the residual category, the time left over after all the necessities have been taken care of.

Contrary to the common refrain, these time diaries show that American leisure time is fairly plentiful. The 2005 data shows that the average person over the age of 15 had five hours and eight minutes of leisure time on any given day. Men, with five hours and 30 minutes had a bit more than women, who had about four hours and 48 minutes of free time. Although there are, of course, some who have too much time on their hands—the unemployed come to mind—very few people seem to have five hours each day to do with as they wish. Still, the Canadian data show much the same puzzling pattern. The last time the data were compiled, in 2005, the results showed that free time averaged five hours and 30 minutes a day, with men getting five hours and 48 minutes "off" and women getting about five hours and 12 minutes.

Compared to the data on working hours, and compared to what seems like everyone's experience, the numbers feel wrong. "How much leisure time does the government say I have? Four or five hours? To sit and do nothing?" That's the reaction of Lisa, a sales manager at a high-tech company as well as the mom of two children, both under two years old. She describes her day.

"I get up when the kids get up—between 6:45 and 7:15 a.m. Then my husband and I care for them. We have a nanny, but she gets here about 8:30. I work at home, so as soon as the kids are settled, I head downstairs to my basement office, and then I'm busy all day. Sometimes I go out to see clients; other times we do "webinars." There are days I don't even get upstairs to grab lunch. At 5:00 I call it quits. The kids nap in the afternoon, but they get up around 5:00 and we play a bit. Then I have to cook dinner, and my husband comes home and we eat and clean up. Then baths and all that, and the baby goes down to sleep at 8:00 p.m. My 22-month-old goes to bed closer to 9:30. 'Leisure' is whatever is left over, and I don't have much left after that."

Few would likely agree that we have more leisure time now than was true in earlier generations, yet a thorough examination of the data by two economists leads to just that conclusion. In a paper for the Federal Reserve Board of Boston, economists Erik Hurst and Mark A. Aguiar argue that since 1965, leisure time for adult Americans below the retirement age has grown by four to eight hours a week, depending on just how narrowly "leisure time" is defined.

How to explain the sharp increase? Part of the reason supposedly comes from a change in the way that Americans divide their work time in the labor force and in the home. Since 1965, women have entered the workforce by the millions, taking their aggregate labor force participation rate from 39.3 percent in that year to 59 percent at present. Although they are more likely to be working outside the home, they have theoretically been compensated by working less at home. You can see this most clearly by looking at the data for married women. According to Hurst and Aguiar, between 1965 and 2003, labor market work rose by 9.3 hours a week on average, but was offset by a decline in non-market work of nearly 13 hours per week,[6] and married women's leisure increased by somewhere between 1.3 and 3.5 hours per week. People eat out instead of cooking, they hire Molly Maid to clean, they buy no-wrinkle clothing instead of pulling out the ironing board. Overall, that carves out a bit of household time. Even Lisa, the sales manager, admits that she is able to farm out some of her at-home work. "I do all the cooking myself, and I do make most things from scratch, although I'll buy prepared marinades and things like that. But I'm lucky in that the nanny helps with some of the chores—one day she'll dust, another she'll get laundry done. So I do less of that stuff than I would otherwise."

Still, nobody feels like they have much leisure time, maybe because leisure is not really "leisure." According to the ATUS data, Americans spend about half of their leisure hours watching television—about two hours and 40 minutes a day in front of the tube. If that seems like a lot of time, it should be noted that it is pretty low-quality leisure. TV

6. Aguiar, Mark and Erik Hurst, "Measuring Trends in Leisure: The Allocation of Time over Five Decades." Federal Reserve Bank of Boston working paper, No. 06-02, January 2006.

is a passive and cheap leisure activity, especially in terms of energy spent. "The more tired you are, the more you are likely to choose television as a leisure activity," says John de Graaf, the founder of Take Back Your Time, a national organization designed to fight overwork and time poverty. "It is no coincidence that the Americans and the Japanese work the longest hours and watch the most television. The Norwegians work the least and watch the least." At any rate, watching television is not likely to be an exclusive activity. According to BIGresearch, when watching TV, 66 percent of people regularly or occasionally read the mail, 60 percent go online, and 55 percent read the newspaper.[7]

So which is correct, the overwhelming opinion among North Americans that they do not have much leisure, or the numbers that say they do? Anecdotally the numbers do not seem to mesh with the reality. One way to deal with that is to say that the figures are correct, and people are under-estimating the amount of free time they have. Another way is to take a look at how the economy has changed over the past three decades, supposedly the time during which leisure has grown. If leisure has actually increased, these should have been boom times for cooking slow meals and spending time on the golf course, playing 18 holes and then sipping drinks at the 19th. However, a surge in meals eaten outside the home and a drop in the numbers of rounds of golf being played tell a different story. Indeed, what we have these days is not at all a leisure boom economy: it is a time-crunch economy and a rather sophisticated one at that.

THE TIME-CRUNCH ECONOMY

"And when you're finished with the mixing bowls, well, just leave them," instructs Holly, a bright-eyed 20-something with an upbeat manner. "You can walk away from all the dirty dishes, and we'll clean them up." Her audience is Gail and Donna, two 40-something working moms clad in jeans and sweatshirts. They giggle guiltily at the thought of walking away from the cooking debris. Leaving the dishes is not

---

7. "Simultaneous Media Usage Survey." BIGresearch, January 5, 2005.

something they could do at home, which is why they are spending a Saturday morning at Super Suppers instead.

Tucked away in a strip mall in the Bethpage, New York, Super Suppers is an example of an "easy meal prep" center. In a large, airy room decorated to look vaguely like a Tuscan restaurant circa Long Island, six separate meal preparation stations, each resembling a salad bar, have been set up. A simple recipe is taped at the top of each station above a selection of meats, chopped vegetables and sauces. Gail and Donna make their way around the stations to put together meals of their choice—Tarragon Chicken with Lemon and White Wine Sauce, Stuffed Manicotti a la Marinara, Asian Chicken and Veggie wraps. *Put together* is a more appropriate way to describe what they're doing than *cook*. Everything has been shopped for; everything is chopped; everything will be cleaned up later. "You just put it in your containers, and you have a home-cooked meal waiting for you any night you want," says franchise-owner Holly.

Super Suppers is a part of a North America-wide chain of "meal-assembly" stores sprouting up at an astonishing rate. Designed to help busy people "make" dinner with minimum time investment, the idea has found a grateful niche, particularly in the ranks of time-crunched working women striving to avoid take-out food. "I get off the train from Manhattan at 6:15," says Donna, an office worker as well as a mom to three teenagers. "Sometimes I cook, but we eat pretty late if I do that. Gail, who works at a mortgage company closer to home, is every bit as time-crunched. "I have four kids," she says with a wry smile. "A couple have left home, but they all seem to eat there anyway."

It is the first time at Super Suppers for both women, but they love the concept. "I just wish they had late evening drop-in sessions," sighs Donna. "Saturdays are already crammed with ten thousand other errands. I might do better getting here during the week." No wonder then that the U.S. Easy Meal Prep Association reports that as of 2007, there were 1346 meal prep centers in the United States, representing 431 companies. Meal prep centers are a time saver, and time savers are a necessity in a time-poor society. Indeed, people have become so busy that cooking is getting crowded off their schedules altogether. The ATUS data shows that on any given day in 2005, only about 37 percent of men and 66 percent of women reported doing *any* meal preparation. In contrast, about half of all food dollars spent in the United States are for food eaten outside the home: the restaurant industry is the biggest private-sector employer in the country.

Home cleaning services, once the exclusive property of households rich enough to afford a "Hazel," have expanded to include anyone who wants to pay a service to come in every couple of weeks. And the biggest growth industry in some swish neighborhoods may be dog walking. From dog walking services to full-time doggy daycare, pet sitting is now one of the fastest growing areas of the pet service industry in the United States. As well, the industry has also created a variety of pet toys, such as mechanized tennis ball throwers, that do not require any human involvement.[8]

Of course, the data from Hurst and Aguilar suggest that one of the reasons there is more leisure time now (according to their calculations anyway) is that people are availing themselves not just of services like Super Suppers, but of technological advances from dishwashers to microwaves that make meal preparation quicker and easier. It is a bit of a chicken-and-egg situation, though, and not much of a leap to suggest that the services have sprung up simply because so many other demands on our time have also blossomed.

You can see this trend in many other service industries. Even banks, once the least flexible of institutions, became kinder to their time-crunched customers in the 1980s and 1990s. Hours were expanded to include weekends and evenings, instant tellers and drive-through banking found a foothold, and customers were urged to bank from home using the Internet. To be sure, such initiatives reduced the labor costs to banks, but they also found an audience in households who, once they got over any initial resistance to technology, were glad to find ways to speed up the banking process.

---

8. Fox, Camilla H. "What About Fluffy and Fido?" in *Take Back Your Time: Fighting Overwork and Time Poverty in America*, John de Graaf (Editor), San Francisco, Berrett-Koehler Publishers Inc. 2003, p.7.

Interestingly enough, the leisure industries have also done extremely well in general over the past few years. According to data from the U.S. Craft and Hobby Association (CHA), as of 2006, the craft industry in the United States was a $30 billion industry. Some sectors like scrapbooking have seen phenomenal growth already, to the extent that one in four households in the United States now includes someone who "scrapbooks." How to reconcile that with the perceived time crunch? To an extent, the time-intense activities are fueled firmly by more mature households, and by those who have less intense demands on their time.

Other industries have also adapted themselves to those with little free time by creating ways to make people feel like they have accomplished something, without actually having had to invest very much time. There are adult versions of the old "Paint by Numbers" sets, that let people create their own version of a Vincent Van Gogh masterpiece— all in the span of an evening. At the extreme, time-crunched consumers are also happy to pay for someone else to take care of their hobbies: you can now give your box of photographs to someone else who will make up the scrapbook for you.

The sports and fitness industry has been affected by the time crunch. The past few decades may have seen the advent of everything from Pilates studios to special shoes for jogging, but for every person who won't miss a day at the gym, there are a couple of others guiltily calculating the cost-per-use of their gym membership, given that they've worked out four times over a year. The ATUS data shows that on average 0.3 hours—about 18 minutes—a day is devoted to participating in sports or exercising, considerably less than the two hours and 35 minutes spent watching television. And of course the result of that decrease in physical activity is evident in the fact that 66 percent of Americans are either overweight or obese, and their health is declining as a consequence. There has been particular success in the fitness industry, however, in those facilities that promise a quick in-and-out experience. Curves, a chain of fitness centers for women that started in 1992, specializes in 30-minute workouts for time-crunched women. By 2007, the chain had over 4 million members and 10,000 locations worldwide; one of every four fitness centers in the United States is a Curves.

The golf course industry knows all about the problem of the time crunch. In the 1980s, the industry seemed poised for a huge increase in interest and in golfers. Spurred by everything from an aging population to the popularity of Tiger Woods, golf was poised to be the hot sport of the new millennium. Golf courses were built at a rapid clip in the 1990s, and expectations were high that they would fill up with eager golfers. One study, presented to the National Golf Federation in 1986, said that by 2000 there would be 26.8 million golfers in the United States, a projection that turned out to be very close to the reality (by 2003, there were 26.2 million golfers in the U.S.[9]). There's only one problem: golfers have no time to play golf. The U.S. National Golf Federation notes that the number of rounds played dropped off in the later 1990s and have stayed flat since.

So what other businesses have thrived in the time-crunch economy? Anything that promises to make time management easier has been a hit. From BlackBerries to workplace dishes specially designed to fit in front of a keyboard so you don't have to take a meal break, much of what is designed and sold these days is manufactured for those who simply cannot spend the time to do one thing at a time. Time management consultants are a growth industry too.

Not that all the innovations reduce our stress, however. One study, published in the *Journal of Marriage and Family*, showed that increasing use of cell phones and pagers was linked to a decrease in family satisfaction and increased stress at home, as both men and women carry over job stress into their family lives. Women with pagers and cell phones reported an extra problem: they carried over more stress from their home lives into their workplaces.[10]

Among the biggest growth industries, thanks to the time crunch, are those that help people "de-stress" from all of the demands of their lives. The spa industry has grown by leaps and bounds, with locations expanding by an unbelievable 51 percent in the year 2000, then moderating to about 12 percent growth between 2002 and 2004. Between 1997 and

9. Murphy, Mark, "Why are we Playing Less?" *Golf World*, Number 7, November 2003.

10. Chesley, N. *Journal of Marriage and Family*. Volume 67, December 2005, pp. 1237–1248.

2001, aggregate revenue growth doubled every year, although that has plateaued recently. With the expansion of day spas—those that you can be in and out of in a few hours, rather than the old style "health farms" that require a larger time commitment—spas have become the dominant player, accounting for about 41 percent of the industry. "There's a need for people to take mini-breaks with the stress levels we are all under," one spa owner says. "It's not very often that we can afford to take the weekend or go away for three to four days to just do nothing. That's where the day spa fits [in]."

Maybe the best way to see that the time-crunched economy is now in force is to look at the fact that civic involvement has faltered in recent years. Volunteerism has actually been on the upswing for the last several years, perhaps because of President Bush's call to community service, following September 11, 2001. However, much of that has been spurred by large-scale programs, particularly those that require high school students to participate in volunteer activities as a condition of graduation. Old-style, grassroots community involvement, though, has certainly been on the decline. "We used to have a big fair in our church every year," says Marie, a 75-year-old congregant of a Greek church in suburban Long Island. "We'd always make a lot of spanakopita; everyone would bring a batch. And then, maybe 10 years ago, less and less people were able to participate. Everyone was working, busy. So now it's all catered ... but it's not exactly the same." And pastries for the church are only the tip of the iceberg: civic involvement in things as simple as casting a vote are also on the decline.

So there it is: the statistics say one thing, but the economy says something else and those figures—tracked by the flow of money on goods and services to deal with the time crunch—do not lie. Good or bad, the time-crunch economy is an economic phenomenon. Started, perhaps, by the fact that people are spending so much of their time at work, it has snowballed into many parts of our lives and in the process it has caught the attention of business. We buy the calendars and tack them up, and hope that not too much will get lost in the shuffle. We feel more time-crunched than ever.

But concentrating on the time-crunch economy may mean missing the next major shift. The leisure economy is ahead, and its economic reach will be every bit as powerful as what came before it. Understanding why that is going to happen means first understanding exactly how we got to the point where room for pictures on our calendars has come to seem like an unaffordable luxury.

ECONOMIC PROGRESS AND LEISURE RUIN

Adults in higher-income households perceive more time stress...
Time stress is part "time crunch," but much is also part "yuppie
kvetch."

> — *Daniel S. Hamermesh and Jungmin Lee in*
> *"Stressed Out on Four Continents: Time Crunch*
> *or Yuppie Kvetch?" National Bureau of Economic*
> *Research, 2003.*

In one sense it defies logic. Whatever the official numbers show, the time crunch has become increasingly pronounced over the past decades. The previous chapter documented its progression: from ready-to-go suppers to drive-through banking, companies have reacted to the reality of what their customers told them about their time-impoverished lives. At the same time, North America has a record of centuries of economic progress, and in the 1990s polished off the longest economic expansion experienced since the end of the Second World War. That progress has made possible creature comforts that in many ways have made our lives better—while at the same time leaving us less time to enjoy them.

True, the gains in income have not been evenly shared, particularly over the last few years. But the signs of prosperity abound. From the proliferation of middle-class households with flat screen televisions to the fact that the homes they put those TVs in are now frequently big enough to house a media room, there are plenty of examples showing that material wealth is high. Indeed, more than 70 percent of all Americans now own their own homes, and about half have a stake in the equity markets. Leisure, though, has proved to be the elusive luxury item, the one that has actually diminished as material wealth has increased. It's as if we have all fallen down the rabbit hole that is North America in the 21st century. If you make the right educational and career choices, you can make money, and with that money you can buy more and more things that you want. What you cannot buy, however hard you try, is leisure time.

To understand exactly how this has happened, you have to look at how the economy has developed over time. The reasons for the time-crunch economy cover a broad spectrum, including everything from an unfriendly economic environment to, ironically, an appetite for high-cost leisure pursuits. Together they have ensured that not only have the past decades not brought about a leisure boom, they have come together to create the time-crunch economy.

NORTH AMERICAN WORK— A LONG HISTORY OF LONG HOURS

Whether we are talking about today's time crunch or that of two hundred years ago, we have to start with the world of work. True, the issue of time stress now is complicated by many more things than just working hours—from commuting to getting a book read for a book club or getting snacks organized for a child's soccer tournament. But the biggest chunk of many people's time is still devoted to making a living, and it always has been. In fact, in a historical context it could be argued that we are already enjoying the leisure economy even though it doesn't feel like it to us. Although it has happened in fits and starts, economic progress in North America has generally meant more time for leisure—at least until the last decade or so.

Going back a few centuries, North America barely bothered to separate work from leisure. From colonial times up to about the second half of the 19th century, agriculture was the dominant occupation for most North Americans. Some estimates suggest that workers put in long days, perhaps to the extent that some form of work filled all their waking hours.[1] At that point, there was really not much of a split between work and leisure, or at least the demarcation between the two was not that clear.

Drawing a line between leisure and work really started to happen at the end of the 19th century. The Industrial Revolution was launched in Britain in the late 18th and early 19th centuries, and the late years of the 1800s are sometimes dubbed "the Second Industrial Revolution." Those years were a time of rapid industrialization across North America, as huge breakthroughs were made in the processing of resources like coal and iron, and factories started the mass production of consumer goods. Productivity was on the rise and prosperity was, too, meaning that workers could share in some of the improvements through shorter work weeks that did not also mean smaller paychecks. Records of hours of work in the U.S. manufacturing industry are available from about 1830. They show that in that year, workers put in a week of an estimated 69.1 hours.[2] By 1860, this had slipped to about 62 hours, and by 1880 to about 60.7 hours.

The middle class suddenly had more time off, and more money to boot. Pastimes like going to the theater or listening to the newly developed gramophone were in vogue, and the leisure industries flourished. Ironically, the new menu of leisure pursuits meant that workers had a new incentive to work even harder so as to be able to afford them. It was the start of something that would really take hold later: leisure became more expensive, so working became important in the sense that it could pay for pleasure.[3] Workers, at least those in the higher income

1. Much of the following discussion is based on information from Robert Whaples's "Hours of Work in U.S. History." EH.Net online Encyclopedia of Economic History. http://eh.net/encyclopedia/article/whaples.work.hours.us

2. Ibid.

3. www.wikipedia.org/wiki/Leisure.

brackets, had moved beyond working just for necessities. In response, Thorstein Veblen wrote his famous work, *The Theory of the Leisure Class,* where he introduced the idea that leisure was a non-productive use of time. Published in 1899, it was specifically concerned with the upper classes, those who could afford "conspicuous consumption"—spending to have better things than your neighbors, not just to buy necessities.

But if Veblen saw pure leisure as a pastime for the rich, those further down the income scale were also getting a bit of it too. In the years before the First World War, the eight-hour day came into existence. It was a direct response to the strength of the economy: the United States was growing at a rapid clip, and some of the wealth made its way back to workers. By some estimates, manufacturing wages rose by over 11 percent in inflation-adjusted terms between 1914 and 1919.[4] At the same time, labor force growth slowed, partly because of a decline in immigration, as well as the effects of war and of the 1918 influenza epidemic. For all these reasons, a push by workers—partly through their new, strengthened unions—was successful in reducing the length of the workweek. By the beginning of the 1920s, a 48-hour workweek—six days a week at eight hours a day—was becoming the norm. But after nearly a century of progress in reducing the workweek, another shift in the economy was about to halt the progress.

If in the two decades prior it was prosperity and productivity that bought shorter hours for workers, in the 1930s, it was economic weakness that threatened to shorten working hours. The boom of the 1920s was effectively wiped out in 1929, along with $13 billion of value in listed stocks on the New York Stock Exchange. From a rate of 3.2 percent in that year, the unemployment rate in the United States climbed to 8.7 percent in 1930 and to nearly 16 percent by 1931. In an effort to "share the work," President Herbet Hoover encouraged shorter hours for employees and, in time, companies like Sears Roebuck, General Motors

4. Garrett, Thomas A. "War and Pestilence as Labor Market Shocks: Manufacturing Wage Growth 1914–1918." Federal Reserve Bank of St. Louis—Research Division, Working Paper No. 2006-018A, March 2006.

and Kellogg cut working hours, sometimes to 30 hours a week. A formal bill to reduce working hours, the Black–Connery 30 Hours Bill, was introduced under the tenure of Franklin Delano Roosevelt, but was ultimately defeated. Income stress, not the length of the workweek, was the preoccupation of the workers, at least for those lucky enough to be employed.

During the years of the Second World War there was pressure for working hours to rise. Labor continued to press for shorter work hours, but the argument for sharing the work no longer held when every bit of labor was needed to create machinery and weapons and generally keep the war machine operating. In an effort to lift war production, entire campaigns were run to increase working hours, with the implication that working less than flat out was unpatriotic. Indeed, the move to get women into the labor force for war production was successful. In the United States, 6 million women moved into the workforce, mostly taking factory jobs that were vacated when men left to fight overseas. In the enthusiasm to get the job done, working hours rose and incomes did too. Early battles to achieve a shorter workweek were forgotten, and they tended to stay forgotten when the war ended.

The two decades following the war were heady economic times for North America. It was a "guns and butter" economy: spending on defence was high in the United States, but domestic spending was high too. People were acquiring more education, partly thanks to the GI Bill in the United States, and there were plenty of jobs for them to fill. The middle class expanded, and they bought up houses in newly built suburbia just in time to house their baby-boom children. Average working hours stabilized at about 40 hours a week, and they paid for a host of consumer comforts, from backyard barbeques to television sets.

The availability of jobs enticed many into the labor force. A 1954 story in *Woman's Day* magazine reported that twice as many young Americans were taking summer jobs as in 1940. Interviewing a score of young people, including a waitress, a junior cowboy and a farm cadet, all of whom were happy to be tasting some economic independence, they pronounced that "working beats loafing."[5] And, despite the stereotype of June Cleaver in the kitchen, women in the 1950s were more likely to hold a job than they were a decade earlier. In the United States, the labor force participation rate among women was 24 percent in 1940; it rose to 30 percent by 1950. It continued to climb through the decade, reaching 33 percent by 1960. The rate was lower among married women and women with children: in 1955, 27 percent of women with children under the age of 18 held a job.[6]

Still, despite what might have seemed like all-out contentment with the work–leisure trade off, the increasing demands put on workers by corporations were noted, and resented by some. Sloan Wilson's 1955 novel, *The Man in the Gray Flannel Suit* (later made into a movie starring Gregory Peck), told the story of Tom Rath, a suburban-dwelling father of three with a stay-at-home wife, three children and a house that needed a lot of money for repairs. In an effort to boost his income, Rath takes a job with a large television station but is soon taken aback at the hours that success in the industry demands. By the end of the book he makes his decision: "It's just that if I have to bury myself in a job every minute of my life, I don't see any point in it," he tells his boss, a man so committed to his own work that he has let his family be destroyed. In contrast to what would probably happen in such a situation today, Rath's decision is apparently fine with his employer, who tells him that the company needs men like him just as much as they need workaholics. Work–life balance, in the 1950s, was something that apparently still could be achieved—and encouraged.

By the time the 1960s rolled around, there was great hope that a leisure boom was but a few years away, courtesy of technology. After all, the economy in North America continued to prosper through most of the decade. In the United States military spending for the Vietnam War provided a boost to the economy, and in both Canada and the United States government spending rose. At least through the first part of the decade, the gleam of the 1950s still abounded.

---

5. Kinard, Epsie. "Working Beats Loafing." *Woman's Day,* June 1954.

6. U.S. Department of Labor and Women's Bureau. Information Please database, www.infoplease. com.

Corporate profits soared, reaching a level of 10 percent of gross domestic product by mid-decade—a level that would not be seen again until 2006.[7] And consumers did fine too. If the previous decade was notable for enabling North Americans to get new homes and new cars, the 1960s saw a rise in the services they consumed. Travel and tourism became accessible to more and more people, as did other leisure pursuits.

These were the years when policymakers had to tussle with the promise and the threat of automation on the workplace. Blue-collar workers and their unions were justifiably frightened by what machines might do to their jobs. In response, in 1962 the *Manpower Development Training Act* was passed in the United States with the backing of the AFL-CIO, America's largest federation of unions. It promised retraining for workers who lost their jobs because of technological improvements, a promise that in practice was combined with phased retirements. Author Jeremy Rifkin depicts this time period as the moment that labor made their big mistake by pushing for retraining instead of for a share of the gains from any increases in productivity. After all, the reason to automate was to improve the profitability picture for the companies. Instead of insisting on retraining, workers could have instead demanded that the work be shared, possibly through shorter workweeks.[8] Whether this might have been a sustainable arrangement is a source of debate, but regardless, it was an avenue not pursued.

The more optimistic believed that productivity was going to bring about a society where work did not take up nearly as much time as before. Thanks to great innovations, workers were supposed to be freed of working 40, or even 20, hours a week. The spectacular failure of that particular set of projections is one reason why it is now very difficult to get anyone to believe that the economy may ever move from a time-crunched state to a leisure one. Still, the average workweek during those years drifted down a little. Data from the U.S. Bureau of Labor Statistics show that as of 1964, workers were putting in about

7. U.S. Department of Commerce Data. "Not Sharing in the Gains." *The New York Times,* August 28, 2006.

8. Rifkin, Jeremy. *The End of Work.* New York: G. Putnam and Sons, 1995, p. 86.

38.5 hours a week, and that by the end of the decade the average had slipped to 37.5 hours.[9]

By the 1970s, the North American economy had shifted again, and it was not in favor of workers. Deficits rose and economic growth slowed down as the 1960s ended and the 1970s began. Then, in 1973, an oil embargo by the newly formed Organization of Petroleum Exporting Countries (OPEC) caused energy prices to shoot through the roof. North America learned a new word—*stagflation*—to describe the atypical unappetizing mix of rising prices and stagnant economic activity that had taken hold. Government spending rose in both the United States and Canada as a way to jumpstart the respective economies, and both countries toyed with forms of wage and price controls to keep inflation in check. On both sides of the border, however, the remedies had little success.

In the late 1970s, the task of reversing spiraling North American inflation shifted squarely to the central banks. In the United States, the Federal Reserve tightened monetary policy, which caused interest rates to ratchet higher, and in Canada the Bank of Canada did the same. The results hit consumers hard. A conventional U.S. mortgage rate, for example, averaged 9.6 percent in 1978. By 1981, it had surged to 16.6 percent, which for many consumers meant a difference in mortgage rate payments of hundreds of dollars a month.[10] The results were swift and powerful. A recession in the housing sector spread throughout the economy of North America, and for the first time ever, U.S. and Canadian unemployment rates headed into double-digit levels.

For workers at all levels, their biggest concern was first to hold on to their jobs, and second to secure some kind of inflation adjustment to their pay that would at least allow them to maintain their standard of living. If they had ever been on the table, shorter working hours got shoved firmly off. Indeed, in many families a second wage earner—usually a former stay-at-home mother—re-entered the labor force to try to keep up with ever escalating costs and mortgage payments.

9. From Survey of Establishments. The Current Employment Statistics Program, U.S. Census Bureau.

10. U.S. Federal Reserve, www.federalreserve.gov/releases/n15/data.htm.

Things turned around somewhat as the 1980s progressed and "the Reagan Revolution" brought about lower tax rates, albeit accompanied by rising deficits and interest rates that never dipped below double-digit levels. The 1980s were also notable for signaling new worries about North American competitiveness in relation to the rest of the world. Japan became a major rival to the United States for manufactured goods such as cars, and there were real worries in North America that manufacturing jobs would disappear for good. The service side of the North American economy prospered, though, and the U.S. unemployment rate slipped into the 5 percent range by the latter part of the decade.

As the decade ended, however, economic activity boomed and inflation bounded back too. Once again, monetary policy was tightened in the United States and Canada, and once again the results were predictable. The 1990s started with a deep recession, as well as with weak economic activity in almost every area. As a way to boost their bottom lines, companies started to make big investments in capital equipment. Partly as a result of their investments, things turned around in the second half of the decade to the extent that people began to talk about the "productivity miracle." Something had changed: the unemployment rate had slipped to a level not seen since the 1960s. Normally that might not be thought of as a sustainable situation, but this time around it was a bit of a puzzle: low unemployment that did not trigger inflation, and thus the need to have interest rates rise to slow things down. Of course, the "Goldilocks" situation—an economy that was not too hot, not too cold but "just right"—did not last long: a pronounced correction in the stock markets and the events of 9/11 saw to that. Interestingly though, even though the U.S. economy lost thousands of jobs between 2000 and 2003, the unemployment rate never rose to the old levels.

In the heady days of the stock market boom, the U.S. unemployment rate had fallen to 3.8 percent in 1999, the lowest since the late 1960s. Even as the economy cooled following the tech wreck, the U.S. unemployment rate did not climb much, increasing to only 6.2 percent at its peak in 2003. A similar pattern was seen in Canada, which, although it did not experience the same decrease in the rate during the late 1990s, by 2006 had reached its lowest unemployment rate in more than three decades.[11] The tight labor market of the 1990s continued into the new century, with good workers still strongly in demand. Through it all, however, more leisure simply did not seem to be an option for workers.

A DECADE WITHOUT LEISURE

One of the real paradoxes of the last decade is why economic growth has been paired with so many extra hours of work. True, not all workers are in high demand, but in many occupations they are. And true, not every worker wants to put in less time, but many, especially those with young families, continually express a desire for more leisure. And yet the time crunch, much of it stemming from the demands of the workplace, has continued to worsen over the past decade.

The answer may be that although the unemployment rate is low, in many senses the situation for workers has worsened rather than improved over the last few years. To start with, some of the decline in the unemployment rate has been illusory and has to do with demographics. The baby boomers, after all, shifted the unemployment rate higher when they entered the labor market, because there were so many of them looking for work at the same time. In addition, there is always a higher unemployment rate among younger workers than there is among older ones. But by the 1990s even the youngest boomers were headed for their 30s; inevitably, the unemployment rate got pushed down as the boomers settled into jobs. Economists Lawrence Katz and Alan Krueger estimate that of a decrease of 0.8 percent in the U.S. unemployment rate between 1989 and 1998, about one quarter of the decrease was simply the result of the population aging. Another unlikely factor reduced it by a further 0.1 to 0.2 percent, namely an increase in the U.S. population incarcerated during the time period.[12]

---

11. The Canadian and U.S. unemployment rates are tracked by different methodologies and are not directly comparable.

12. Katz, Lawrence F. and Alan B. Krueger. "New Trend in Unemployment? The High Pressure U.S. Labor Market of the 1990s." Brookings Papers on Economic Activity, 1999, p. 1.

Other factors have also made the decrease in joblessness look better than it actually is. Temporary help agencies have proliferated in the past two decades and in one sense have gone a long way toward making the economy more efficient. Agencies screen workers and offer them to employers at a set fee, saving the companies the expense of benefits. Workers are able to pick up short-term assignments that keep them from joblessness. In many cases the workers may like the flexibility of working on a contract basis, which gives them the opportunity to choose some leisure time between assignments. In other instances, however, the temporary agencies are a barely acceptable alternative to unemployment. Katz and Krueger calculated that in 1999, the unemployment rate had been lowered by 0.4 percentage points because of the proliferation of temporary help agencies.

Then too, the boom years of the 1990s have been accompanied by a boom in technology that has meant workers can work wherever they are—in their offices, in their homes or on the road. Take a commuter train out of a big city on any weekday and you can see this in action: workers texting their assistants on their BlackBerries, phoning clients on their cell phones, or industriously keying reports on their laptops. Jill Andresky Fraser detailed the phenomenon in her book *White Collar Sweatshop*, making this grim assessment: "Technology has done more than simply facilitate the current trend of working longer and harder ... It may, indeed, have exacerbated patterns of overwork and job stress by broadening many white-collar staffers' (and their employers') definitions of 'on the job' to include areas far beyond the traditional ... office space."[13]

Finally, the rosy unemployment rates also mask an increase in job instability. From the 1970s on, layoffs have risen in Canada and the United States. Just how many people have actually lost their jobs is in question. In the book, *The Disposable American*, Louis Uchitelle, economics writer for *The New York Times*, estimates that, based on the worker displacement surveys from the U.S. Bureau of Labor Statistics, at least 30 million full-time workers have been laid off in the United

---

13. Fraser, Jill Andresky. *White Collar Sweatshop*. New York: Norton & Company, 2001, p. 75.

States since the early 1990s. That works out to an annual average of about 4 percent of full-time workers in the United States each year. Although a similar study is not available for Canada, the anecdotal evidence certainly suggests that layoffs have gone from being a rarity to something of the norm over the same period.

The layoff phenomenon has definitely hiked worker insecurity, and with good reason. Layoffs were not the norm before the 1970s, but economic circumstances arguably made it necessary to resort to layoffs at that time. More recently, "downsizing" workers has simply become part of the way that business is conducted. A study by economist Henry S. Farber looked at the experience of workers who lost their jobs during the period from 1981 to 2001.[14] He found that job losses during the 1990s were higher than might have been expected, given the strength of the economy at that time. In addition, job losses among more educated workers rose, although less educated workers continued to have the highest probability of losing their jobs. When the economy cooled again in 2001, workers were in for another shock. Although in the 1990s they generally were able to find other jobs when the economy picked up, this time finding work got progressively more difficult. When they did find work, it was likely that they would have to settle for a lower wage—a trend that started in the 1990s and has continued since. The Canadian figures show a similar pattern. A 2004 study by Statistics Canada[15] concluded that while the chances of losing one's job did not rise sharply in the 1980s and 1990s, the chance of finding a new job in the event of a layoff fell markedly.

The increase in job insecurity goes a long way towards explaining why a seemingly healthy labor market has not helped North American workers negotiate their way out of the time crunch. Add to that the fact that despite a decade or more of low unemployment, the North American economies have been rocked by roller coaster business cycles

14. Farber, Henry S. "Job Loss in the United States, 1981–2001." Princeton University Working Paper #471, Industrial Relations Section, January 2003.

15. Morrissette, Rene. "Permanent Layoff Rates." *Perspectives*. Statistics Canada Catalogue no. 75-001-XIE, March 2004.

and external shocks for most of the past two decades. From the stock market correction in the late 1990s to 9/11 to the most recent spike in oil prices, workers have had reason after reason to worry about their jobs and their prospects.

So they have been holding on, asking for and generally not getting much in the way of improvements in the pay that would improve their material well-being. At the same time, there has been a legitimate drive to improve competitiveness in the United States and Canada so that North America can better compete globally. Workers and management have thus had something in common: from both sides of the table, they have agreed that cutting the workweek seemed like a bad idea all around.

THE NORTH AMERICAN AVERSION TO LEISURE

Even if there were the chance to have a lot of leisure time, it is not clear that North Americans would want it. True, from time to time when the economic circumstances have permitted it, workers have seized on the opportunity to enjoy shorter working hours. But it has happened in fits and starts, and with mixed emotions. Unlike other parts of the world such as Europe where there has always been a premium put on leisure, free time has always been a source of mixed emotions in North America.

The all-work-no-play ethos goes back several centuries. Colonial America believed in it passionately—or at least those who set the laws did. Yet the earliest settlers did understand about taking time for leisure. As early as 1611, there are accounts of almost starving colonists taking time out to play bowls. The first Thanksgiving, at Plymouth, is the stuff of legend, complete with food, wine and a maypole. But the idea of settlers frittering away their time when the nascent country needed a big infusion of productivity was clearly an unsettling one for some. Bowling was forbidden, and as for the maypole, it was cut down, with the Governor of Massachusetts Bay Colony warning that "no person, householder or other, shall spend his time idly or un-profitably, under paine of such punishment as the Courte shall thinke meet to inflict."[16] And so the die was cast. From the discouragement of holding church meetings in mid-week in the 1700s, to the guilt that many 20th century North American workers feel when they take their allotted two weeks a year, the paradigm was readily understood: labor market work is good and leisure is for the idle.

Then too, mechanization may have helped workers draw stricter lines between what counted as work and what as leisure, but it also ushered in an era when standards inside the home started to rise. Unlike the era of agriculture where everyone pitched in, industrialization meant that men went out to work and women stayed home. "Women's work" became better defined, and by the late 19th century North American women were under more pressure to keep their homes up to better standards than their grandmothers ever had to meet. As more men moved to work in factories, women's role in the home was intensified. As well as the basic baking, cooking, childrearing and cleaning, many women still had to haul water in from a well and tend the fire in the stove. They were also becoming inundated with advice on how to run their homes better. Catherine Beecher, the half-sister of the abolitionist Harriet Beecher Stowe, had written the definitive work on the subject, a book called *The Treatise on Domestic Economy for the Use of Young Ladies at Home* in 1841. Its influence swept through the U.S. population. "Scientific housekeeping" was in vogue, and women were encouraged to increase their knowledge in all areas and apply their skills to the households. Newspapers gave out helpful tips too, and with innovations in printing, recipe books began to circulate. All in all, it meant that work for women inside the home was on the upswing.

Male or female, though, Americans began to take more vacations as the 19th century progressed. Before that time, vacationing was mostly a pastime for the rich, and even they did it with an eye to finding cures for whatever ailed them. As a new, white-collar middle class flourished, they ventured out to new vacation spots. By the 20th century, they were joined by blue-collar workers. Still, as historian Cindy S. Aron writes in *Working at Play: A History of Vacationing in the United*

---

16. Dulles, Foster Rhea. *A History of Recreation: America Learns to Play.* Second edition. New York: Meredith Publishing Company, 1965, p. 5.

States, "Vacationing ... exposed the contradictions at the center of the middle class: industriousness and discipline helped to make people middle class and thus entitled them to vacations, but vacations embodied the very opposite of what the middle class most valued."[17] As Aron details, self-improvement vacations—sojourns that allowed them to do some religious work while taking time off, for example—flourished along with the vacation culture.[18]

It's an observation that has often been made. In 1962, *Of Time, Work and Leisure* by Sebastian de Grazia was published as basically a lament against the shift to work that had made many societies fail to appreciate leisure time. Quoting Aristotle, the author points out, "The Spartans remained secure as long as they were at war; they collapsed as soon as they acquired an empire. They did not know how to use the leisure that peace brought." America, de Grazia concluded, was also a society that had made a decision to be a society without leisure.[19]

Philosophical arguments aside, the most compelling reason that North Americans have these days to choose work over leisure is this: it is the only choice they can afford. Leisure is an unattainable luxury for workers who have trapped themselves into endless work hours because of a penchant for every kind of consumer gadget. On top of that, many leisure pursuits have become relatively pricey. The price of plasma televisions sets may keep dropping, but it still costs to upgrade your TV to the newest model every year. And every hobby—from scrapbooking to deep-sea diving—has its own set of special paraphernalia to go with it, and not for free either.

If you want to point fingers as to where this particular trend to spend started, a good place to start might be in the 1920s. That's the era that some call the first "decade of the consumer." The rise of the consumer was in some ways a reaction to the push by workers for more time off. If people worked less, went the argument, then they

17. Aron, Cindy S. *Working at Play: A History of Vacations in the United States.* New York, New York: Oxford University Press, 1999, p. 9.

18. Ibid.

19. De Grazia, Sebastian. *Of Time, Work and Leisure.* New York: Vintage Books, 1962.

could buy less, which would stall economic growth. Accordingly, there was a push to convince workers that with their efforts they could make enough money to improve their standard of living. Whether it was as calculated an effort as that, or whether workers just responded to increasingly sophisticated advertising, is not clear. What is clear is that before the First World War, workers wanted more time off; by the 1920s, they wanted everything they saw, whether it was a new Ford or that other marvel of the 1920s, a radio. Workers started trading off work for leisure, because working hours bought more in terms of consumer goods—and they never looked back.

Leisure was getting pricey too. Automobiles were suddenly available to the middle class, and they scrambled to get them. In the late 1920s, the sociologists Robert Staughton Lynd and Helen Merrell Lynd put together a case study of a town in Indiana (called Middletown in their book but later identified as Muncie), chronicling the use of the residents' time, including leisure. Noting that taking drives (along with listening to the radio) had become the most popular leisure activities in the town, the Lynds wrote, "Group sanctioned values are disturbed by the inroads of the automobile upon the family budget ... a case in point is the not uncommon practice of mortgaging a home to buy an automobile ... the automobile has apparently unsettled the habit of careful saving for some families."[20] Families wanted an automobile for more than leisure pursuits, of course, but as they acquired them (helped by Henry Ford, who believed that if he paid his workers enough to afford the cars they produced it would be good for the economy) they changed the way they spent their time—and their money.

More recently, of course, the interest in acquiring goods has been blamed for everything from the increase in debt loads to the slump in leisure hours. The evidence is pretty compelling. According to the U.S. Commerce Department, between 1992 and 2005 the U.S. savings rate slumped from 9 percent to –0.3 percent—signaling that consumers were spending more than they were receiving in income. U.S. personal bankruptcy rates rose to a record level in 2005, and more than 2 million

---

20. Lynd, Robert S. and Helen Merrell Lynd. *Middletown: A Study in Modern American Culture.* New York: Harcourt Brace and Company, 1929, pp. 254–55.

Americans sought protection from Chapter 7 and Chapter 13 bankruptcy. The numbers are even clearer on an aggregate level. According to the Federal Reserve, U.S. consumer debt nearly doubled between 1998 and 2006. Perhaps most chilling is that much of that debt has come out of Americans' homes, which for many have become the equivalent of a giant ATM. As a result, the ratio of homeowners' equity to their homes' value had fallen to an all-time low of 54 percent by 2006.

But you do not need reams of statistics to show that spending is in fashion: when Veblen defined "conspicuous consumption" a century or so ago, he would not have been able to imagine the array of all-wheel-SUVs, "average" homes of 3,000 square feet, and $200 sneakers for high school athletes. Even a generation ago, eating out was more of a treat for a birthday than something that consumers routinely did when they did not feel like cooking. Not that spending money on any of these things is necessarily wrong; indeed, in many ways they enhance the perceived quality of life for consumers and in many cases can be considered money well spent. At the same time, they do take up a lot of space in family budgets and thus reduce freedom—and savings.

Some of the more recent spending pressure has come about simply because "basic" goods have now shifted themselves into the luxury category. The growth in a category called "premium denim"—jeans that cost $75 or more—is a case in point. According to NPD group, a market research group that tracks clothing sales, the upper end of the market has been the fastest growing part of the jeans market since 2002. Brands like 7 for all Mankind, Paper, Cloth and Denim, and True Religon are now everywhere, all sporting price tags upward of $150 a pair, and mall staples like Banana Republic now routinely stock jeans with price tags of over $100. Who's wearing them? Sure, celebrities are, but celebrity followers are too, whether or not they would characterize themselves as such. Is it necessarily bad? Of course not. If people are happier with larger homes or nicer jeans, then it is their choice. But when a pair of jeans costs roughly 10 times the average hourly pay rate (which was around $16 an hour as of 2006), then something in the buying equation has changed, and inevitably it is going to affect the amount of leisure time that people can afford to take.

Then again, some dispute whether we are actually as oriented to conspicuous consumption as we are made out to be. In *The Two Income Trap*, writers Elizabeth Warren and Amelia Warren Tyagi argue that in real terms workers are not spending more on most categories than they ever were. They calculate that after paying for such basics as house payments, car payments and insurance, the average two-income family in the United States has less in inflation-adjusted dollars left over than their counterparts had three decades earlier.[21] And indeed, it is a boom in the housing market that many families would point to as the reason that they are working flat-out, frequently with both partners in the job market.

But whether the lack of leisure is about their work ethic, the amount of money they like to spend or simply the amount they have to spend on basic shelter, the fact is that the majority of workers have not cut themselves much slack in terms of time off. That's true whether we talk about their working hours or the vacation time they take. More than that, though, in general they have simply become "busier" over the past few decades. You hear the lament everywhere: too many things, too little time. Interestingly, the problem may be one of affluence more than anything else.

THE "YUPPIE KVETCH"

"Steve and I fight about only two things," sighs Robin, a working mom of two preschool sons. "Dirt and time. The house is too dirty, and we don't have time to clean it. That's really it. The household organizational stuff is the stuff we just cannot get to." Money, although like everyone she says she could use more of it, is not really a problem. As an investment advisor married to an architect, her household income has steadily climbed over the past few years. As a result, her family has been able to renovate their home in a trendy area as well as do things like take a Christmas trip to Australia. When her older son turned three, the party had a sailing theme and was held at a nearby yacht club. "It was so cute; they had the kids out on little boats. And it was

---

21. Warren, Elizabeth and Amelia Warren Tyagi. *The Two-Income Trap: Why Middle-Class Mothers & Fathers Are Going Broke*. New York: Basic Books, 2003, p. 51.

fun doing the loot bags to match ... although I admit I got a little carried away on the whole thing," she laughs.

Some economists would point to her situation as a symptom of the growing income divide in North America, whereby highly skilled and educated workers like Robin and Steve do very well, while those in middle and lower income brackets struggle to just get into the housing market. That may be, but Robin and Steve are also on the wrong side of another distribution: the leisure divide. "There is not enough time," she says. "Although I already work an abbreviated day—I leave work at 3:30 and take over the childcare from the nanny then, I have to hit my numbers like everyone else. I'm up at 5:30 in the morning and I keep going until late at night, but that's not enough time to do it all." And indeed, the time crunch for people like her has now gotten so pronounced that *The New York Times* recently declared, "The act of canceling a meeting or dinner date can constitute the most precious gift one busy professional can bestow on another. Both parties tacitly acknowledge that the empty calendar is the greatest luxury of all, one that even the rich—especially the rich—can't buy."[22]

If the unemployed are disproportionately leisure-rich and income-poor, time-crunched professional households are in another category: income-rich and leisure-poor. Although there are no specific boundaries to define this group, it is typified by people like Robin or Allie, the woman with the color-coded refrigerator calendar. Neither may consider themselves rich, but as members of dual-income households, they are doing better than most. According to the U.S. Census Bureau, as of 2005 married-couple households made an average of $66,067 a year, a figure over 40 percent higher than the all-households median of $46,326.[23] They are also the households that consider themselves disproportionately time-stressed. By every measure, they are also the ones that have seen the biggest drop in their leisure hours over the past two decades. Between 1970 and 2000, the combined workweek for married couples rose by 10 hours to 63 hours. In 1970 only one in four

22. Williams, Alex. "Pencil It In Under 'Not Happening.'" *The New York Times*, June 18, 2006.

23. DeNavas, Walt, Bernadette D. Proctor and Cheryl Hill Lee. "Income, Poverty, and Health Insurance Coverage in the United States: 2005." U.S. Census Bureau, August 2006.

American married-couple families had two earners, while by 2000, it had risen to one in two. Two-earner families worked an average of 82 hours in 2000, up from about 78 hours in 1970.[24]

The 2005 ATUS data shows the same time crunch for working parents. Compared to the 5.1 hours of leisure for those aged 18 and over seen across the economy, men with children under the age of 18 at home typically had 4.7 hours of leisure a day, while women in the same situation had 4.1 hours. Those with younger children were even more time-crunched. Men with children under six typically had 4.39 hours of leisure, while women had 3.8 hours.

Professional occupations like "investment advisor" or "architect" or "lawyer" are also red flags for signaling a time crunch. According to a study by the American Sociological Association,[25] managers and professionals put in the longest work weeks. As of 2003, more than one in three men in that occupational group worked at least 50 hours a week, compared to about one in five for men in other categories. About one in six women in these occupational groups worked the same long weeks, compared to about one in 14 for all other occupations. This highly skilled cadre is where education levels tend to be the highest, and also where overtime tends to be expected, though not necessarily directly compensated. These days, the longer you went to school, the less leisure you can count on getting. According to the ATUS data, those with less than a high school education typically got 6.3 hours of leisure a day; those with a bachelor's degree or more got 4.3 hours.

It's not hard to think of examples of professions where the norm for working hours has reached incredible standards. In law, for example, what is thought of as an "acceptable" work day has mushroomed over the past few decades, according to Karen MacKay, a member at Kerma Partners, a global consulting firm that specializes in the legal profession. "Twenty years ago, the hardest working associates at New York City law firms were putting in maybe 1,500 billable hours a year," she says. Now, they—and by this I mean the hardest working

24. Gerson, Kathleen and Jerry A. Jacobs. "The Work-Home Crunch." *Context*, Volume 3, No. 4, Fall 2004.

25. Ibid.

associates—are being asked to put in something like between 2,200 and 2,600 billable hours. That means they are easily being asked to work 11-hour days, which was not the norm in the 1970s."

In the tech sector, the 80-hour workweek has long been taken as a given. During the boom years, workers traded in every waking hour for such perks as fully vested stock options, free snacks and the option of bringing their pets to the office. For many companies who got their start a decade or so ago, the majority of their workers were in the early stages of their careers. They were also in a different phase of their lives. Today, five years or more after the dot-com boom collapsed, the picture is a little different. One company, Electronic Arts Inc., recently lost a lawsuit filed by its video programmers, who claimed that they were entitled to overtime pay. The company complied with the ruling, and now pays extra wages, an option apparently preferable to cutting back worker hours. That means that the workers (who as hourly-paid employees have had to sacrifice the bonuses they formerly received) are a little bit richer but as time-crunched as ever. In describing the ruling, one news story noted, "Many tech professionals who began their careers as singles now have families, making them more eager to leave the office in time for dinner at home"[26]—a desire no court could apparently enforce.

But it is not just work hours that have filled up the lives of the income-rich and leisure-poor. The frequent lament is that they have too much to do in general. "We have always considered ourselves time-crunched, even before we had children," says Robin. "A lot of it was work, but I have to admit we were fitting in a lot of fun too. We were making it to the gym every day, and going skiing every weekend. And even now there is some of that in our lives. Steve will tell you he had a 'hectic' summer, but partly that was because he managed to do a lot of sailing."

As the notion of a time bind filled up newspaper lifestyle sections in the 1980s and 1990s, some analysts examined the situation and took a pretty dim view of the whole thing. A decidedly unsympathetic analysis came from University of Texas economists Daniel Hamermesh and

26. Frauenheim, Ed. "More Overtime Tussles for Tech Companies?" www.cnetnews.com. May 17, 2005.

Jungmin Lee. In a paper for the National Bureau of Economic Research published in 2003, they referred to the notion of a time crunch as simply "yuppie kvetch."[27] After looking at data from four countries—the United States, Canada, Australia and Korea—they did not find much to actually refute the idea of a time crunch, but did find it was mostly limited to those in upper income brackets. The reason? The more money you have, the more goods and services you can afford to buy, and the more those things fill up your time.

To use one of their examples, an upper income family may have to juggle arranging home renovations at the same time they are getting ready for a trip to Europe. A poor family simply would not be able to do either of those things. Work played a part, but was not the only driver of time stress. When they looked at the German data, they found that among non-working women, those with rich husbands were more likely to be time stressed than those whose husbands made less money. In all countries, time stress came disproportionately from higher-income, two-earner families. Hence, in their view, the whole time-crunch problem is yuppie whining, and not worth serious consideration in a world where real problems, like poverty, exist. They also suggested that, if anything, people were going to get more stressed in future. After all, as economies expand, there will be more opportunities for people to try new things—whether windsurfing or traveling to China—and those things were going to fill up their calendars even more.

A more charitable way to look at the situation is to acknowledge that while Hamermesh and Lee may have a point, perhaps it is more about general affluence. A generation ago, kids may have had swimming or violin lessons, but families could not routinely put them into swimming and soccer and gymnastics and ballet and junior gourmet cooking and music appreciation all at the same time. It is not necessarily bad that many middle-class children are exposed to all these things now, but it does inevitably mean that parents must spend their time

27. Hamermesh, Daniel S. and Jungmin Lee. "Stressed out on four continents: Time crunch or yuppie kvetch?" NBER Working Paper Series. Working Paper 10186, December 2003.

running their children to these activities. And true, it is a stress that lower income families simply do not have. In Hamermesh and Jungin's study, they found that lower income households were stressed too, but they were stressed, not because they did not have enough time, but because they did not have enough income.

The yuppie kvetch argument goes some way towards explaining why we have fashioned a time-crunch economy, even though more people are apparently stressed over money than are stressed over time. If the most time-crunched households are the most affluent, it stands to reason that they are also the biggest spenders. The data bears that out. According to the U.S. Department of Labor, households headed by someone between the ages of 35 and 44 (households which typically included at least one child and more than one earner) had annual expenditures of $55,190 in 2005. The households with more leisure time typically had less income. Seniors, for example, spent just $32,866.[28] In the eyes of those that market leisure services, leisure time has not been in the "right" hands—not in the income and demographic groups that make a difference. The time crunch, conversely, has been in the hands of the group with the biggest power to buy.

The time-crunched yuppie kvetchers are also the societal leaders. They are the managers and professors and politicians and lawyers and decision makers. Television shows model characters on them, and journalists quote them when they are writing stories. They set the fashion, and at this point in the early 21st century, the fashion they are somewhat reluctantly setting is this: to be time-crunched is the only cool way to be.

ESCAPING FROM THE NEO-LEISURE WORLD

Affluent we may be as a society in North America, but in recent years we have been struggling to hold on to our economic strength and affluence. And so leisure time, at least in its traditional form, has ended

28. "Consumer Expenditures in 2005." U.S. Department of Labor, U.S. Bureau of Labor Statistics, Report 998, February 2007.

up as the bargaining chip we have given up in the fight. In the battle, however, workers have created their own form of stolen leisure, mostly while on their employers' payrolls.

Ironically, much of the phenomenon can be attributed to the same technology that means workers are always "on," whether that means checking their email late at night from home or getting and sending text messages while at the beach. But it works the other way too, as anyone who has ever monitored their Ebay "watch list" at work knows only too well. In a 2000 article, *Fast Company* magazine termed the phenomenon of surfing the Internet and playing solitaire at the office *neo-leisure*. "Neo-leisure, formerly known as goofing off, is what knowledge workers do for R & R . . . It's why bean counters have been trained to check office phone bills for 1-900 phone-sex calls." Neo-leisure also means workers are getting some of their chores done at work. The U.S. National Retail Federation reported that as of 2006, over half of all consumers with Internet access at work planned to do some shopping from their desks.[29]

And so the line between work and home is blurred a bit more; work encroaches into home and home encroaches into work. Although there is no official way to judge whether the overall effect is positive or negative for productivity, no one seems especially happy about the development. Erica is a marketing manager at an insurance company who figures she has no choice but to do some things at work. "Sure I spend gobs of time on the phone figuring out the soccer schedules or whatever," she says. "I take work home, I travel, I stay late—and I have no choice but to do some personal stuff at work."She's a yuppie kvetcher too, a member of a two-earner family that juggles work responsibilities along with getting the kids to all their activities and planning family events and occasional holidays.

But her situation, like that of all those who are time-crunched, is a particular product of time and circumstances. The beginning of the 21st century has begun with a mish-mash of economic events that have effectively created a world where leisure is in short supply for many. It

---

29. "A Spy in the House of Work." *Fast Company*, October 1993, p. 26.

was almost a perfect storm of circumstances that took the time-crunch economy to its peak over the past decade, but those conditions are clearing. The next set of conditions are going to bring us the leisure economy, although just exactly when that happens will depend on how quickly and astutely people eventually figure out that they have traded away their leisure and the price is too high.

TIME OFF FOR GOOD BEHAVIOR

"Yeah I work a lot of hours. In the course of my career, I've been caught in three mergers where people lost jobs, and it had nothing to do with their job performance. The way I see it, it is in my best interest to spend quality time with my BlackBerry."

— *Jim, Management Consultant and baby boomer*
on why he is a workaholic

It is a glorious Friday afternoon on the cusp of autumn and things are quiet at the Oakville Club. The blazing heat of the summer is past and the air is soft; a gentle breeze rustles the surface of the aquamarine pool. The club, a yacht and social organization in the wealthy Toronto suburb of Oakville, is the perfect place to appreciate the beauty of the day as it draws to a close, but unfortunately few seem to be around to do so. A mother and her toddler splash in the pool, and in the bar a few older gentlemen kid each other about their golf games. Around the pool, though, all but one of the umbrella-topped tables sit empty.

To the teenagers folding towels at the side of the pool, the quiet is a welcome respite. They know the peace will not last. Soon, the hordes of baby boomers that make up a chunk of the club's membership will get off the commuter trains carrying them home, and perhaps head there for cocktails and dinner. Others will be working too late to make it on Friday, but on Saturday they'll be splashing in the pool and filling the tennis courts. But what the towel folders do not know is that the afternoon peace will not last much longer either. Soon, when the boomers get off the trains it will be for good. The baby boom is about to parachute into the world beyond work, and when they do, the leisure economy will begin.

THE TIME CRUNCH: A MATTER OF DEMOGRAPHICS

One of the reasons we have become such a leisure-poor society is simply a matter of demographics. As waves of baby boomers entered their adult years and started families, they entered the most leisure-poor time of their lives. With kids to raise and jobs to do, they had limited time to participate in sports or sip drinks in the sunshine. Indeed, that the leisure industry has done as well as it has over the past few decades is something of a minor miracle: the demographics have been firmly against it. As well as being in the leisure-poor years of their lives, the boomer generation has also demonstrated a particular, generational distaste for taking time off. Maybe it has something to do with their sheer size. After all, boomers are such a large generation that they have always effectively competed for what they wanted, and then worked as hard as they could to pay for it. That, in turn, has meant a vicious circle in terms of the time crunch.

As this huge cohort has moved into their busiest years, society in general has become rushed and competitive, and that trend has spread through society just as surely as did their penchant for rock and roll, free love and bell bottoms. As boomers move out of the high-stress years, however, the reverse will happen. A significantly larger proportion of North Americans will soon have more unscheduled time than they have had for decades. Once they get used to that, they'll deem that leisure is cool—and cool it will be.

After all, first-wave baby boomers made a star out of Captain Kangaroo and later made one out of Janis Joplin. Their numbers forced the creation of suburbs for their parents to raise them in, and encouraged the construction of universities where they could be educated. When as a group first-wave boomers converged in their 20s, there was talk of a "youth culture." And, when they hit the labor force in a big way— in high-pressure jobs and often in households where both partners worked—they created what seemed like an economy-wide time crunch. Whatever the boomers have done has tended to define how we see our society, and boomers are now about to define the new leisure economy.

THE AGE–LEISURE EQUATION

If you really want to observe people with all the time in the world, check out preschoolers who are told that it is time to leave the park. "Why do we have to go now?" is the most common response you'll hear, and it is a pretty rational one to come out of a three-year-old's mouth. After all, they don't have to read anything for work the next day or get dinner started or pick up the dry cleaning or anything else. For the most part, their time is their own. They should probably enjoy that time while they can, though, because it certainly will not last. Leisure time fluctuates with age, and the beginning and end of your life is where you tend to get the most of it.

The data from the American Time Use Survey (ATUS)[1] shows the flow of time over a life cycle very clearly. In truth, ATUS data does not include estimates for those who are under the age of 16, but it is not hard to construct a typical day for those in that age group. For the young, most time outside of school is effectively "leisure." Homework and chores take up some time, of course, as does getting to and from school. The rest of the time, however, is pretty much taken up by playing, and perhaps by spending time in organized sports or activities. Of course, there is the debate about over-scheduled children, and perhaps there are those who figure that their lives being shuttled from one soccer field to another are more like work than a life of leisure. But without a job to go to and with summers pretty much free, those under the age of 15 have almost the most leisure-filled lives of anyone.

---

1. The data in the following sections refers to the United States only, primarily because the data is updated annually. Statistics Canada last looked at Canadian leisure time for the General Social Survey conducted in 2005, and prior to that in 1998. Although there are some small variations from the American survey, the Canadian data generally show the same age–leisure correlation.

Those aged from 15 to 24 do pretty well in the area of leisure too. According to the ATUS data, in total they had five hours and 33 minutes of leisure time a day as of 2005. Interestingly, even at this early age, males, with six hours and 14 minutes of leisure, had more time than females, who had about four hours and 52 minutes. Part of the gap likely comes because women in this age group are more likely to be parents (or single parents) and thus spend a disproportionate amount of time in childcare or household activities.

Leisure Over the Life Cycle

Hours of Leisure per Day, by Age

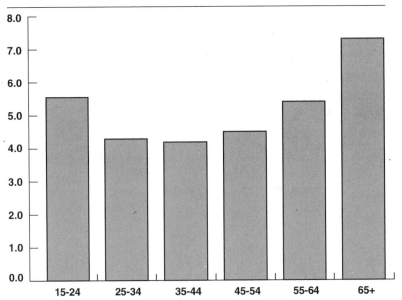

Source: American Time Use Survey, 2005

Get out of school and get a job, though, and you'll see your leisure time evaporate: from the age of 25 onwards, leisure time starts to spiral downwards. For the most part, this is the period of life when work becomes full time and then some. According to the official figures, for the group aged 25 through 34, average leisure hours are four hours and 17 minutes a day, with men getting about four hours and 40 minutes and women getting about three hours and 55 minutes.

Although the leisure estimates sound a bit hefty, they may not be a bad approximation of the time that many in their late 20s have to play with. Jodie is a case in point. A 28-year-old personal trainer who also manages her own gym, it is not unknown for her to put in workweeks of 70 hours. Lots of things get crowded off her busy schedule—as much as she tries to eat healthy food, actually cooking is not something she has the time to do, and scheduling a vacation has turned into a nightmare. At the same time, she is able to make it a priority to spend time with her friends and even play soccer twice a week. "I do that for me," she says. "I'm busy but I don't have kids to take care of so I do have some freedom."

But it may soon be "last call" for her leisured days. According to the ATUS data, those aged 35 through 44 have the worst leisure dearth of any age group. On average, this cohort gets just four hours and 12 minutes of leisure a day in 2005. Women in this category get just about the same as their 25- to 34-year-old counterparts, at about three hours and 55 minutes. Men, however, are more likely to slide into parenthood at this time of their lives, making this the 10-year period when they are likely to have the least time of all: just four hours and 28 minutes a day of leisure.

Not surprisingly, there is a skewed distribution of leisure time between households that have children and those that do not. The divergence shows up in all households, but is especially pronounced for this group. Of all men and women in this age group, those in households with no children under the age of 17 have an estimated 5.66 hours of leisure a day, while those with children have 4.37 hours of leisure. Who are the most time-crunched of all? Working women with children under the age of six. Lisa, the sales manager and mom quoted in the first chapter, would be gratified to find that her own estimate of time off is quite close to what the government says she has in terms of free time. By the ATUS estimates, she has 2.1 hours of "free" time a day on weekdays, almost exactly what she estimates herself.

Based on the age–leisure distribution alone, it is easy to see why North America has become the time-crunch economy. As the baby boomers entered their time-crunch years, over the past few decades the number of people with very little leisure time has grown exponentially.

In 1975, there were about 22.8 million people in the United States aged between 35 and 44—the time-crunched years. By 2000, this demographic had risen to 45.2 million people, an increase of 97 percent. As a percentage of the population, this cohort went from a 10.6 percent share to 16 percent over the time period.[2] All things being equal, a large population that is scrambling to get to work, get home and get everything else done in whatever waking time is left is going to feel time-crunched.

It's not just that the boomers shifted into their crunch years: as they did it, they redefined just how time-crunched a household can be. In 1970, the average number of working hours of a married couple household was 53 hours; by 2000 it had increased to 63 hours.[3] The increase had nothing to do with the length of the average workweek, and everything to do

Population in 'Time Crunch' Years Rose in 1990s

Percentage of U.S. Population Aged 35-54 as % of Total Population

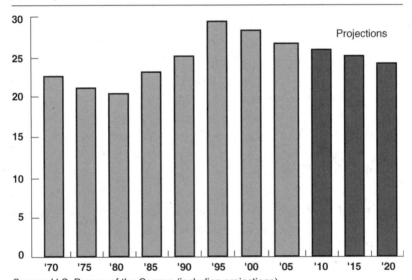

Source: U.S. Bureau of the Census (including projections)

2. U.S. census data (www.census.gov). Calculations are by the author.

3. Gerson, Kathleen and Jerry A. Jacobs. "The Work Home Crunch." *Contexts.* The American Sociological Association. Volume 3, No. 4, Fall 2004.

with the fact that women were entering the labor force in droves. This shift created an attractive target for marketers, particularly since many of the baby-boomer women were working in professions that gave them less time and more disposable income than women had ever seen in the past. Although it is easy to see why the phenomenon hastened the creation of the time-crunch economy, it is also important to realize this was a once-in-a-generation growth phenomenon, and the percentage of the population that holds a job is not likely to grow anywhere near as quickly in future.

Then again, today's time crunch did not come about just because the baby boomers were in a certain age group: it was also created because baby boomers had a certain mindset. Being time-crunched, it could be argued, fit in nicely with the baby boomers' worldview. Indeed, the time crunch is every bit a boomer phenomenon, in much the same way that hula hoops, Barbie dolls and yo-yos once were.

GENERATION: THE DEFINING ROLE

But let's back up from talking about the boomers for a minute. First of all, it is important to establish that there is a strong generational influence on the subject of leisure time—both how much we get, and how much we want. In fact, there is arguably a strong generational influence on everything we do. Our attitudes towards everything, including leisure, are shaped by when we are born, and the economic and other influences to which we are subjected. Authors William Strauss and Neil Howe explored the issue in their book *Generations*, first published in 1991. According to their theory, each of America's generations is one of four archetypes that repeat in sequence—Prophets, Nomads, Heroes or Artists. As they see it, the cycle of history also repeats, going through a cycle they call a "turning," which lasts about 20 years. Each generation gets molded by where they are age-wise when the different events that mark a turning occur. For example, what they call the "GI Generation" was young during the Second World War, which means that they would have come of age trusting and respecting conventional institutions, and consequently develop a respect for team work and civic responsibility.[4]

4. Strauss, William and Neil Howe. *Generations: A History of America's Future*. New York: William Morrow and Company, 1991.

Whether or not you believe that generations repeat over time, it is hard to disagree with one of Strauss and Howe's other points: North America's generations have been shaped by events that have marked the various stages of their lives. For those raised in the Second World War era, a defining moment may indeed have been the bombing of Pearl Harbor or the end of the war. For baby boomers, the defining moments in their early lives would have been different ones—perhaps the flight of the Apollo astronauts, the assassination of JFK, or more likely the advent of a television set into their home. For Generation Y—born since the beginning of the 1980s—their defining generational moment may be the events of 9/11.

What generation you belong to tends to play a role in how much leisure time you get. All things being equal, the bigger a generation, the more they have to compete with each other for resources. If they have to compete in the job market to get entry-level positions, they do so by promising to work harder than their competitors, and then following up. That means a large generation probably will end up with less leisure time than will a smaller one. A larger generation will also have to compete with each other for assets like houses. If they are all clamoring to get into the starter-home market at the same

The Generations

U.S. Population by Age, 2006 (millions)

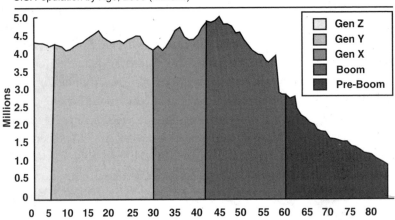

Source: U.S. Census Bureau, author divisions

time, then they will push up the price for starter homes. In turn, that will mean they have to work lots of hours—and hang on to the jobs they have—to pay for them. Leisure will be something of a luxury for them, compared to generations that have an easier time in terms of competition.

PRE-BOOMERS: SETTING THE STAGE

For the generations born before the baby boomers, leisure time was more or less seen as a luxury.[5] For the most part, they led what would now be considered fairly modest lives, where things like vacations and second cars were considered extravagances or treats rather than necessities. Their work lives typically spanned four decades, and they did most household chores rather than contracting them out. Indeed, just the amount of time earmarked for household chores as recently as a few decades ago is eye-opening. In 1965, women between the ages of 18 and 64 were putting in a total of 26.9 hours of housework a week— or about 3.8 hours a day. Frozen foods had made their debut by then, and housewives were also able to take advantage of things like electric washing machines, which were in three-quarters of American homes by 1960.[6] Still, flipping through women's magazines from the 1950s and 1960s, one sees references to products such as Linit perfect laundry starch ("with Linit there are never any spots or streaks ... makes ironing fast, easy!")[7] or Coats and Clark's Sewing Thread ("gives you hours of sewing without rethreading the machine"[8]), which were apparently in common use in the mid-1960s. Both starch and thread are still available, of course, but you will not find them advertised in full-page ads in any mainstream women's magazines today. The number of hours spent doing housework, by the way, had dropped to 21.3 hours

---

5. Exactly where to cut off a generation's birth years is the source of some debate. Using the Strauss and Howe definitions, there are two pre-boomer generations still alive: The "GI Generation" born from 1901 to 1924, and the "Silent Generation" born from 1925 to 1942.

6. Bowers, Douglas E. "Cooking Trends Echo Changing Roles of Women." *A Century of Change in America's Eating Patterns.* USDA, January–April 2000.

7. *Woman's Day.* October 1956, p. 106.

8. *Woman's Day.* May 1956, p. 11.

in 1975 and to 18.7 hours by 1985.[9] By the time of the 2005 survey, the equivalent figure for housework was 12.5 hours.

Still, in the post-war years the time and money that North Americans had for leisure would have startled their grandparents. In 1958, *Life* magazine devoted an entire issue to the subject of "The Good Life," marveling that Americans "now enjoy more discretionary time than any civilized people ever."[10] The memory of Saturday as a workday was still recent enough that *Life* followed two families around as they did chores, errands and shopping, not lamenting the work that had to be done on a weekend, but instead marvelling that "Today, thanks to mass production methods, including automation, the free Saturday morning is pleasant and practical proof that Americans are living better than ever before."[11]

Life also chronicled what was a boom in spending on leisure, which by their estimates had created a $40 billion leisure industry. As calculated by economist Dora Costa four decades later, that spending was taking up an increasing share of family budgets. By her estimates, in 1930, about 3.5 percent of a family's budget was being spent on "recreation." By 1950, this had increased to about 4.5 percent, and it stayed in that range until the early 1970s.[12]

Money spent aside, in many ways the pre-boomer generations have led fairly leisured lives. For one thing, they were predominantly single-earner families, meaning that the extra stress that comes with two working parents was absent from their lives. Second, their children led less structured lives than later generations have done; they were more likely to play ball on the street than to need chauffering to ball tournaments and formal play dates.

In some ways those generations had a fair amount of economic stress in their lives, especially since many were born into or raised

9. Robson, John P. and Geoffrey Godbey. *Time for Life: The Surprising Ways Americans Use Their Time.* University Park, Pennsylvania: The Pennsylvania State University Press, 1997.

10. "Leisure Could Mean a Better Civilization." *Life* magazine. December 28, 1958, p. 62.

11. "Time: Saturday AM, Place: Elm Street." *Life* magazine. December 28, 1958, p. 54.

12. Costa, Dora. "Less of a Luxury: The Rise of Recreation since 1888." National Bureau of Economic Research, NBER Working Paper 6054, June 1997. Costa's data shows that recreation's share of the budget was 3.5% in 1934–35, 4.5% in 1950 and 4.6% in 1972–73.

during the Depression and the War Years. In other ways, however, the pre-boomer generations have had fewer economic difficulties than later generations. To get into the housing market, for example, took significantly less of one's income in 1960 than it does now. In 1963, the median home price in the United States was $18,000, and in 1970 it was $23,400. Converting those figures into 2006 dollars gives estimates of $119,940 and $122,970 respectively—a far cry from the median U.S. new-home price of $225,000 posted in August 2006.[13]

ENTER THE BABY BOOMERS: A SPECIAL CASE

Unlike their parents, the baby boomers have seen a different reality. Born from 1946 to 1964, they are the numerous and infamous generation that has dominated the years following the Second World War. Their choices have set the fashion—and they have predominantly chosen work. To the chagrin of their elders, they grew up taking many things for granted. They got to travel younger and further than the generations before them, and they typically got more education than their parents. They have also acquired a lot more material goods. When boomer couples got married in the 1970s and 1980s, their wedding presents typically included the appliances and luxuries that it took earlier generations a lifetime to acquire. But what the baby boomers have not had much of is leisure time, and they have tended not to ask for it, either.

Work Ethic or Workaholic?

Never mind that baby boomers are now in their most time-crunched years and have been for a couple of decades; if they were more laid back about work and leisure, we probably would not have anything close to the time-crunched economy that we now have. Baby boomers are by nature goal-oriented and work-oriented, and they tend to run the rest of their lives on tight schedules too. No wonder, then, that as they have reached adulthood, they have taken the time-crunch economy into high mode.

---

13. Median home prices come from the www.census.gov/const/uspriceann.pdf. The August 2006 figure is as per the U.S. National Real Estate Association. Historical data was converted to the equivalent in 2006 dollars by using the consumer price index calculator from the U.S. Department of Labor. http://data.bls.gov/cgi-bin/cpicalc.pl.

For whatever reason, baby boomers have turned out to have a strong work ethic. As a generation, they have been asked to make many sacrifices for their jobs, and to a large extent they have done it. "They had the example; then they had the opportunity," says Jordan Kaplan, Associate Professor of Management at Long Island University. "They were given the chance to pursue education and they took it. They became the most educated generation ever. And for others, they also had access to well paying blue collar jobs. The boomers had it pretty good."

In some ways, though, the baby boomers have had to hustle pretty hard to get ahead. As a huge generation, they have had to compete against each other their whole lives. Baby boomers have grudgingly accepted a bundle of other inconveniences, minor and major, from the time that they were born. When they headed to kindergarten, many had to spread out their blankets for quiet time on tiny squares of floor, so as to make room in their overcrowded classrooms. There were always more of them than the resources really provided for. It was no different when they entered the workforce. Although the first-wave boomers generally started work in a robust economy in the late 1960s and early 1970s, they always found themselves up against a wave of other workers in their age group. Subsequent waves of workers, of course, came up against such treats as the 1973 oil shock, inflation and rising unemployment rates, even before they got to the recession of the early 1980s and its aftermath.

An ever increasing workload and a perpetual time crunch were the inevitable results of a work life that has always meant competition. Indeed, if advertisers competed to woo the boomers because of their large numbers, employers always took the opposite tack. There was always another boomer coming along, so employers did not need to compromise much in the way of what they offered employees, particularly those at the entry level.

And boomers took to their jobs with zeal. The word "workaholic" first showed up in 1971 in the book *Confessions of a Workaholic*.[14]

---

14. Oates, Wayne Edward. *Confessions of a Workaholic: The Facts about Work Addiction.* Nashville: Abingdon Press, 1971.

A play on the term "alcoholic" as a way to describe someone addicted to alcohol, it was used by author Wayne Oates to describe his own obsession with work. In the next two decades, it was often used as a way to describe the way that baby boomers approached their work. Over the past two decades, baby boomers have become the workaholics, or at the very least the good soldiers of corporations. They have created the climate where weekend work, 10-hour workdays and putting off vacations has become *de rigueur*, especially for professionals. Just exactly *why* is a subject for debate.

The baby boomers' work style can partly be credited—or blamed—on their parents. Some think they have a strong work ethic because, at least for the first wave of baby boomers, their role models were their Depression-era parents, and that strongly shaped their values. For one thing, they grew up with a fair bit of structure in their lives, typically as the children of traditional families with one breadwinner. First-wave boomers in particular (those born from 1946 through to the end of the 1950s) grew up amidst a booming economy and were told that if they worked hard, success would be theirs. No wonder, then, that they have tended to be an optimistic and hard-working generation. But whatever their early lives might have given them, as they hit the workforce they got hit with some fairly tough economic times. They may have gotten into corporations when they were hiring, but they have also watched layoffs blitz their friends' jobs, or perhaps their own.

As a generation, baby boomers pioneered concepts like two-working-parent households, latchkey kids and high stress. "We went to college, and the expectation was that we'd work," says Jane, 52, a teacher who had her first child in 1977. "But we were kind of in-between any real changes within the household ... our husbands did some stuff at home but not that much." Still, Jane is happy with her career choice, one that at least gave her summers off and a week to spend with her kids during Christmas and Spring holidays. "I saw a lot of my friends leaving for work at 7:00 [in the morning] and getting back home at 6:00 and having to deal with everything. That was not for me."

Boomers at Play

Ironically, as the data quoted in Chapter 1 shows, baby boomers have in some sense had more leisure time than their parents. Their quest to shake off some of the more mundane tasks of everyday life has created many of the time-crunch economy's time savers, from home cleaning services to drive-through fast food. And boomers have definitely spent hefty amounts on the leisure they managed to get. Costa calculates that as of 1991, when the boomers were raising their children, 5.6 percent of family budgets went to spending on recreation, up from 4.6 percent in the early 1970s. Although it is not captured well in these figures, the boomers also ushered in the era of what futurist Faith Popcorn once dubbed "small indulgences," including indulgences in leisure activities. While a middle-income golfer might have been content with middle-of-the-road golf clubs a decade or two ago, boomers who take up golf frequently want something more top-of-the-line.

Travel has also been a big budget item for baby boomers. As the Association of Travel Marketing Executives says, "Boomers consider travel a necessity, not a luxury." As children, their holidays might have consisted of car trips to the beach, but by the time they were young adults the cost of air travel had fallen in real terms, and incomes had increased, too. Accordingly, many took their first trips to Europe as young adults, or at least set out as soon as their budgets would allow. For their parents' generation a trip to the Caribbean may have been an impossible dream unless they were in a certain income class; for the boomers, even those in the middle-income group were able to take advantage of deregulated fares and package holidays to head to the sun. Yes, taking a week or two of leisure may have been a problem, but when they did take it, they made the most of it. "Work Hard, Play Hard," became their mantra.

That focus on travel plays into the "yuppie kvetch" argument mentioned in the previous chapter. As their wealth has grown, many boomers have started to take several vacations a year, some of them of short duration. Each trip has to be planned for and executed, often with the help of the Internet. In one sense, of course, this is quicker than having to visit a travel agent to find a hotel or get airfares; in practice, it often means that consumers devote far more time to finding the perfect hotel (based on reviews posted on any number of websites) and the lowest airfare than they ever did before. Does it result in a better holiday? Quite possibly. Undoubtedly, though, it also means that there are more tasks added to the "to do" list, which adds to the ongoing feeling of time stress that is the main theme among boomers.

Boomers and their Children: The Echo

If baby boomers have felt the need to be competitive at work, that competitiveness and workaholism has also extended into the way they have structured their children's lives. Only too aware of the cutthroat world of work, boomers have been eager to give their "echo boom" children every advantage that may help them succeed. The term "hyper-parenting" is sometimes applied to their tendency to play Mozart to their offspring before they are even born and to prop them up in front of Baby Einstein DVDs soon after. By the time the children are in school, the children and parents are often embroiled in a frantic dance of activities and carpools to get them where they need to be.

"I had my kids in the early 1990s," says Jill, a marketing manager with an MBA. "It was the whole era of 'superwoman' and 'superkids.' I felt so pressured to do it all … including get them to whatever activities they needed to be in. I'd work all week then have to be up to get Caitlin to music at 8:00 on Saturdays, and usually somewhere else after that. The whole thing hit a peak last year when both kids, who are teenagers now, started playing rep soccer. That means six days out of seven we had to get them to something, including practices that were about two hours in length. Either I had to drive them, or I had to arrange the carpool to get them there, which believe me takes just as long."

Atlhough Gen-X parents have picked up on these practices, the "soccer mom" is very much a boomer stereotype—no doubt started with the best of intentions. "In many ways today's parents are the most self-sacrificing ever, willing to sacrifice their personal happiness if that helps their children become "winners,"[15] says Dr. Alvin Rosenfeld, author of

15. Rosenfeld, Alvin. "Stressed, Overscheduled Families." Keynote address delivered to the Adelphi University Institute of Parenting at the First Annual Conference on Effective Parenting. Garden City, New York, June 2, 2006.

The Over-Scheduled Child and an authority in the field. Whether it is a good or bad thing for the children is a separate discussion. Unambiguously though, the "hyper-parenting trend has meant that boomers have in some senses devoted far more time to getting their children from activity to activity than their parents would have dreamt possible.

All in all, these trends have created a generation that is time-poor: too much work, too much commuting and too many activities that have to be scheduled and ticked off the list. As a result we have had a few leisure-poor decades, but the end is in sight.

AGING INTO LEISURE

Baby-boomer aging will be a major force in propelling the time-crunch economy into the leisure economy. Boomer retirements will not hit the economy in a gusher; they will be like a slow trickle that eventually turns into a flood. Right now there are about 77 million baby boomers in the United States. The oldest of them—born from the late 1940s through the early 1950s—are already close to exiting the labor force, or have already done so. As each successive baby boomer retires, a chunk of time gets opened up for leisure pursuits.

As of 2006, baby boomers made up nearly 40 percent of the U.S. labor force.[16] Now in their early 40s to about age 60, they are in senior positions and exercise a great deal of influence in terms of their attitudes. Some even refer to them as the "gray ceiling"—the mass of workers that has been glued in place for years and is preventing those further down the ladder from being promoted. But retirement is looming, and for many it will come quickly. Consider that every eight seconds, a U.S. baby boomer is turning 60. That means that over the course of the next two decades, virtually all boomers in the United States (and in Canada too) will enter the age group typically associated with retirement.

Even for those who are not in the workforce, huge changes lie ahead. For example, many boomers still have children who are teenagers or younger. Over the next two decades, the echo boomers will presumably leave home, or at the very least will no longer need

---

16. Calculated by the author, using the definition years 1946 to 1964, using single-year of age data from the Current Population Survey of the U.S. Bureau of Labor Statistics.

day-to-day support from their parents such as rides to school or meals prepared for them. That means a huge shift in the lives of the boomers will happen within a few years.

Baby-boomer aging alone will mean a big increase in leisure hours, both to the boomers and to the economy as a whole. Just think of how leisure flows over a lifetime. According to the ATUS figures, individuals aged between 45 and 54 were getting about 4.5 hours of leisure a day in 2005. By the time they hit the 55 to 64 age group, it grew to 5.4 hours, and by 65 plus it spiraled up to 7.3 hours. Assuming that those estimates of leisure are reasonable for the future, you can get an idea of how much extra leisure time is going to be dumped on the economy over the next couple of decades as the baby boomers reach the end of their working lives. Between 2005 and 2015, all things being equal, total leisure hours in the United States will rise by about 12 percent. Leisure hours for those aged 55 to 64 will grow by 33 percent, and for those aged 65 plus by 28 percent. The leisure gains will continue for another decade after that. Between 2015 and 2025, total leisure hours in the United States will grow by a further 11 percent. At this point, the

Leisure Hours are Set to Soar

Total U.S. Hours Spent on Leisure Activities (billions)

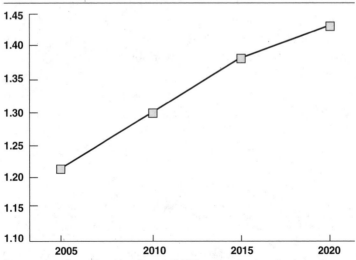

Source: American Time Use Survey (2005) and projections by the author

increases are firmly for the over-65s. In that cohort, leisure hours will grow by 36 percent over the decade, while they will increase 2.5 percent for the 55- to 64-year-old group.[17] Any business person who wants to be ahead of the curve would do well to read the signs. It's time to stop catering to the time-crunch economy and prepare for the leisure economy—the baby boomers are about to get time off for good behavior.

Then again, boomers have always defied straight-line forecasts, and on the subject of leisure hours that may also be the case. Since they did not behave like other generations through the earlier part of their lives, they are unlikely to be carbon copies in retirement either. One major difference is that boomers typically had children later than did earlier generations, and many divorced and created second or even third families. That means that although almost all earlier generations had raised their children by the time they turned 65, many boomers will still have financial obligations to younger children. According to a survey by Pew Research, as of 2005 about half of all boomers were raising one or more young children and/or providing primary financial support to one or more adult children. In addition, another 17 percent of boomers with children over the age of 18 were providing some financial support to them. That's an important point: with today's 20-somethings now more likely than in the past to be burdened by college or other debt, boomer parents may be on the hook to provide their children financial support for significantly longer than was true for earlier generations, meaning that they may be inclined to stay in the workforce longer.[18]

And even assuming their children end up eventually supporting themselves, boomers may still have difficulty paying for their own retirements. Just how well the boomers are set up for retirement is covered in depth in Chapter 5. For now, it's enough to say that there are huge disparities in retirement wealth between boomers. Some boomers

---

17. Unless otherwise noted, all projections are by the author and have been generated using data from the American Time Use Survey and population projections from the U.S. census bureau. Projections were generated by holding constant time use by age estimates and using them as coefficients. These coefficients were then applied to projections of population by age calculated by the U.S. Census Bureau (base case projection). The resulting calculations show the total number of leisure hours for each demographic cohort.

18. "From the Age of Aquarius to the Age of Responsibility." Pew Research Center, December 8, 2005.

may indeed have to work past 65. Then again, many boomers who can afford to retire routinely profess a desire to keep working. According to a survey done by Challenger, Gray and Christmas, as of 2006, 70 percent of baby boomers planned to work beyond the age of 65.

But even taking all of these factors into account, there is every reason to believe that the baby boomers will indeed retire over the next two decades, even if they go kicking and screaming into a retirement that is less well-financed than many would have liked. Indeed, some first-wave boomers have already retired. According to a study by the U.S. Congressional Budget Office, as of 2004, over 4 million U.S. baby boomers had already left the labor force, some because they were disabled, but others simply because they had the means and could. By their estimates, if boomers continue to follow the pattern set by the oldest of their generation, approximately one-third of boomer men and about half of boomer women will have exited the U.S. labor force by their 62nd birthdays.[19]

Maureen and Paul are typical of the trend. They started their careers as typical baby boomers with conventional careers: she as a journalist and then a PR specialist, he as an urban planner. They traveled a bit for their work, at one point heading to Canada's North for Paul to take a planning contract. In general, they found success in their fields. In the 1980s, when both were in their early 40s, they decided to switch tacks and go into business for themselves, opening a store that specialized in high-end linens. Despite fighting through two business-cycle downturns, the store did well and they were able to add to their retirement stash. And so they decided to do just that: retire. To their surprise, they like the retired life very much, perhaps more than they ever imagined. These days Maureen is involved in volunteer work, writing press releases for a charitable organization, and Paul is able to spend more time on home renovations, a passion that had been put on hold for a few decades. "I enjoy doing PR work much more now than I did a few decades ago," says Maureen. "It's for an organization I believe in, and I enjoy the work."

---

19. Smith, Ralph. "Disability and Retirement: The Early Exit of Baby Boomers from the Labor Force." Congressional Budget Office, November 2004.

Like Maureen, other baby boomers are likely to enter the next stage of their lives filling their calendars with lots of activities, which, of course, brings up another point: there is a fine line between having lots of time and no longer being time-crunched. Unlike the retired from earlier generations who alternated hobbies and activities like running errands and enjoying their grandchildren, boomers may indeed create a different kind of time bind for themselves, simply because they are used to it. But it will be a gentler time crunch, one less focused on getting the work done to pay the mortgage and getting the kid to soccer and picking up the other kid from karate and making everyone's lunch for the next day. Maureen is a case in point. "It's a very busy life and a very relaxed one too, if that's possible." Apparently it is possible, and this new lifestyle lies ahead for a very large and influential part of the population.

MAKING LEISURE COOL

If the baby boomers are doing it, then you can bet that they are going to market it as the cool thing to do. That was true when they were driving Ford Mustangs in the 1960s and when they moved into minivans in the 1980s. It is still true about how they view their music choices. Teenagers desperately looking for the latest music on the radio are barraged with oldies stations that still play boomer favorites from the 1960s and 1970s. No wonder so many teens have eschewed radio altogether and stick to their iPods!

The boomers, after all, have set trends their whole lives. For several decades, their lifestyles have been the ones the media have promoted and told us to emulate. Not to mention that the boomers' influence has been amplified over the past decade as they have moved into their power years. Bill Clinton, elected in 1992, was the first baby-boomer president, and George W. Bush is a boomer too, as are Canadian Prime Minister Stephen Harper and British Prime Ministers Tony Blair and Gordon Brown. So are Katie Couric, Michael Jordan, Bill Gates, Oprah Winfrey, Tom Hanks, Jay Leno, Condoleezza Rice, Hillary Clinton, Prince Charles, filmmaker Michael Moore, musician Bono and Federal Reserve Chairman Ben Bernanke. Although not every famous boomer is known for his or her workaholic tendencies, those that are not have frequently met with criticism. George W. Bush, a baby boomer who has dared to take frequent vacations, has met with frequent unflattering comparisons to his predecessor, the workaholic boomer stereotype, Clinton.

But Bill Clinton is semi-retired now. Although still extremely busy with speeches and charity work, the former president has already raised his child and put his most challenging job behind him. He will soon be followed by successive waves of boomers, the youngest of whom are now in their early 40s (the baby boom ended around 1964) as they move into their high-leisure years. Microsoft Chairman Bill Gates is moving towards retirement from his main job and has made it clear that he will be spending his leisure time concentrating on philanthropy through his charitable foundation. Other boomers are trickling out of the labor force too, and are making their own choices as to how to spend their new leisure.

A commercial for make-up in the 1970s used to show a harried young career woman rushing through a brutal day at the office. "Who has time for touch-ups at lunch?" asked the voice-over, praising the staying power of the particular brand of liquid foundation. "Who has time for lunch?" If you did, was the intoned message, you were out of sync with how things were done. Now, that same generation will soon have time for lunch—or for charity work, or anything else they want to do.

And perhaps it is important to realize that the definition of leisure, which has meant different things over time, will evolve once again as the boomers leave their working lives. The time-crunch economy will still live on in some ways; retiring boomers may still be as time-crunched as ever as they juggle golf games or book clubs or head up volunteer organizations. The leisure economy may dredge up images of scores of people stretched out on a hammock, immersed in a good book as they sip lemonade. And although that may be part of the new reality, let's not forget that the leisure economy will be mostly defined and crafted by the baby boomers. It will be a unique invention influenced by a generation that has always had a big impact on the economic times in which they live: the leisure economy is more likely to be one part time crunch and one part hammock.

IN PRAISE
OF SLACKING

I get home most lunch hours and I take a couple of days a week off.
I spend a lot of time with my kids and that's the way it should be. If
you have to work a zillion hours a week to prove you're cool then I'm
really un-cool ... slacking is good.

> — *Jeff, optometrist and Gen Xer, explaining why he*
> *is not a workaholic*

"Well, maybe we are kind of a lazy demographic," says 29-year-old
Melissa, only half in jest. "I mean, I see boomers who have had to work
really, really hard to get where they are. We can kind of just be."

As a project manager for a non-profit organization, Melissa is
acutely aware that she has been blessed: finding a job has never been
particularly difficult for her. She took a little time off after high school,
trying out various jobs in the hospitality sector, mostly in places that
offered good skiing. Her first post-college position was working for a
politician, and when she felt she had gone as far as she could with
that, she segued into her current job. She's bright and educated,
but she knows she owes her good fortune to more than her bubbly

personality. Born late into Generation X, Melissa has been part of a fortunate demographic group, one that is small enough to not have faced massive competition in the job market.

Still, she is not using her post-boomer freedom to get rich. In fact, living as she does in Vancouver, a booming city with one of the tightest housing markets in North America, she does not have much cash left over after paying the rent. But as much as she thinks the kind of job that gives you a signing bonus would be nice, she figures she has something better: the ability to intersperse her work life with large doses of leisure. Driving a couple of hours takes her to Whistler-Blackcombe—a mountain resort so magical that it has been chosen as the home of some of the Winter Olympic events in 2010. There, she is able to put balance in her life, which has certainly become a casualty of the time-crunch economy. Lifestyle is important to her and if it takes a few trade-offs to get the life she wants, she's happy to make them.

Welcome to the leisure economy, a place that is already taking shape thanks to the generations born after the baby boom. Whether we talk about Generation X, those that directly followed the boomers, or Generation Y, those that have been born since the 1980s, we are dealing with a slice of the population with a very different outlook than the generation that preceded them. Already they are demanding that their lives be about more than work. As they become ascendant in the workforce, they will shape work to be more in sync with their beliefs than the baby-boomer workplace they have inherited. While they're at it, they may dismantle other parts of the time-crunch economy too.

THE SLACKER GENERATION(S)

If the boomers have been the workaholics of corporations, the generations that followed them have been tagged by a less flattering moniker: the Slacker Generations. Although the term was originally used to describe Generation X, some managers have been only too happy to extend it to Generation Y as well. "It's like pulling teeth to get them to work a Saturday," says Janice, the baby-boomer manager of a high-end spa that has an endless client demand for manicures and pedicures on the weekend. She's frustrated by what sometimes seems like apathy on the part of newly hired aestheticians, many of whom are culled from Generations X and Y. "I work weekends. My other aestheticians work weekends. Getting one off is a big deal, but they want them off all the time," she fumes. And perhaps it is telling that for many in the post-boom generations, the slacker moniker is not even that off-putting. "Boomers have had so much to prove, especially some boomer women," shrugs Melissa, the project manager for a non-profit. "I know I work hard, even if it's not on their terms."

Generation X (1965–1976)

To understand how things got to this point, we have to rewind the tape and look at economic history first. Let's start with Generation X. Actually defining when this generation started is a bit tricky. Although the term "Generation X" had been used a bit prior[1] to its popular use, it was Douglas Coupland's 1991 novel, *Generation X: Tales for an Accelerated Culture*,[2] that made the term a household one. At the time, Coupland was referring to the last wave of baby boomers, those who were too young to remember the glory of the 1960s protests and who by and large tended to resent the huge baby boom and their influence. Coupland's Gen Xers were basically baby boomers, those born from 1958 to 1964 in the United States or through to 1966 in Canada (the Canadian baby boom ended later than the U.S. one).

There are many other definitions, though, of when this generation's birth years began and ended. In *Generations*, Strauss and Howe put the birth years of this generation from 1961 to 1981, based on the cultural events that define them, rather than when births peaked and ebbed. Economist and demographer David Foot, author of *Boom, Bust & Echo: Profiting from the Demographic Shift in the 21st Century*, calls the last wave of the baby boom, those born between 1960 and 1966, "Generation X,"

---

1. Wikipedia. The term "Generation X" originated in 1964, when a filmmaker named Jane Deverson conducted a series of interviews of teenagers for *Woman's Own* magazine in Britain. It then resurfaced in 1976, when it became the name of a punk rock band featuring Billy Idol (the band disbanded in 1981). Douglas Coupland first used the term in 1997, for an article in *Vancouver* magazine.

2. Coupland, Douglas. *Generation X: Tales for an Accelerated Culture*. New York: St. Martin's Press, 1996.

emphasizing the fact that while the number of births was still high during those years (in contrast to the following decade), this birth cohort has had a very different life experience than the boomers had. (Foot refers to those who were born from 1967 to 1979 as "the baby bust," because they represent the years when birth rates plummeted). Others have different definitions. Consulting company Rainmaker Thinking Inc. defines Generation X as spanning the years from 1965 to 1977; Yankelovich Partners, another large consumer research company, says it is 1965 to 1978. Claire Raines, CEO of Generations at Work Inc. and the author of *Connecting Generations*[3] puts the Gen X boundaries at 1960 to 1980. For the purposes of this book, Generation X is assumed to start in 1965, and to end in 1976 when births started to ebb. Any definition of Generation X is arbitrary, but the end points more or less capture the grimness of the Generation X birth years. The Gen Xers were born after the first couple of waves of boomers and their we-can-change-the-world mentality, and before Gen Y with their slightly different brand of optimism.

GENERATION X (1965–1976)	GENERATION Y (1977–1999)
Cynical	Indulged
Watched their parents get laid off	Diverse
Never welcomed into the labor market	The dot-com generation
Wary of the 'gray' ceiling	Optimistic—with less to prove
Team-work oriented	than boomers or Xers
Family oriented	Praise-driven
About to be promoted—and not sure they want to be	Want a life!

Unlucky and Cynical

Everyone seems to agree that Generation X has not been the most fortunate of generations. Strauss and Howe dubbed them "The Thirteenth Generation," partly because they were indeed the thirteenth since

---

3. Raines, Claire. *Connecting Generations*. Menlo Park: Crisp Learning, 2003.

American independence, but also because they have tended to be a bad luck generation on many scores. Foot, too, agrees with Coupland and Strauss and Howe that those born in these years have tended to be unlucky in their economic prospects. Coming after the waves of earlier boomers, they have faced everything from housing prices that have been bid up to unprecedented highs to a labor market that has typically not been that enthusiastic about making space for them. In Coupland's book, the main character is a university educated but marginally employed 25-year-old named Kevin who is part of a circle of young people who are income-poor and cynical about the world around them. Although Coupland himself later tried to distance himself from some of the generalizations that later sprang up around Generation X, he was definitely on to something with his characterization.

Much more so than the baby boomers, Gen X got caught in some harsh economic realities at the beginning of their careers. Those who entered the labor market in the 1980s did so in a decade when the North American economy was bookended by two severe economic recessions. As a result, Gen X developed a thick skin about economic reality that was sometimes labeled as cynicism. The television series *Friends*, which debuted in 1994, had a theme song that was meant to capture the angst of a generation: "Your job's a joke, you're broke, your love life's DOA," sang the pop group, the Rembrandts.

From Divorce to Family First

In other ways too, Generation X has encountered challenges that the boomers by and large did not. More than any other generation before them, they were likely to grow up with divorced parents or with two working parents and the experience of being latchkey kids. As a result, many Gen Xers want to approach parenthood differently by making more time for their children and making sure there is always one parent at home. They are sometimes called the Family-First Generation. "These were the kids of the earliest boomers and from day one you saw surveys with them saying stuff like 'If I had kids I'd spend more time with them than my parents did,'" says Claire Raines. "It's no surprise that you look around now and it's family, family, family." Jennifer, a corporate lawyer who dropped out of the workforce in order to spend more time with her children, concurs. "My mom was a hairdresser, and she worked all the time … evenings, weekends, whatever. We were total latchkey kids. So sure, that did factor into my decision to be home."

Like the characters on *Friends*, who by the end of the series had hit their 30s and were not in loser jobs anymore, Generation Xers are now headed for the mid-point of their careers, and are within a few years of their power years, when they will replace retiring boomers in the most senior roles within their organizations. That shift will be complemented by the fact that the workers they will be managing will come mostly from Generation Y.

Generation Y (1977–1999)

Generation Y is the group that might catapult North America into the leisure economy. It is significant that Generation Y had its origins in 1976. It was a notable year. Flags waved throughout the United States as the country celebrated its bicentennial, marking its 200th year of independence from Britain. The Concorde began flying from New York to Europe, and in a daring raid, Israeli commandos rescued hostages from Entebbe, Uganda. In entertainment, *Rocky* was the top grossing movie and *Charlie's Angels* made a mega star out of a toothy blonde named Farrah Fawcett-Majors. In Canada, the CN Tower in Toronto opened—and another cultural icon, the Eaton's department store cata-logue, was discontinued.

Not generally noted in the "it happened when" summaries is the advent in 1976 of a company called Gymboree Play and Music. It began as a sort of organized form of indoor play for children. For a fee, parents could enrol young children—still in diapers—for classes. The concept worked. By 1986 Gymboree entered the retail market, manufacturing and selling high-end clothing for children aged seven and under. The previous generation of parents were happy to clothe their children in generic jeans and shorts from department stores and take them to play in a park. This company tuned in to the needs of these new boomer parents, whose children sported distinctly pricier merchandise from lines with names like "Forget Me Not" or "Country Club" and enjoyed mind-enhancing, carefully choreographed fun—provided by Gymboree, of course.

Enter Generation Y. Gymboree was one year ahead of the trend: Generation X births were officially finished in 1976, and Generation Y (sometimes called "The Millennium Generation" or "The Echo Boom") births began in 1977. Largely the children of the baby boomers, this is the group that has been brought up with lots of self-esteem (too much, say some recent evaluations), lots of activities and a huge appreciation of what technology can provide for them in terms of improving efficiency. They are what writer Don Tapscott in 1997 termed "Generation Net," a wave of people who not only grew up as likely to work a computer mouse as a telephone, but to navigate everything from DVD players to BlackBerries to iPods. They programmed their parents' VCRs for them, so they have no illusions about the tech savvy (or deficit) of older generations.

Educated and Diverse

As a group, Generation Y is extremely educated. Among the baby boomers, many had the experience of being the first in their families to go to college; not so for Generation Y, which has grown up viewing college attendance as the norm. As of 2003, 64 percent of U.S. women and 60 percent of U.S. men headed for college after high school graduation, and 85 percent of them attended full time.[4] But making generalizations is a bit tricky when it comes to Generation Y. As a group, they are diverse, ethnically as well as in attitude: in the United States, one in three is not Caucasian. Still, like every other generation, they have experienced common life events that give them a sense of cohesion as a generation. They have many characteristics in common, some of which are still being uncovered by the marketers and academics that are at work trying to figure out what makes this generation tick.

---

4. "The Millenials: Americans Born 1977 to 1994." U.S. Census Bureau, 2002.

Tech Savvy and Then Some

Generation Y's familiarity with and respect for technology tops the list of what Generation Y is all about. Unlike Boomers, or even Xers, Gen Y would be hard-pressed to tell you when they first touched a computer. They have embraced and picked up how to use every technological innovation that has come their way, usually faster than their parents. On the plus side, that has tended to make them adaptable and accepting of change on a wide scale. On the down side, it has not made them patient. Instant messaging and cell phones with their instant gratification have not made them very good at waiting. Some think that characteristic also makes them less likely to want to pay their dues in the labor market. Senator Hillary Clinton perhaps united a generation of baby boomers, whatever their political affiliation, when she asserted in a June 2006 speech: "We have a lot of kids who don't know what work means. They think work is a four letter word … (kids) think they're entitled to go right to the top with a $50,000- or $75,000-a-year job, when they've not done anything to earn their way up."[5] Although the Senator later took back some of her remarks, prompted in part by an admonition from her own Gen Y daughter, her remarks were an accurate reflection of the thinking of many baby-boomer managers.

Super-Parented or Spoiled?

In many ways, Generation Y is a very spoiled generation. True, like Generation X, they have only just entered the workforce—long after the myth of lifetime employment had been destroyed. Still, as the children of the baby boomers, they have enjoyed many luxuries—everything from Gymboree clothing to $45 logo tees and $20 flip-flops hawked by Abercrombie & Fitch. Their parents have been super involved in their upbringing and in all aspects of their lives. This is the group whose overscheduled lives ate up their parents' free time as they were shuttled from place to place and activity to activity. They have gotten to try a lot of things, and as a result, they tend to be more confident and optimistic than the two generations that preceded them. Parental

---

5. Clinton, Hillary. Speech to the U.S. National Chamber of Commerce, May 2006.

involvement may be a large part of that: many of these young people feel that their parents will always be there to back them up.

"They were taught they were special from the word go," says Claire Raines. "And the way that their parents are still involved in their lives is crazy—the 'helicopter parent' thing. For example, a lot of college kids have cell phones with a local number, and their parents take advantage of that to talk to them a couple of times a day. And it is not a myth—we have people in their 20s, who, when they run into problems at work, have their parents calling their supervisors."

That overwhelming attention and care by their parents has sometimes earned Gen Y the moniker of being lazy, a term that even some members of the generation do not dispute. "Yes, I think we're a lazy generation," says Ashley, 25, an esthetician. "I'm not, and my boyfriend's not, but let me tell you, my friends are. Their parents have always given them everything. I know one guy who keeps getting laid off from jobs he's basically responsible for losing, and his parents keep letting him live at home and giving him money. I have another who gets his beer delivered to him. They sit on the couch, and let other people—me—make their plans for them, even though everyone's got three phones or whatever, and then they'll go out. And it's a good thing everyone has a car—and they all do—or else they'd have to get public transit to get places and believe me they'd never leave their houses in that case."

Christine, 21, a university student, agrees that her peers are lazy. "It gives me an advantage actually, because I'm the same age but I have a different work ethic. But they are so lazy ... they have a real sense of entitlement. I guess we've all had our parents very involved in our lives and we kind of all know that they're there for backup. For some people that has really destroyed their sense of responsibility."

Whatever words best describe Gen X—unlucky, cynical, family-oriented—and Gen Y—tech savvy, educated and spoiled—they are totally different from the best words to characterize the baby boomers. The Slacker Generations' attitudes towards leisure have already shaken up the work world a bit, and they are set to shake it up much more in the years go to come.

THE SLACKERS GO TO WORK

Generation X wants "a life" and has made a few strides towards getting one; Generation Y wants a life and fully expects their employers to give them time off to pursue one. No wonder, then, that baby boomers in the workplace are confused by the picture they see around them. Somewhere along the line there was apparently a shift in values that made the subsequent generations want different things from their lives and their workplaces. As Generations X and Y move into their power years, they may well shape the workplace into something more akin to their values.

Gen X at Work

Generation X's attitude towards leisure is all about their economic history. They entered the workforce in the late 1980s and early 1990s, and the economy was less than welcoming. The recession of the early 1980s was a deep one, and even when the economy recovered, many industries were wary about taking on more staff, particularly those at the entry level. For many Gen Xers, that meant a prolonged period of not being in the kind of job they wanted to be in or anything close to it. Even for those who did make their way into corporations, the atmosphere was a grim one. "When they walked into their workplaces, they saw baby boomers who had been there for years being let go and everyone being told, 'It's time to get lean and mean.' Historically, they were the first generation to know right from the start of their careers that job security did not exist," says Carolyn Martin, principal with management training firm Rainmaker Thinking and the author of *Managing the Generation Mix: From Urgency to Opportunity.*[6]

It was the start of a new era in the workplace. Generation X may not have had much choice but to blend into the prevailing culture in the workplace, but they had a different agenda. When management guru Tom Peters wrote an article called "The Brand Called You" in *Fast Company* magazine in 1997,[7] his message was lapped up by Gen Xers

6. Martin, Carolyn A. and Bruce Tulgan. *Managing the Generation Mix: From Urgency to Oppourtunity*, 2nd Edition. Amherst: HRD Press, 2006.

7. Peters, Tom. "The Brand Called You." *Fast Company*, August 1997, p. 83.

who wholeheartedly agreed with him: "Today in the age of the individual you have to be your own brand." With perhaps limited success, Gen X asked for flexibility in the workplace, for telecommuting, for the opportunity to take leaves from work. "Gen X understood that the paradigm of work for however many years, followed by go into retirement and your leisure years, was over," says Martin. "They looked at jobs as a 'value transaction'—they started wanting to find the best deal for them as well as the best deal for the company."

Generations in the Workplace, 2006

U.S. Labor Force by Single Year of Age, 2006

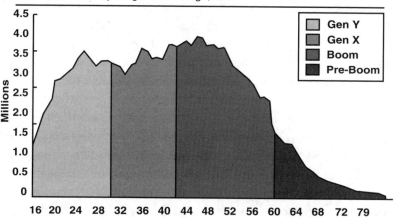

Source: U.S. Current Population Survey, author divisions

But if Generation X has wanted to create a different kind of workplace from the one they inherited, they have had limited means with which to do it. The first part of their work lives has happened against the backdrop of a traumatic time for the North American labor economy, one that has contained everything from massive industrial restructuring to a meltdown in the stock market. In addition, Xers have had a hard time making it into managing positions, blocked by the wave of baby boomers just above them. That's set to change: now, Generation X accounts for 27 percent of the U.S. labor force, compared to 40 percent for the boomers.[8] As boomers retire, however, Generation X will ascend in the labor force and will be able to bring their own values to the table.

Gen Y at Work

Generation Y has experienced a different reality than Generation X in the job market. By and large, they have grown up not just knowing decent economic times, but have also been told that the world has in fact been waiting for them. This is partly because of the way that their parents raised them, of course, but it is also because of the demographic realities. The aging of the baby boom as a phenomenon has been well understood since Gen Yers were toddlers. As a result, they have frequently been assured that there would be jobs for them, and indeed, for many, that has been true of their first forays into the labor market. The surge in service jobs during the 1990s, for example, has meant that many had no problem getting part-time positions while they were in school. Despite the turmoil in the economy following 9/11, new graduates were also fortunate enough to enter a U.S. labor market that was relatively welcoming. In contrast to previous economic cycles, the U.S. unemployment rate did not rise sharply with the decline in the economy, and young adult Gen Yers, with their brand new degrees, found that there was decent demand for their skills. It was a similar situation in Canada, which for the first time in memory did not slow along with the U.S., and in fact created a record number of jobs in the post–9/11 years.

So perhaps it should not be a surprise that newly minted Generation Y graduates tend to be pretty picky about what they want in a job. Heading into a job market with unemployment rates for college graduates at around 2 percent,[9] they know they have some bargaining power.

8. Based on data from the Current Population Survey, U.S. Bureau of Labor Statistics, which uses the birth years of 1946 to 1959 for the baby boomers, and 1960 to 1979 for Generation X. It should be noted that the data from the Bureau of Labor Statistics is available in five-year increments, meaning that the baby boomer estimates encompassed labor force participants from the age of 46 through 60, rather than the correct 47 through 61, while Generation X estimates were for labor force participants 26 through 45, rather than the correct 27 through 46.

9. According to the Bureau of U.S. Labor Statistics, the unemployment rate for college graduates was 1.8 percent as of October 2006. U.S. Bureau of Labor Statistics, Current Population Survey.

Universum, a research and consulting firm, conducted a survey of 29,046 undergraduates in the 2006 academic year. Recent grads, apparently wanted a lot more from their employers than any other graduating class in the 11-year history of the survey. (In 2006, graduates would have been born in the mid-1980s, making them firmly Generation Y. The early years of the survey would have included Generation X). This first wave of Gen Y frequently asked about health insurance and retirement plans, something new grads were not apt to do just a few years ago.

"They run spreadsheets on benefits," says Kate, a college liaison manager for a major financial services company. "It's unreal—and it's very different from what we saw a decade ago. There is this incredible sense of entitlement. Just in the past few years, we have had a real problem of people saying 'yes' to us then rescinding the offer because they found something better. I know it's a strong statement to say this, but even a few years ago graduates had more personal integrity. And we are seeing it everywhere—there is no difference between California or Iowa or Massachusetts."

Melissa, the non-profit manager mentioned at the beginning of the chapter, admits that she is pretty fussy about what makes a job acceptable to her. "I want to give a lot of input as an employee," she says. "I want a job where I can continue to learn, and to keep being stimulated and challenged." A study by Deloitte Human Resources[10] reiterates that this is a priority. "Gen Y believes it can learn quickly, take on significant responsibilities and make major contributions far sooner than baby boomers think." Houston Brown Manager of Graduate Recruitment for Shell Oil in Texas agrees: "That's the biggest challenge we have with Generation Y ... have to keep them challenged or they're unhappy, but you do have to teach people a few things before they are really able to do all they want to."

According to that 2005 study by Deloitte Human Resources, Gen Yers have very different priorities from the generations that preceded them. Their ease with technology has made them believe that work can

---

10. "Connecting Across the Generations." Deloitte Human Resources. Talent Market Series, Volume 1, 2005.

be done anywhere, and that what counts should be the final product, not face time. The study did not find that Generation Y was more likely than other generations to want to leave their employers particularly quickly. Instead, it found: "They want long-term relationships with employers, but on their own terms. The 'real revolution' is a decrease in career ambition in favour of more family time, less travel and less personal pressure."[11]

And there it is in a nutshell: Generation Y treasures their leisure time. Recruitment managers are dazed by just how far some take that desire for work–life balance. "They care about this a lot," says Kate. "I had one candidate—and I'm not making this up—tell me that if I couldn't guarantee that he'd be out of the office every day for 4:30, he wasn't interested." Those companies that have initiated programs to provide work–life balance often find that they have a big carrot with which to attract Gen Y graduates. "It's very competitive to get the right people, and the fact that we as a company embrace the work–life issue is a strong selling point for us," says Houston Brown. "We have a program where every second week people take Fridays off by working nine hours a day Monday to Thursday. Managers do it too. That's very popular with Generation Y."

The myth of lifetime employment having been destroyed long before they set up their first lemonade stands (supervised carefully by anxious parents who ensured the operations were set up safely away from the road), Generation Y seems more likely than either the boomers or Generation X to chuck their jobs, if necessary, to glean a bit of leisure. "Generations before them, studies have shown, valued tenure and career advancement," wrote Anna Bahney in *The New York Times* in June 2006. "But this group sees the chutes in the world as interesting as the ladders."[12]

"I think one thing making quitting easier for us is that we do have less loyalty to our employer than our parents' generation did," says Ella, 26, who works serving coffee, despite having a degree. "We saw

---

11. Ibid.

12. Bahney, Anna "A Life Between Jobs." *New York Times*, June 8, 2006.

them get laid off, have their plant close down, or whatever, and [so we] have a healthy sense of watching out for ourselves instead of giving everything to the company and expecting something in return. And I do think there is this myth that we will always be able to find another job. I say myth because I don't believe it. I do think our economy is struggling, jobs are disappearing, and college graduates are way too educated for the positions that are open, but a lifetime of hearing 'you'll have no problems finding a job' made an impression and now we're failing to wake up to reality."

It is partly in order to manage their time—and especially their leisure time—that Generation Y is apt to give entrepreneurship a try. *The Boston Globe* has reported that among graduates from affluent colleges like Harvard and Carnegie Mellon, 30 to 40 percent end up starting their own businesses within five years of graduation.[13] However, for now, Generation Y has not been able to wholeheartedly head for entrepreneurship, in part because of the start-up costs, and especially the cost of providing health insurance. A 2003 study by the U.S. Bureau of Labor Statistics found that as of 2003 only 1.9 percent of workers under the age of 25 were self-employed, although the figure jumped to 5.3 percent for those aged 25 to 34. As they age and build up some resources, more and more may choose to go this route.

"I think of myself as having an incredibly strong work ethic," says Jeannie, a make-up artist who chooses to juggle freelance work rather than take a full-time job in her field. "I've been out on jobs the last few weekends. Sometimes I'll take an early morning assignment at a television station then head out again in the afternoon and keep going until into the evening. It can be crazy." When asked why she has chosen freelance work, a look of almost guilty recognition spreads over her face. "Ah," she says, "well I guess that has to do with my leisure time. My passion is really riding horses—I did [ride horses] from the time I was nine—basically after nine years of begging for riding lessons—through to the time I finished school. Then I knew I had to make a living but I wanted to make sure I could ride

<hr />

13. "The Ladder Isn't the Only Way Up." www.bostonworks.com. February 19, 2006.

in the summers without anyone telling me I couldn't get the time I wanted off."

The focus on work–life balance is shaking up some of those professions that have traditionally been the most rigid about working hours. In 2004 a survey of lawyers conducted by professional services consulting firm, Edge International, asked those aged 25 to 30 to look at a list of 17 "motivators" ranging from "autonomy" to "financial reward" to "security" and rate them according to importance. Not surprisingly, "Developing as Professionals," "Opportunity for Advancement" and "Job Security" took three of the top four spots, but none made the top of the list. That honor went to "Time for a Personal Life," which was cited by one in three associates in North America as extremely important. When partners were asked how important "time for a personal life" was to the associates they worked with most closely, only one in five saw it as extremely important, compared to one in 2.4 associates worldwide.

The medical profession is seeing this shift in priorities too. In an article for the *Group Practice Journal*, authors Carol Westfall, President of search firm Cejka Search, and attorney John Powers examined the way that, in their words, "times are a changing in the medical profession." Speaking to older physicians hoping to find the right graduates to take over their practices, Westfall and Powers admonish the older physicians to back away from the view that because they "paid their dues" when starting out that a new generation of physicians are going to be happy to do the same. "...Young Gen Xers and emerging Millenials carefully guard their time, often choosing to diversify their time commitments as they do their other investments. While strongly loyal to their principles and their families, they are less loyal to their employers than their parents were to theirs. Rather than viewing the practice opportunity you offer them as the start of their lifetime career, your young recruit may see it as a means for building a personal—and portable—portfolio of career assets."[14]

Those who have studied Generation Y doubt that they will be willing to give up their various passions and devote themselves wholeheartedly

14. Westfall, Carol and John Powers. "Beyond the Labels: Lessons for Physician Recruitment in Changing Times." *Group Practice Journal*. Final for Submission 9-18-2006.

to corporate life any time soon. "They have been raised with all these activities [and] all these interests," says Claire Raines. "They are not going to say sure, that's fine; I'll make my life all work." Jim Lanzalotto, Vice President of Strategy and Marketing for YOH Associates, agrees that Generation Y wants a different kind of workplace, and that they may get it. "You remember those companies we had during the dot-com years, the ones that let you bring your dog to work? That's the kind of thing that Gen Y wants, and we'll see some version of that come back. Don't forget, they have demographics on their side. When I was a kid—I'm a baby boomer—I remember schools kept shutting behind me because the population wasn't there to support them anymore. Well, that's what we'll soon have with the workforce, a real lack of supply, and Gen Yers' demands may well be met."

Another consideration with potential workplace ramifications is that Generation Y has also been raised with a strong volunteer ethic, frequently because of mandated volunteer programs in their schools. A study by the federal Corporation for National and Community Service shows that between 2002 and 2005, volunteerism by college students increased by 20 percent in the United States. As a result, for many being part of the volunteer sector is also part of what they see valuable in their lives—and a valuable way to spend their leisure time. "I'm more likely to pick a company or stay with a company if they have a volunteer program, and if they show me they have a sense of corporate responsibility," says Christine. "I did volunteer work all through high school and I loved it. That's important to me." Kate, the college liaison manager, admits that the Gen Y graduates she sees are concerned and caring about the world and community. "I have to say that they are not selfish in that way. They are interested in a lot of causes, and they are willing to put time into them."

All in all, it seems that all-work-and-no-time-for-leisure is a bad fit for Generations X and Y. To date they are trying to cram their values into a world that is perhaps not ready for them, but in time it might be more open to their point of view. That's likely to be especially true for Generation Y, which is hefty in numbers and will have some extra bargaining power when baby boomers start leaving the labor force. "Maybe they will end up achieving real balance," says Kate. "Maybe they can figure out how to have lives where they have work and a family and a social life and they spend time volunteering. Because I think it's quite possible that companies like mine will end up buckling and giving in to what they want in terms of balance, simply because with boomer retirements they will not have much choice."

OPTING OUT OF WORK

Changing the way work is done is one thing, but what about giving up on work altogether? That's what we are seeing at the extreme: people who have completely traded work for leisure and are dropping out of the labor force altogether. In the United States, the labor force participation rate—the number of people either working or looking for work as a percentage of all who are eligible to do so—declined from 67.1 percent in 2000 to 66.2 in 2005, taking it to the lowest it has been since 1989. It may not sound like a big deal, but think of it another way: if the participation rate had remained constant, just for that five-year period, there would be 1.7 million more people working in the United States than there are right now.[15]

Breaking it down by age shows that potential workers in virtually every age group are less apt to choose to be in the labor market than they were a few years ago. According to the U.S. Bureau of Labor Statistics[16], from the onset of the U.S. recession (in 2001) through to the end of 2005, the total labor force participation rate for all those aged over 16 dipped by 1.1 percentage points. The biggest decrease was for those aged between 16 to 24, where the participation rate dropped by a huge 5.2 percentage points, basically because the weak labor market made more young people apt to prolong their education. More interesting is that the participation rate dipped among those groups where it is traditionally the highest. For men between the ages of 25 to 54, the participation rate was down by 1.2 percentage points, while for women in the same age group it decreased by 1.5 percentage points. The only increase in labor force participation was in the group aged

15. U.S. Bureau of Labor Statistics. "Current Population Survey." Calculations are by the author.

16. U.S. Bureau of Labor Statistics.

55 plus, where labor force participation for both sexes grew by 4.8 percentage points over the period—partly because baby-boomer women were hitting that age group, and they were more likely to be in the labor force than the cohort of women they were replacing.[17]

To be fair, the decreases have not exactly meant there has been a rush to enjoy a more leisured life. Part of the decline has been due to what are termed "cyclical" factors, or basically gyrations in the economy. All things being equal, the better the economy, the more people are apt to join the labor force. University graduates will find it worth their while to forgo graduate studies and just look for work, for example. That's why a decrease in labor force participation over a period when the economy is in recession or recovering from recession is not that surprising. But several analyses[18] suggest that the decrease because of the sagging economy can explain only part of the decrease in labor force participation.

"I don't want to sound ungrateful or like I'm complaining in any way," says 36-year-old Jennifer. She's multi-tasking as she speaks: one hand is on her one-year-old, a big-eyed baby girl named Olivia who has her eyes on the staircase just ahead of her. Jennifer's other hand is still dabbing at her three-year-old son David's nose, trying to make sure a nosebleed is at bay. "I feel very fortunate, very lucky. I had great opportunities in terms of education and great opportunities when I was a lawyer. And I feel really lucky that I was able to do this." "This" refers to being a stay-at-home-mom to Olivia and David, something no one would have foreseen Jennifer doing a dozen or so years ago when she was getting through law school with flying colors, picking and choosing among the firms that wanted to bring her on as a corporate lawyer.

Walk around the playground of any affluent neighbourhood these days and along with the nannies pushing the swings you'll find a gaggle of used-to-bes: "used to be a lawyer," "used to be a PR executive,"

---

17. "Charting the U.S. Labor Market in 2005". U.S. Department of Labor. Bureau of Labor Statistics, 2006.

18. Aaronson, Stephanie, Bruce Fallick, Andrew Figura, Jonathan Pingle, and William Wascher (Board of Governors of the Federal Reserve) *The Recent Decline in the Labor Force Participation Rate and Its Implications for Potential Labor Supply,* Brookings Paper on Economic Activity, vol. 1 (2006), pp. 69–154.
   McEwen, Helen, Pia Orrenius and Mark Wynne. "Opting Out of Work: What's Behind the Decline in Labor Force Participation?" *Southwest Economy,* Issue 6, November/December 2005.

"used to work on Wall Street and I kind of miss the bonuses." Like generations before them, these women traded in work outside the home for what might be termed a more leisured life, in as much as childcare and running a household do not have to take place around a structured work day. Unlike other generations before them, however, they left a lot more in terms of cash and time put into careers on the table when they left. The cost of their leisure is high, but they are paying it just the same. This is the group that *New York Times* writer Lisa Belkin was describing when she penned the term the "Opt-Out Revolution" in 2003. Writing in the *New York Times Sunday Magazine*,[19] Belkin asserted, "It was not just that the workplaces have failed women. It is also that women are rejecting the workplace." Citing such lofty examples as Karen Hughes, President Bush's former advisor who left the White House because her family was homesick for Texas, Belkin made the case that high-profile women were increasingly deeming the sacrifices asked of them to maintain blazing careers unacceptable. As it happens, Hughes, a baby boomer, was a poor example of an opt-outer, returning as she did to full-time work within a couple of years of leaving it. But Belkin had tapped into something. Among Generation X women, at least, there has been a steady exodus from the labor force over the past several years.

Among women, there has been a fairly startling change in the labor force participation rate. For those aged between the ages of 25 to 34, the labor force participation rate slipped from 76.0 in 1997 to 73.9 in 2005. For the slightly older group, the 35 to 44 age group, the participation rate went from 77.7 in 1997 to 75.8 in 2005. Somebody was dropping out—or at least deciding not to participate. There are a host of factors explaining the dip—an increase in women with disabilities, for example, as well as a rise in the number of Hispanic women, who as a group tend to have a lower labor force participation rate. However, a study by the Federal Reserve Bank of Boston[20] also found that the decline in participation rates has been concentrated among

---

19. Belkin, Lisa. "The Opt Out Revolution." *New York Times Magazine*, October 26, 2003.

20. Bradbury, Katharine and Jane Katz, "Women's Rise—A work in Progress: Are Professional Women Opting Out? Recent Evidence on College-Educated Women's Labor Force Participation," vol. 14, no.3 (Quarter 1, 2005). .

college-educated women, and the biggest declines have been for college-educated married women who have children under six and/or a high-earning husband, in other words, women like Jennifer with plenty of education and great futures, who have decided to chuck it. This marks a contrast of a sort, between Generation X and baby-boomer behavior. In the 1980s, highly educated women with children—primarily baby boomers—decided to stay in the labor force, causing the labor force participation rate to rise. In the years since 2000, highly educated Gen X women are causing the labor force participation rate to fall.

"I worked so hard to get where I was," says Jennifer. "I was in corporate law and I managed a group. And it was exhilarating for a lot of the time that I was there ... I understood that the culture demanded 10- or 12- or 14-hour days or whatever and I did that. I had been with my firm for close to a decade and we had a lot invested in each other. But I finally had no choice, or I felt I had no choice but to leave. If I could have worked normal hours, left at 5:00 every night, I might have been able to work, but my firm has never been very happy with the part-time thing. Once I had my second child, I knew I didn't want to be there anymore."

This may not be a group that wants to be in the leisure economy wholesale, but it is one that wants to intersperse their working lives with meaningful leisure experiences, a large dose of them involving their children. Other generations may have wanted the same things, but Gen X appears ready to articulate their needs more clearly, and to bargain for time away from the workplace. They have already created the beginnings of a leisure economy for themselves, and as their bargaining power increases, they will increase its breadth. That may mean choosing to spend some time outside of the paid labor force, or it may mean adapting their workplaces to better meet their needs for a rich life outside of work.

The evidence is more than anecdotal. A study from the Work and Family Institute looked at different workers and classified them as either "work centric," those placing a higher priority on work than family, "family-centric," those placing a higher priority on family than work or "dual-centric," those placing the same priority on their job and family. According to their interviews, 22 percent of boomers are work-centric compared to 12 to 13 percent of other generations. In Gen X, 52 percent are family-centric compared with 41 percent of boomers and 50 percent of Generation Y.[21] This finding suggests that there is a *generational* difference between boomers and Gen X rather than a life cycle difference related to parental responsibilities.

Even more eye-opening is the hint that Gen Y college-aged women are already planning stints outside of the workforce. A *New York Times* story published in late 2005 created some shocked buzz when it stated that among women at elite colleges approximately 60 percent planned to exit the workforce either temporarily or permanently and stay home when they have children. Although based on a small sample (the researchers had sent out emails to 138 young women) the conclusions were powerful in their impact. This, after all, is the elite group, the one that has the most to gain, at least on a financial basis, from being in the labor force. They were training for challenging careers, ones that could make them among the leaders of their generations. And yet this particular group seemed ready to trade it all in to be some form of 21st century soccer mom. "I'll have a career until I have two kids," one of the young women in the article was quoted as saying. "It doesn't necessarily matter how far you get. It's kind of like the experience: I have tried what I wanted to do."[22] Of course, what these young women end up doing career-wise is yet to be seen; life (or the economy) may overtake them and they may find they work more than they had planned. A more hospitable workplace could also keep them working, even if they had originally planned to leave to raise their families.

But maybe the worry should be over the "Parent Drain" rather than just the "Mommy Drain." Continuing a trend started with baby boomer fathers, Generation X dads have increasingly become hands-on parents, to the extent that they spend far more time on child care than fathers a generation or so ago. True, according to the ATUS data, as of 2005, women still spending far more time involved in child care than

21. Bradbury, Katherine and Jane Katz. "Women's Rise—A Work in Progress: Are Professional Women Opting Out?" Federal Reserve Bank of Boston. *Regional Review,* First Quarter 2005.

22. "Generation & Gender in the Workplace." An Issue Brief by the Families and Work Institute, New York, 2004.

men—2.5 hours of primary care versus 1.3 hours per day. But other research suggests that since 1965, the time that married fathers spend on child care has more than doubled to 6.5 hours a week from 2.6 hours a week.[23] And, both men and women now acknowledge that to some extent child care is at least shared, compared to a generation ago. A study by Reach Advisors showed that of 3,000 surveyed parents, Gen X fathers were spending twice as much time on parenting as their own fathers did. That higher involvement in their children's lives has already meant some shifting in the labor market. According to the Census Bureau, as of 2005, there were approximately 147,000 actual full-time, stay-at-home fathers in the United States—a 40 percent increase over 105,000 in 2002.[24] Although that number is still relatively small, it could spike up incredibly quickly as Generation Y, with their looser attitudes towards who does what as long as it gets done, start their families.

Gen Y may also push for public policy changes that make it easier to opt out to be with their families, whether for short or long durations. Indeed, if family leaves were available to them, it could be assumed that they would take advantage of them with alacrity. You can already see a taste of this in Canada, where "parental leave" has been available to moms *or* dads since 2001. Maternity leave—to be taken strictly by mothers—is between 15 to 18 weeks in Canada, depending on the jurisdiction. For a further 37 weeks, either parent is then eligble to take a leave from work and be paid an allowance of 55 percent of insurable earnings (subject to an income ceiling). As of 2005, approximately 15 percent of men took some leave, albeit generally much less than their wives. In the U.S., the legislation for paid parental leaves is much less generous. Unpaid maternity or paternity leaves of twelve weeks duration are available to workers in covered companies (generally all public sector employers or companies with 75 or more employees) under the *Family and Medical Leave Act*. It is a matter of time before Gen Y politicians—or Xers or Boomer politicians who understand Gen Y—tap

23. Story, Louise. "Many Women at Elite Colleges Set Career Path to Motherhood." *The New York Times*, September 20, 2005.

24. Bianchi, Suzanne, John P. Robinson and Melissa Milkie. "Changing Rhythms of American Family Life." Russell Sage Foundation, 2006.

into the desire in both countries for legislation that supports Gen Y values.

Finally, it should be noted that opting out is not just about women, and it is not just about Generations X and Y. Slacking, so to speak, has also become the province of many who never expected to leave the labor force prior to retirement, but found once they did leave that they liked the involuntary leisure.

"Men Not Working, Not Wanting Any Job" said the front page story on *The New York Times* on July 31, 2006. Inside, economics writers Louis Uchitelle and David Leonard told the stories of men who, having lost blue-collar jobs, had more or less opted out of the paid labor force rather than take work they deemed beneath their abilities or tolerance. Although discussions on the article quickly turned into something called "the lazy man crisis," in the media and in blogs, the authors had articulated a trend visible to economists for years: labor force participation rates for what used to be called "prime aged-men"—traditionally the most stable portion of the labor force—had been trending down for years. The most recent peak of U.S. male labor force participation was in 1984, when about 76.4 percent of all men aged 16 or over were either employed or looking for work. At that time, 94.4 percent of men aged 25 to 34 were in the labor force, as were 95.4 percent of those aged 35 to 44 and 91.2 percent of those aged 45 to 54. By 2005, the overall participation rate was 73.3 percent, while the participation rates had fallen to 91.7 percent, 92.1 percent and 87.7 percent for the three age groups respectively. That means there are 1.94 million men who would have been working had the labor force participation rates stayed constant, but who as of 2005 were neither working nor looking for work.[25]

The reasons for the decline in labor force participation in this group are varied, and to a large extent have to do with what has become a much weaker labor market for blue-collar men over the past couple of decades. But there are other reasons too, including everything from the rise in dot-com millionaires to the increase in stay-at-home dads who

----

25. U.S. Census Bureau. www.rebeldad.com (analysis of U.S. census data).

were able to leave the labor market. The more interesting phenomenon may be that for many of those who have left the labor market, there has been a new recognition that time outside of the labor market can be as fulfilling as time inside the labor market. Indeed, it is not nearly as socially unacceptable as it might have been 20 years ago to be a man in the prime of life who decides to do something that does not involve working for money, whether it is raising your children or running a non-profit foundation. The leisure economy, it would seem, is already affecting some of those who did not plan to be a part of it until much later in their lives.

CRAFTING A LEISURE ECONOMY

Many unanswered questions remain as to how Generation Y will allocate work and leisure through the rest of their lives. Up to now, they may have been adamant that they "want a life" and will not allow the forces of work or anything else to put them into a high-stress, baby-boomer kind of time bind. Having said that, there are also many challenges ahead for them that might make them, as a generation, have to compromise.

To be sure, both boomers and Xers have crafted some changes in the workplace already. "It's not really about people wanting to work less," says Roy Krause, CEO of Spherion, a staffing and recruitment company. "It's that they're saying, 'Look I have to go to my kid's kindergarten on Friday morning, and that's it; I'm going to go. And it shouldn't affect my salary or my bonus or anything else." He thinks that there has been a change in the workforce since 2000, and credits it to technology. "Everyone has computers; everyone has email. So companies are allowing people to spend some time working from home, for example." At a time when the average commute takes 25 minutes each way in the United States[26] and over 30 minutes in Canada,[27] just working at home one or two days a week means workers have snatched back some leisure.

---

26. U.S. Bureau of Labor Statistics. Calculations are by the author and were derived by applying the 1984 participation rates for men aged 25 to 34, 35 to 44 and 45 to 54 to the civil population for each age group as of 2005, then calculating the total.

27. "Commuting in America." U.S. Census Bureau, August 2006.

For Generation Y, the biggest question is how they will parent. The surveys may show that some or all are likely to want to stay home, but it will be many years before we see whether they ultimately make that part of their reality. Despite the surveys that suggest parents might opt to stay home, there seem to be plenty of Gen Yers who say they want to repeat what they considered a positive experience as the child of a working parent. Heather, born on the cusp of Generations X and Y, is a new mom and a social worker, and she is eager to return to the workforce. "My mom was a working mom and I know I want to go back to work too. I know my daughter will be better for it, more socialized. And I remember that I used to go to after-school care and I loved it." Others may simply realize that their aspirations to have a parent home are out of sync with their financial realities. Ashley, the aesthetician, wants to be home the same way that her mom was home for her. "I work crazy hours now ... I'll get in to work in the morning and not leave till 8:00 at night. There is no way I want to continue doing that when I have children." At the same time, she concedes that she probably will end up working, at least part time. "My boyfriend and I can barely pay our bills now," she says. "Realistically, we are both going to be working when we have kids. But if there was a way I could avoid it—if I could say okay, I'll never take another vacation just let me be home—I would do it."

It is unclear what aspects of their own experience as the children of baby boomers Gen Yers will bring to their own childrearing. Hyper-parented to an extent themselves, will they choose to involve their children in fewer activities and perhaps insist on more of a leisure life that includes their own families? Dr. Alvin Rosenfeld, author of *The Overscheduled Child*, thinks it is far too early to predict which way Gen Y might go when they raise their own children. "It's too early to know ... and as with everything else, there is going to be a statistical distribution with some thinking the scheduling was great and others wanting to do it a different way. But I see the stress and the over-scheduling as getting worse, not better, for the present. We are all aware that our standard of living could well go down. Wealth is getting transferred to places like India and China, and to keep up, we have to be more competitive. So the drive to put your kids in as many activities as possible will still be there." Claire Raines adds, "Whatever the complaints kids have about their parents, I don't hear much dissatisfaction about the amount of time and attention they got. So I imagine that will continue to be part of the experience."

The final tally of who stays home and who works, and who enjoys the full leisure economy experience and who does not, is likely to depend on not just the decisions of any generation but on the way that the economy performs over the next decade or so. That is hard to predict, but barring a severe change in economic circumstances that forces everyone back into the labor force, it would seem that North America is inching towards the leisure economy slowly and generationally.

Julian, a 29-year-old on the cusp between Gen X and Gen Y, sums it up well. "I guess I'd really rather have a job that lets me live my life instead of my job being my life. And I feel wimpy saying that because my dad and many others (today and before us) have had it far worse, but I'd like more leisure time and lots of it. And I'm not work-shy or lazy. I grew up on a dairy farm and have worked six-day weeks, 70-hour weeks and all night to get various projects done or meet deadlines, but in the end, it doesn't go anywhere. Family and friends do."

5
THE NEW HAVES
AND HAVE-NOTS

Wealth may be an excellent thing, for it means power, and it means leisure, it means liberty.

— *James Russell Lowell*
poet and satirist (1819–1891)

"I spoke to the bank and we have some hard decisions to make," says a husband to his wife in a commercial for a financial services company. The couple, an attractive pair of 50-somethings, are seated in an upscale restaurant where they fit in perfectly amidst the crisp white tablecloths and the bottles of mineral water. The premise is that they are discussing their retirement, and she looks anxious at what he has to say. Having enjoyed her discomfort for a minute, his face breaks into a huge smile as he tells her what they will have to decide: "Will it be Provence, or will it be Tuscany?" Sighing with relief, they hug, their future settled. They have plenty of years ahead, and plenty of money to enjoy them with. Their leisure will be long and well-financed, and the tourism officials from both Provence and Tuscany would be well advised to court them assiduously.

The couple in the commercial are part of what is turning into an elite in-group we can call the "Golden Leisurites." This fortunate sub-group of baby boomers will be the trendsetters in the leisure economy just as they have been for most of their working lives. Well educated but affluent, they will be able to continue their fulfilling careers if they want and stop working if they feel like it. They may take up hobbies ranging from gourmet cooking to model train collecting, spending lots of money on their new pastimes in the process. They can travel if they choose, or spend time and money adding new media rooms or wildflower gardens to their homes. They are a marketer's dream, but they do not by any stretch of the imagination represent all of the baby boomers now freewheeling towards 60. A significant number of boomers will not be able to afford high-priced leisure in retirement, and some will barely be able to afford to retire.

But the boomers will hardly be the only group who find themselves divided into leisure haves and have-nots. At the other end of the age spectrum, Generation Y will also face a divide. As a generation they repeatedly profess their interest in balance, and as they form families they are likely going to want to achieve that balance by taking time away from the workplace to spend it with their children and to create a life with varied interests. But only a select group will get to do so: the rest will find themselves trying to pay off the mound of debt they amassed early in their lives, through tuition or credit card purchases. Indeed, many may find they are digging themselves deeper and deeper into the debt morass, with the result that they will have to work longer and harder than their parents before them, whom they had hoped not to emulate.

It won't be fair, but it never is. Not everyone made a killing in dot-com stocks either. Not everyone saw the value of their home double in the first two years they owned it, and then double again in the two years after that. There are plenty of ways that the economy has divided North Americans into haves and have-nots. Since the 1980s, one of the biggest divides has been income, and plenty of studies have shown that however strong the economy has gotten, all boats have not been lifted equally, and some not at all. The stock and real estate markets have also created some lottery-type wins for some, while leaving others out in the cold. Now, however, it is time to add another source of divide and envy to the list of things that create haves and have-nots among North Americans: leisure time. Leisure is about to be perceived as a must-have commodity, but there will be definite haves and have-nots among those that manage to achieve it.

The leisure economy will be powered by a new surge in leisure time, but it will not be any more evenly distributed than Microsoft stock bought in 1986 (the year it went public). A big chunk of the population will find themselves with unstructured time, to either leave as hammock time or fill as they wish with family time, community work, hobbies or measured forays into the labor market: they will be the haves. There will also be a group we can call the "double-haves": the ones that have hefty income to go along with their time.

Another chunk of the population will find themselves working more than they care to; that group will encompass those on all ends of the age spectrum. Some of these will continue to be part of the old time-crunch economy, the group that spends their money buying conveniences, and plans spurts of leisure when they can. Some may not even consider themselves to be have-nots, but many—such as potential retirees who have to keep working, or parents who wish they could be home with their children but find that an impossible dream—will indeed be unhappy about their leisure situation.

There will also be a final group of leisure economy have-nots: those with time but not money. In this group will be younger people, who have opted to perhaps cut down their household working time, as well as boomer retirees at the bottom rung of the income spectrum. They will have some adjustments to make, paring back their spending levels from what they spent as part of the time-crunch economy. For business, the key may be in realizing that if we are talking about baby boomers in retirement, we may be talking about a group of people who will want different products than they did when they were younger. Some may still be willing to pay for cleaning services to blitz their houses once a week, as was necessary when they were working; other households may find that as still healthy 60-year-olds with no children underfoot, the cost of bi-weekly cleaning can be put to much better use. Business should also realize that the ranks of young families may increasingly be filled by those who are making income sacrifices to have a parent home with their children. That may mean that they too will give up their cleaning service, or never engage one in the first place.

The divide will mean brewing resentments in different classes of people. Some of the young, working population, bogged down with long commutes and precious little time off will look enviously at their boomer colleagues putting in a couple mornings a week then heading to catch a movie matinee in the afternoon. Nothing will make them more angry than knowing that the matinee tickets will be bought at seniors' discount rates—and they will make their feelings known to retail establishments and policy makers alike.

Within generations there will also be splits and divisions. Generation Y has made it clear that they want balanced lives, a conviction that is likely to grow when they get around to forming families. But having time off is a value that is out of sync with the reality for many in that generation: modest paychecks and huge debt payments. For those who started their working lives with the right conditions—manageable student debt (or preferably none at all) and the right (read high-paying) professions—everything may fall into place. No matter what their generation, plenty of have-nots will look at the haves and be unhappy with their own situation. The boomer split over leisure time will at once be more subtle and more brutal as a dividing line. Some will sail into the leisure economy earlier, then literally sail off (on newly purchased boats) for happier climates if they like. Others will find themselves working well beyond the age they foresaw, frequently because of the dividing lines in their earlier lives. Those divisions are the same ones that in the past two decades have created a polarization of income levels: things like being white collar or blue collar, highly skilled rather than low skilled, or having an advanced degree rather than minimal education. The cost up to now might have been perceived as money only, but in the leisure economy it will be time as well as dollars and cents.

WAYS FOR BUSINESS TO ATTRACT POST-BOOM HAVES AND HAVE-NOTS

Post-Boom Haves:
Leisurites with Time and Money

These Gen Xers and Gen Ys will have negotiated time off (one parent home, longer vacations, flexible hours) and with their high income they'll want to find the best uses for their leisure:

- *Experiences, especially experiences for their children, will be most important to them.* From family adventure travel to Saturday fencing lessons to mother–daughter learn-to-knit programs, they'll be willing to put in the time and money to learn something and use their time in ways they consider meaningful.
- *They'll buy leisure equipment for their homes—and use it too.* Home gyms, swimming pools, home art studios—all will be priorities that they'll enjoy with their families and friends.

Post-Boom Haves-Nots:
Plenty of Time but Little Money

These Gen Xers and Gen Ys will have tight budgets, but won't want to lead the kind of time-stressed lives the boomers did, so they'll make sacrifices to be part of the leisure economy.

- *Family volunteering will be cool.* Like the haves, they'll want to give their children experiences but will need to be creative about them. Volunteering as a family will fit the bill nicely, and fit in well with their values.
- *They'll be harder consumers to hook.* Money will be tight so they'll be doing more of what their older brothers and sisters paid someone else to do—cleaning their own houses, mowing their own lawns, making their own food and entertaining at home. Forget the hundreds of dollars others are spending at all-inclusive party centers for their kids' parties: they'll want a do-it-at-home kit, including a recipe for the birthday cake.

And of course there will be those in the post-boom generations who are not part of the leisure economy at all—whether Gen X or Gen Y, they'll stay firmly part of the time-crunch economy and will keep the market for "convenience" products an important one—although more of a niche market than previously.

LOFTY VALUES, GIGANTIC DEBTS

"I would definitely not return to the office environment until my youngest child was out of elementary school," says Sarah, a recent college graduate with ambitions to enter the publishing industry. "After having a job in the publishing industry for at least five years, I don't see any reason why I wouldn't be able to work from home with the contacts I establish." Sarah's life is relatively well mapped out. She and her fiancé are planning a wedding after they have worked for a couple of years, and then plan to have their first child three or four years into their marriage. They are also eager to get into the housing market around the time they start a family. Lofty ambitions, but Sarah figures she is well positioned to achieve them. "Luckily, because of my parents' income and a hefty academic scholarship, I was able to attend four years of college without any student loans, a very unique situation in this day and age … We'll be able to afford a home and children on his [Sarah's fiancé's] salary alone, based on the job he has now and the typical promotion cycles his company goes through." In a generation about to divide into haves and have-nots, Sarah is a definite have. Although it is not clear just how big a house she's likely to get, or how high her standard of living will be, she does seem on track to achieve what many in Generation Y would like.

"Their values are really not about money," says Steve Rothberg, founder and president of CollegeRecruiter.com, an online job posting and career resources site. "They want to be around their families. What they'd like, and what I'd expect, is all kinds of innovative arrangements that allow them to be home with their kids. Job-sharing between partners, moms staying home, dads staying home, part-time work. This is not the baby boom. They are not going in wanting to or expecting to have to work all-out." In one sense, Gen Y is well equipped to structure that kind of arrangement. After all, at least at the entry level, it appears that they are in demand. They are also telling employers what they want in terms of a work–life balance, and perhaps, with a labor shortage looming in North America, they will be able to get the arrangements they want. But here's the catch: even if the companies offer up the deals, a large chunk of Generation Y will not be able to accept them, simply because they cannot afford to.

What Cost Education?

Generation Y faces economic circumstances that make them even less likely to acquire the mix of work and leisure than the two generations that preceded them. Cognizant of the need to achieve a post-secondary education in order to compete in today's economy, they have been hammered by the cost of achieving that goal. Julian, 29, a Gen X–Y cusper who wants to balance work and family, is typical. "I am very much interested in working part time professionally," he says. "I have worked as an English teacher and an editor, and with both jobs I have wished it was possible to split the job between two people and just take half the salary, giving me half the year off. The only problem: debt. Right now, it's no big deal, but I do have 40K in school loans, 12K to pay on my car, and 5K in credit card debt." Like many, Julian is to a degree hamstrung by the amount of debt he has collected even before his work life has really kicked off. For him, and for others in the same situation, paying back their loans will mean accepting more and different labor market work than they had planned at the beginning of their careers.

The cost of education is the real problem for Generation Y. According to figures from the U.S. College Board, the real cost of an education has increased stratospherically over the last few decades. For a student going to school in the 1976–77 academic year, the total cost of tuition, room and board and other charges at a public four-year institution was $6,877.[1] By the 2006–07 academic year, the typical cost at a public institution was $12,796—an increase of 86 percent over the 20-year period, or 4.3 percent per year. Costs have increased even more quickly over the past decade. The College Board calculates that over the past decade, total charges for full-time students at public four-year colleges have increased at a 6.3 percent clip per year in nominal terms, or about 3.3 percent per year after adjusting for inflation.[2] In Canada, the cost of a post-secondary education has increased even more sharply. According to Statistics Canada, between 1990–91 and 2006–07, undergraduate

---

1. All figures have been inflation-adjusted into 2006 dollars.
2. "Trends in College Pricing 2006." The College Board, 2006.

tuition fees at Canadian universities increased at an average annual rate of 7.0%.[3]

Not surprisingly, the increase in costs means that student debt for Generation Y is climbing. A 2006 poll of 20-somethings by credit-reporting agency Experian for *USAToday* found that over the previous five years student loan debt had grown by 16 percent to an average of $14,379. Approximately 3 percent of 20-somethings owed $20,000 or more in student debt—a small percentage, yes, except that this group of mega-loan holders is growing in numbers faster than any other group of debt-holders.[4] In Canada, the most recent data available is for the class of 2000, which represents the first wave of Generation Y. In that year, 53 percent of those graduating with a bachelor's degree had some debt, with the average indebted graduate owing over $20,000. By two years after graduation, only one in five of those who had graduated with debt had managed to become debt-free.[5]

What Cost Credit?

Generation Y has also made some hefty inroads into acquiring debt for things other than tuition. Brought up in an age of consumerism, they have been indulged and have now moved on to indulging themselves. Credit cards, after all, have made it easy. According to college loan provider Nellie Mae, as of 2004, 76 percent of U.S. college undergraduates began the year with credit cards and 56 percent of students said that they got their first credit card at the age of 18. The *USAToday* survey showed that revolving debt, including credit card debt, surged over the five-year period to average $5,781. A study by the advocacy group Demos found that as of 2004, the average household in the 18- to 24-year-old demographic group was spending about 30 percent of their income on credit payments.[6]

3. Statistics Canada, "University Tuition Fees." *The Daily*, September 1, 2006.

4. Fetterman, Mindy and Barbara Hansen. "Young People Struggle to Deal with Kiss of Debts." *USAToday*, November 22, 2006.

5. Allen, Mary and Chantal Vaillancourt, "Class of 2000: Profile of Post-Secondary Graduates and Student Debt." Statistics Canada, Catalogue No. 81-595-MIE, No. 016, April 2004.

6. Draut, Tamara and Javier Silva. "Generation Broke: The Growth of Debt among Young Americans." Demos report, October 13, 2004.

Saving: A Lost Art?

The flip side to the spending is an alarming decline in saving among young workers. According to a study by the American Institute of Certified Public Accountants[7] (AICPA), in 1985 about 65 percent of those aged between 25 and 34 (Gen Xers, according to our definition) had some form of savings instrument: a savings account, stocks or bonds or a 401(k) account.[8] By 2000, that percentage had fallen to 59 percent, and by 2004 it had decreased to 55 percent. The study also found that the net worth (defined as their assets less their liabilities) of young Americans also dipped over the 20-year period, decreasing from $7,000 in 1985 to just over $3,700 in 2004 (figures are in constant 2004 dollars). That's a sizeable drop, especially since it happened at a time when net worth among all Americans was actually on the rise.

As a way to counteract the deteriorating financial situation of young adults, the AICPA has started a public awareness campaign called "Feed the Pig" to encourage young Americans to pay off their debts and save for a more financially secure future. "This is the group that wants to buy their first home, get married and start a family, and they still have college debt," says Michael Eisenberg, a Los Angeles CPA and a member of the AICPA's National CPA Financial Literacy campaign. The campaign shows that taking small steps now will make a big difference in the future. We use the example of Starbucks—if you just buy one less coffee a day, then the money will add up pretty nicely over a lifetime, because the goals of this generation are not unattainable. A lot do want to have a work–life balance. And for the ones who get themselves organized early in their lives, they can get themselves to the point where they are in good shape, and they can achieve some kind of financial freedom." Some Gen Yers, particularly the ones who do not have a lot of debt to start with, will undoubtedly heed the message and sock money away early on and find themselves in a decent financial position within a decade or so. Others, however,

---

7. Thornberg, Christopher and Jon Haveman. "Savings and Asset Accumulation Among Americans 25–34." Prepared for The American Institute of Certified Public Accountants, October 13, 2006.

8. The complete list includes traditional savings, money market accounts, certificates of deposit and other financial investments such as stocks and bonds, Keogh, IRA, and 401 (k) accounts.

already dealing with so much debt that having savings seems like an impossible dream, will undoubtedly do little to make their situations better.

Reading the Trends

It all means that Generation Y will have some very defined winners and losers in terms of leisure time. For good or bad, the dip in the percentage of highly educated working mothers observed over the past few years may start to edge up again. After all, for households who start their lives with a ton of college debt, any foray into the housing market will necessarily be delayed. That means that by the time Gen Y has children, even if they become parents later than they had planned, they are also likely to be making mortgage payments later than they had planned. Very likely, they will find themselves forced to emulate the two-full-time-working-parent households that they wanted to avoid. That will leave them firmly in the grasp of the time-crunch economy, perhaps to a worse degree than ever before. After all, barring a drop in housing prices, it is unlikely that commuting times are going to get any shorter. And, if their financial situations do not leave them much bargaining power, they may well have to accept work situations that demand long workweeks.

So will there be a leisure economy for anyone in Generation Y? Absolutely, but it will be selective. Just as many boomer parents bought their Generation Y children riding lessons and Gymboree clothes, some will also be able to buy them leisure, simply because they will be paying their kids' debt, or paying their tuition in the first place, as is the case with Sarah. Other parents, by offering free rent or paying a portion of tuition debt, will also give their Generation Y children a head start in the leisure economy if they want to be a part of it. "Unfortunately, I am in debt to the extreme right now," says Carrie, a recent college graduate. "But I'm fortunate that my parents are covering my loans and not charging me rent, so I have time to figure things out before I move out on my own ... I am in somewhat of a unique situation because my father has offered to continue to pay my bills and in return has asked me to challenge myself to write a book. I'm a bit nervous, but as far as my current situation goes I will just take this time to write and actually try to make a career out of my passion."

Of course, there are ways that Generation Y could regain the leisure they want, but they have economic implications too. The simplest way would be just to cut back on spending, perhaps to fairly austere levels. Indeed, some Gen Yers plan to do just that as a way to get a head start in life. "I have a strategy on how to manage my debt," says Patricia, a newly graduated lawyer. "I'm going to continue to live as I did in law school with minimal expenditures until my debt is paid off so that I can be debt free with minimum interest payments. I will not buy a house until I am debt free—however long that takes. As a lawyer I believe that this is the only way that I can avoid the pitfall of bankruptcy that others in my generation have fallen into." If Patricia and others in her generation stick to this plan, it will have a profound impact on the housing market, and on the consumer sector as a whole. It also means that any foray into the leisure economy, which for Patricia means time spent with her aging parents who live overseas, will have to be put off until her financial circumstances improve.

But many are sceptical that Patricia will have much company in her austerity plan. "Generation Y wants stuff as much as any other genera-tion," says Jordan Kaplan, Associate professor of Management at Long Island University and an expert in generational behavior. "The thing is, they have learned to use credit, but the day of reckoning is going to come." The evidence so far suggests that Generation Y is no less fond of nice clothes or decent cars than were their predecessors. As they age, there is no reason to suggest that they will not want two-car garages and finished decks and baby clothes bought at Jacadi. To get to the point where they can afford the things that they want and have some time to enjoy them, some in Generation Y may choose to wait to start a family. The USA Today survey shows that 11 percent of young people have postponed marrying and 14 percent have put off having children because of their debt situations. And some believe that Generation Y is apt to take a long time to form families, regardless of their debt situa-tion. "Kids are maturing later, not sexually, but socially," says Dr. Alvin Rosenfeld. "Their 20s may be a long period of extended adolescence."

Magic Bullets for Gen Y

Of course, there are a couple of other magic bullets that could help propel some in Gen Y towards the leisure economy.

Grandparents

As well as a bailout by parents, whenever that happens (perhaps when they sell their houses and have some cash on hand), grandparents may help too, perhaps through inheritances. Much has been written about the windfall that baby boomers will experience as their parents pass on and they inherit their assets. However, let's not forget that some of that wealth will land on the children of the boomers, whether directly or through their parents. As well as having been precious and spoiled children, Generation Yers, in particular, have been equally adored as grandchildren. Many of them arrived fairly late in the life of their grandparents, whose boomer children put off forming families until their 30s. Not only are most Generation Xers and Yers the only grandchild—or one of two or three—but thanks to divorces and remarriages, many of them have multiple grandparents. The odds of them getting windfall inheritances could be quite high.

The Housing Market

The other little miracle that could help Generation Y achieve their leisure dreams is the housing market. After all, Generation X wanted some time off too, and after a time in the labor market the boomers also wanted to scale back. What made it difficult for either of those generations to work less—individually or as households—was usually their housing debt. The median price of a house rose from $99,000 to $248,000 in the United States over the period from 1991 through 2006—an increase of about 250 percent, or about 10 percent a year over the 25-year period. Even with a sizeable decline in average interest rates over the same time, it still meant that housing affordability decreased over the period.[9] What could bail out Generation Y is a collapse in housing prices that makes the real

---

9. According to the National Association of Home Builders, as at the beginning of 1992, about 52 percent of households earning the median income would have been able to afford the median home sold. This rose to a high of about 68 percent in the late 1990s before declining as the housing boom went into full force. By 2006, the "Housing Opportunity Index" was 40.4 percent. National Association of Home Builders.

(inflation adjusted) cost of housing decrease over the next decade or so. Whether that will happen is as difficult to predict as whether the stock market will surge or sputter over the same period. But should anything happen to drive down housing prices, then there may well be a scramble among Generation Y to make themselves part of the leisure economy.

The sad truth, however, is that many in Generation Y will not even find themselves as part of the time-crunch economy that we have come to know over the past two decades. During the time-crunched years, the lack of time was driven, at least in part, because there were so many choices that boomers turned into yuppie kvetchers, complaining about trying to find the time to do things like meet with the renovators while getting the kids to ballet and soccer. In the new leisure economy facing Generation Y, some may find themselves choosing thriftier forms of leisure—painting the house themselves and letting the kids, when they are finally born, play in the back yard. In a way, this segment of Gen Y will echo their pre-boomer grandparents, and the simpler approach they took towards leisure: they'll get more of it, but it will not be the same as their affluent boomer parents' leisure. It takes a certain income level to be time-crunched: for the debt-laden in Generation Y, their worries may be about paying the bills rather than finding enough time to get to all the leisure activities that they might like.

WAYS FOR BUSINESS TO ATTRACT BOOMER HAVES AND HAVE-NOTS
Boomer Haves: Money and Time? No Problem

- *High-end leisure pursuits can be run at all times of the day and evening.* From more movie matinees to "opera in the afternoon" they will be open to expensive diversions. Think in terms of "series" though, not one-offs. They may be open to filling up every Tuesday for six weeks, even though it costs a chunk of money.
- *Series selling could be used in all kinds of industries.* A salon could sell a six-session package of hair treatments or spa services (come in every two weeks for twelve weeks to get a gradual make-over).

(continued)

Boomer Have-Nots: Plenty of Time but Still Counting Their Pennies

- *They'll eat up discounted events— whenever they are scheduled.* The "earlybird" special has been around forever, but boomers will need a different take on it. Theaters could offer special showings of boomers' favorite movies or television shows (a blitz of *Star Trek* episodes maybe?) in the mornings or early afternoons, when the theaters are normally empty.
- *A little more prep for a little less money will be a good sales strategy* for this group. They always paid for convenience and figured it was a bargain, but they might be prepared to do a little bit more themselves now, especially if they could be convinced it will give them a better product. The classic example: cooking. Sell them the raw ingredients along with cooking lessons or a cookbook, and explain that it will give them a cheaper and better life—now that they have the time to make it happen.

PLEASING NO ONE: THE BOOMER HAVES AND HAVE-NOTS

"I don't think we plan to retire at all ... at least not in the conventional sense, even though we could probably handle it financially," says Nicole, a 55-year-old professor and textbook author. "My husband is a teacher and we are both on the same academic schedule, so we get time off in the summer anyway. I think spending all our time on leisure activities would be boring." Like those Gen Yers without debt, Nicole and her husband are definitely "haves" in the leisure economy. If they change their minds about working they can stop, and if they want to spend more money on leisure activities they can do that too. Although they may not be leisurites all year, they can certainly travel and enjoy sailing or opera or whatever they please on more or less their own schedule. They even have one advantage that many in the leisure economy will not have: they can choose not to spend time on leisure too, since their careers can apparently span as much time as they would like.

Within the boomer population, people like Nicole are more than lucky: they are almost exceptional, In the leisure economy, they will be among the few boomers that are completely happy with the combination of time, money and leisure activities they have achieved. Other boomers are going to be unhappy with the menu of choices in front of them. Some will want to keep working, only to find that their jobs have disappeared, the new mandatory retirement laws notwithstanding; others will want to retire and find that they have to keep going much longer than they would like thanks to their losses in the stock market or the inadequacies in their pension coverage or inadequate healthcare coverage. After all, even though the U.S. has Medicaid for seniors and Canada has nationalized health care, the inadequacies of coverage in each system are well known. But when they all eventually do retire, boomers will find that their personal leisure economies differ wildly. From those with lots of time and lots of money, to those with time and no money to speak of, the leisure economy will not be one single entity but a series of realities and niches. This has huge business implications. Rather than targeting what are sometimes termed "retiring boomers" savvy businesses need to know which segment of the boomer market they want to go after, and target their offerings accordingly. Among baby boomers headed for retirement, there are actually four separate groups.

1. **The first group wants to work past 55 or even past 65.** They get a disproportionate amount of media attention and are often used as the argument that the leisure economy is not going to happen because boomers will all be in the labor force forever. We hear things like, "Sixty is the new 30." Such slogans suggest that even at traditional retirement age, boomers are really just hitting the zenith of their careers. Countless analyses have looked at this group as the answer to an upcoming shortage of workers in North America; perhaps there are good arguments for this. But why are boomers so eager to put off retirement? First of all, there is the fact that, for many, work has been their life for so long they can't imagine life without it. Like Nicole, they see a life without work as boring. That perception may change over time and include such things as meaningful volunteer work. For now, however,

first-wave boomers especially seem to view the idea of leisure as a life sentence of playing canasta, and they are recoiling from the prospect.

Baby boomers do not want a frugal existence in retirement. If they are going to eventually be part of the leisure economy, they want to be able to do it in high style. After all, this is the generation that has always had healthy dollops of money to spend on leisure pursuits, from the skateboards they got as children to the trips to Europe after college. In addition, they are bombarded with media images showing retirement as the chance to explore the good life. If there is a role model for this group, it is those retirees who redecorate their homes to include home theaters and gyms once the kids move out. Realistically, that means stashing away a healthy amount of money before retirement, which means more years in the labor force.

Boomers know they are likely to live long a long time. According to the actuarial tables, an American man who makes it to age 60 can expect to live another 20 years, while a woman can expect to live another 23.[10] In all likelihood, however, plenty of boomers figure they will beat the odds and live even longer, particularly given the ongoing advances in drugs and medical technology. While this may or may not be a realistic assumption, boomers are getting increasingly realistic about how much it might cost to keep up any kind of life, let alone the good life, after retirement. The financial services industry frequently bandies around an estimate of $1 million as what is necessary to get through retirement, and many boomers are becoming acutely aware they are nowhere near that goal.

"Financial literacy has really boomed over the past couple of decades," says Jack Cahill, a general partner with financial services firm Edward Jones. "When I got in this business in the late 1970s, you really didn't have great awareness of anything much beyond basic IRA or 401(k)s. It wasn't there in the early 1980s

---

10. Period Life Tables. U.S. Social Security Online. www.ssa.gov/OACT/STATS/table4c6.html.

either. The mom and pop investor—the millionaire next door type—were not reading the *Wall Street Journal*, and maybe they aren't doing that now either. But when we got the explosion of cable networks, we really increased awareness. And the run-up in the stock market—and the bust too—got people even more aware of protecting their financial future."

And so you have people like Nicole, who want to keep working and seem well able to do so. Although it is early in the game—only the first wave of baby boomers have hit 60—some companies have already re-organized to allow workers to remain at their jobs past the traditional retirement ages. To date, however, most of the workers who are making successful attempts to keep working until they choose to leave are disproportionately in the public sector, health, education, or professions. These workers are leisure-economy haves—those who get exactly the amount of leisure that they want and in the process have some control over their income too.

2. **The second group wants to retire and can.** These boomer haves are a more "traditional" group, similar to those seniors who have come before them. Jane, 52, is happy to call herself a have and typifies this group. A teacher who has been at her profession since her early 20s, she is looking forward to selling her house in a Virginia suburb and finding a rural retreat where she can fulfill a dream to raises horses and take her life down a notch from the time-crunch economy. "My husband may work a few more years than me, so we'll have to pick where we live carefully," she says, "but financially we feel things are pretty solid. I'll have my pension, plus we'll have the proceeds from our house. Our area, which is considered within commuting distance to Washington, D.C., has gone crazy price-wise, so wherever we pick to live is likely to be a whole lot cheaper. So I figure I'll get out of my primary job by the time I hit my mid-50s. Who knows what I'll do then ... Anything is a possibility but I won't have to feel pressured in terms of paying the bills."

3. **Concurrent with the fortunate haves described above are the have-nots.** First in this group are those who do not want to retire (mostly for financial reasons) but find that they are forced into it earlier than they would like. This group is actually large yet gets much less attention. They want to work past retirement but find that their jobs are no longer available to them and alternative work is not easy to find. According to a survey by Pew Research Center[11] only 12 percent of those who had retired as of 2006 were working for pay, and just 27 percent had ever worked for pay. In addition, although the Pew survey showed that the average American surveyed wished to retire at age 61, the average retiree actually retired at age 57.8. Of course, this data relates to pre-boomers, a group that is perhaps not large enough in influence to have made much difference to the way that work is structured. In time, however, the boomers may make much bigger changes to the way that workers past the conventional retirement age are accepted in the workforce. For the first few waves of boomers, however, there are likely to be many who plan to work longer but cannot. This group forced into early retirement will be have-nots with too much time on their hands and not enough money.

4. **The largest category of have-nots may be those who want to retire but find that, financially, they cannot.** Angela considers herself many years away from retirement, if indeed she can ever really leave the labor force. "To tell you the truth the whole thing scares me to death," she says. "I am 48 years old, divorced with two young children. If things keep on like this, I will have to continue to work well past my retirement age ... I do have two jobs now just to keep up the bills, and I have no retirement fund to speak of." Although willing to keep on working as long as she needs to, Angela is also wary of what exactly the work world is going to provide for her. "Yes, when everyone retires there will be more jobs available, but these jobs are hard to get ... I had to

---

11. "Working After Retirement—The Gap Between Expectations and Reality." Pew Research Center, September 21, 2006.

go back to college at the age of 45, change my career, in order to compete with the younger generation."

It may be that workers like Angela will be an important labor source for some savvy companies for years to come, but not in the kinds of jobs they may have envisioned. The trucking industry, for example, has launched a campaign to urge baby boomers to think of careers driving within their industry as a source of both income and freedom. With campaign slogans saying things like "Assembly lines don't give you stories to tell," the focus of the initial campaign has been on luring people dissatisfied with their current jobs to think about trucking as a way to gain some freedom. Realistically, however, their best source of labor may come from baby boomers who cannot afford retirement immediately and see trucking as a way to gain some needed cash. A *Wall Street Journal* article captured the new breed of baby-boomer workers forced to work. It tells the story of Daniel and Becky Ford, aged 57 and 51 respectively, who have started late-in-life careers as long-haul truck drivers. The company that recruited them, Schneider National Inc. of Green Bay Wisconsin, actively recruits drivers 50 years old and over. For the companies, it means they have a new reliable source of labor in husband–wife teams especially. For the workers, the pay and benefits are especially attractive. With pay of $66,000 to $90,000 a year, plus health insurance and a 401(k) plan, it is a good deal for would-be retirees who are unsure whether their pay and benefits are sufficient to get them through a few more decades. "When the money is tight and you have other worries, you can't be too adventurous," Becky, a former hairstylist, is quoted as saying about the occupation that sometimes keeps her in a truck for 22 hours a day.[12] Becky typifies boomers who would like to retire, but can't.

Economist Teresa Ghilarducci has reviewed extensive research looking at whether the elderly actually prefer work over leisure and concludes

12. Chen, Stephanie, "The Over 50 Crowd Finds Second Careers in Big Rigs." *Wall Street Journal,* August 25, 2006.

that people would prefer to retire. Using the time-use diaries as evidence, she notes that once people retire they spend time dong things they like better than work, such as watching TV, cooking, and pursuing hobbies and sports. She goes on to say that the things that make work satisfying earlier in life are generally absent in jobs after retirement. Finally, she argues that retirement is generally good for the health of the elderly, and that putting off retirement is likely to worsen health across the elderly population. Citing a study that looks at workers over a 10-year period, some of whom have retired and some not, she notes that the increase in earlier retirements up to the 1990s may have made a difference to longevity rates. She suggests that if the elderly continue to work, their health expenses could grow and the longevity trends reverse. "People say that they want to work," she says. "But in reality it comes down to the money. If they could totally replace their incomes while not working, they inevitably they choose leisure over work."

Indeed, a study of those who have already retired and then returned to work shows that financial need generally does play a part in the decision. In a 2005 study, Putnam Investments found that about 7 million previously retired Americans had returned to work, most in a job requiring at least the same skill and experience levels that they had previously. In addition, those who came back into the workforce were on average an educated and high-income group, with an average household income of $87,000, a level that is higher than that of 60 percent of non-working retirees. Although this all would argue against Ghilarducci and others who suggest that working in retirement is rarely a matter of preference, the study also found some surprising things about the assets of those who returned to work. Namely, that they were much less likely to own their homes outright. Over half (60 percent) of the returning workers still carried a mortgage, and on average, their equity in their homes was only 47 percent.[13] It would seem, then, that whatever the surveys might say, returning to work after retirement is largely motivated by strong financial needs.

13. "The Working Retired." Putnam Investments, December 2005.

Of course, it is not just housing that can send people back to work: gyrations in financial assets can have the same effect. Rich, a 60-year-old first-wave boomer who spent most of his career in sales, puts himself in that category. "I retired at 55, right around the time that the stock market was at a nice high, in 2001. Then we had that correction in the market, and I lost a ton. So I did go back to work for a while ... I did some market research, some part-time stuff for about 18 months. Then the market came back and I figured I was in a more stable position, so I retired for good."

Eventually, all of the boomers will follow Rich and retire for good. The question is: how many will be leisure economy haves with enough income to enjoy their retirements? In one sense, all the boomers will be haves, in that they will have both more wealth and more income than previous generations. The most comprehensive data on income at retirement for the United States is cited in a paper for the American Association of Retired Persons.[14] Authors Barbara Butrica and Cori Uccello found that median incomes at the age of 67 for boomers (born from 1946 to 1965) will be about $50,000, compared to $36,000 for those born in the years from 1926 to 1935, and $44,000 for those born from 1936 to 1945 (all figures are adjusted into constant 2003 dollars by the authors). It appears that boomer seniors will be able to enjoy the same standard of leisure, or possibly a higher one than their parents enjoyed.

What also comes out of the numbers is a very skewed distribution among the different boomer groups. The Golden Leisurites are quite visible in the numbers, as is the fact that they are a much more visible group than they were in previous generations. The authors demonstrate this by dividing all households into "income quintiles" (basically income groups from the bottom one-fifth to the top one-fifth). They also separate the boomers into two waves, the first-wave boomers, defined as those born from 1946 to 1955, and the second-wave boomers born from 1956 to 1965. For the group born from 1926 to 1935, at the age of 67 those in the top income quintile will have a household income of $86,000. For

14. Butrica, Barbara and Cori Uccello. "How Will Boomers Fare at Retirement?" The Urban Institute. Prepared for the AARP Policy Institute. AARP, May 2004.

the first wave of boomers, that will rise to $125,000, while for the second wave it will be $128,000. That means approximately 17 or 18 million people in the United States entering retirement with a median household income well above the norm for the rest of the U.S. population. Although comparable Canadian statistics are not readily available, assuming that the Canadian numbers are similar, you could add at least 1.5 million more people north of the border. That's enough to be a powerful, elite, group of consumers with plenty of time and money.

Although this is clearly the golden group, the fourth quintile does quite well too, with household income of $74,000 for the first wave of boomers and $76,000 for the second. That also puts them clearly in the realm of affluence. They will not have any particular push to keep working any longer than they choose. Also, assuming that by this time their biggest fixed expenses (housing and child care) are significantly reduced from their earlier years, they will have a substantial chunk of disposable income to spend on leisure activities. It is these first two quintiles of earners—they total about 38.5 million in the United States—who are likely to be the power players in the leisure economy. These groups will be large enough to create a new leisure economy made of the double-haves: those with time as well as money.

The affluent boomers will be the trendsetters, the ones who will create the demand for exotic orchids for their new greenhouses or buy up the property in Tuscany or anywhere else. Not surprisingly, they will be the ones who will catch the eye of businesses who realize their potential. It is important for those businesses to know, however, that this high-income, high-wealth market totals about 31 million in the United States—not the total 77 million boomers, who are sometimes talked about as being the gilded market.

Indeed, income tumbles for the next income quintiles. The middle quintile of earners has a median income of $50,000 at age 67 for both waves of boomers. That income level represents relative affluence as compared to the two prior waves of seniors, who had incomes of $36,000 and $44,000 at age 67 respectively. Still, it represents a much more modest income stream than the boomers in the top two quintiles.

The lowest two quintiles of boomers will have much more modest incomes. The fourth quintile of boomers will have $31,000 and $33,000 a year in income respectively. Although that's significantly below the quintile above them, it does represent an improvement above $22,000 for the 1926–1935 cohort and $28,000 for the 1936–1945 cohort. Any way you look at it, it means that there will be 15 million or so boomers who will have just about enough money to live a reasonable life, but not to regularly indulge in the treats that were supposed to be part of the good life post retirement. It may also mean that for many their standard of living will be pulled down substantially from the days when they were working, and consequently, they will have to adjust their spending.

The fifth and bottom quintile of baby-boom earners will manage to keep their heads above the poverty line, but not by much. The two waves of boomers will have household incomes of $16,000 and $18,000 respectively at age 67—not much above the $12,000 and $14,000 that the lowest income seniors in the previous birth cohorts achieved. This is the group that may well decide they want to keep working as long as they can, through their late 60s or perhaps even into their 70s, simply to fund a better quality of life than the baseline projections would allow them. More likely, they will simply continue working to live frugally, for they are the group that will likely have been at the bottom of the income ladder through their whole lives.

"We probably won't be able to afford not working in some shape or form," says 50-year-old Brenda. "My spouse ... he's 60 ... has a nice annuity and would like to retire before 65. But I've been in and out of the workforce for the past three years and don't have a pension. We don't have any savings either ... we bought our house just six years ago. We can barely keep our heads above water financially, actually. We don't live on take-out, fine dining is a luxury and we haven't vacationed in over three years." When Brenda does retire, she will eventually be part of the leisure economy, but she won't be part of the sipping-chianti-in-Tuscany group. She will be part of the have-not leisure economy, the one that gives her plenty of time and no money to spend on leisure pursuits.

So why all the potential retirement income discrepancies among a generation that was supposed to be wealthy or at least considerably better off than their parents' generation? Most of the inequities come down to the same reasons that baby boomers have been split in terms of earnings for most of their working lives. There is a sharp split between the earnings of those with more education compared to less, as well as a sharp division by race. Perhaps more surprisingly, there is also a pronounced difference in projected earnings depending on marital status. Those who are divorced or who have never been married can expect to have less income in retirement than the married or widowed. There have always been income disparities between baby boomers of course, and these have grown over the past few years. At the same time, the ability to earn income has introduced a dose of equality for some that is likely to be eroded when they retire and have to rely on their assets rather than just their incomes.

The non-golden retirees or have-nots comprise part of another important segment of the leisure economy: those who will have time, but not money. In their own way, they will be as important to the leisure economy as the golden group. This group will slow down the economy. During their working lives, they were happy to spend money on frozen food or take out, mostly because they did not have time to cook. In retirement, which may come much earlier than they had intended, they will make a different series of choices. If they did not have time to cook before, they will now. They will have time to do lots of things they contracted out when they were younger. In terms of leisure, they will have to choose inexpensive leisure pursuits, hobbies that are time-intensive like knitting rather than time-and-cash intensive like collecting antiques. Their economic power will be at least as important as that of the Golden Leisurites. Depending on where you put the cut-off point, they will comprise from 50 to 70 percent of the total baby-boom retirees. Perhaps as important, they will also have among their ranks non-retirees from all age groups, including Gen Xers and Gen Yers.

It is also likely that the leisure economy will be very much a "man's world," a place where being male is an important indicator of whether you can retire and whether you can lead a life rich in high-priced leisure experiences. True, boomer women as a group received more education and spent many more years in the workforce than did their mothers or grandmothers. For professional women who spent most of their lives working, retirement could indeed be a time to experience "the good life," whether they define it as starting the business they always dreamed of, learning to sky-dive or finally taking a biking or art gallery tour of Europe. The signs are good that women, married or single, will create a special group of Golden Leisurites.

Still, as a group, baby-boomer women may find that they face many hurdles that may prevent them from enjoying a well-financed retirement, and many may find that they have more time than money. "Baby-boomer women need to ask some hard questions about how they will survive in old age," according to Estelle James, a visiting scholar at the Urban Institute who in 2004 conducted a study on their prospects. She lists the problems: first of all, although women have been more likely to work than their predecessors, boomer women in industrialized countries, including Canada and the United States, have generally only had labor force participation rates 75 to 85 percent of those of men, and even when they have worked, some of their work has been part-time. Average hourly wages, although they may have risen for women, are still about 15 to 30 percent below those of men, meaning that women are destined to have lower pensions than men after retirement.[15]

In addition, older women are much more likely to be widowed than are men. It costs one person about 70 percent of what it does for two people to run a household, yet this group of women will be doing it on 50 percent or less income. Given that women tend to marry men older than themselves and live longer their spouses, they are likely to be living alone for a decade or longer. So while there may be a group of rich older women who can spend weeks at Canyon Ranch if they want to, boomer women are still more likely than boomer men to be have-nots, both in terms of achieving leisure as early as they want to, and in having a high income with which to enjoy that leisure.

15. James, Estelle. "Financial Hurdles Confronting Baby Boomer Women." *Harvard Generations Policy Journal*, Volume 1, Winter 2004.

Indeed, high-end spas might actually be better off marketing to older baby-boomer men. They may have to be persuaded harder that an exfoliation is good for them, but if they can be sold, they are more likely to have the money to pay the extra for the Desert Herbal Wrap.

Finally, there is the income disparity between the two waves of baby boomers. The first wave of boomers were more shielded from things like radical restructuring of blue-collar positions, as well as from changes to the pension system that would have eroded their benefits. In other ways too, they generally hit a stronger economy throughout their careers. The housing market likely made a difference to their over-all economic well-being. First-wave boomers may have competed with each other to buy their first houses, but they also had a nice big market of second-wave boomers on whom to unload their starter homes. The magic of inflation was theirs too: those who bought houses in the early 1970s then saw the value of their homes rise with inflation, while their payments stayed constant. All in all, these factors made for a nice economic boost for first-wave boomers.

As important as income, wealth also has the potential to be an equalizer among baby boomers. As a group, many boomers were big winners in the housing market, and a few were lucky winners in the stock markets too. Such gains have contributed to overall wealth, which some can potentially tap into to finance a very luxurious and leisured lifestyle. Whatever their respective incomes, there is a big difference between an asset-poor household and one with a multi-million-dollar portfolio.

On net, boomers are a relatively wealthy group. According to the Federal Reserve's survey of consumer finances, as of 2004 the average household headed by someone aged from 45 to 54 (all of whom would be baby boomers) had a median net worth of $144,700 in 2001 dollars. Mean net worth, meanwhile, was about $542,700 (mean net worth is a less reliable measure, given that a few very high income households are likely to skew the entire average[16]). Like income, however, wealth is very unevenly divided among the baby-boom generation.

---

16. Bucks, Brian K., Arthur B. Kennickell and Kevin B. Moore. "Recent Changes in U.S. Family Finances: Evidence from the 2001 and 2004 Survey of Consumer Finances." *Federal Reserve Bulletin*, Volume 92, February 2006, p. A8.

Including everything—housing, retirement accounts and even an estimate of the total wealth that an individual "owns" as part of their social security entitlement, the AARP study estimates that the first-wave of boomer households will have a staggering $859,000 in wealth at age 67, and the second wave will have $839,000. That's a nice uptick from $558,000 for the 1926–1935 birth cohort, and $703,000 for the 1936–1945 cohort. If the figures look high, however, it is because a lump of that money is indeed for social security. The authors define it as the "present value" of the benefits that an individual will receive over a lifetime. Limiting the wealth figure to non-social-security benefits gives a much different reading, but still one that shows boomer households to have better wealth prospects than their elders. Net of social security wealth, first-wave boomers are projected to have $653,000 of wealth at age 67, compared to $632,000 for the second wave. That's quite a bit above previous generations. The 1926–1935 cohort had a calculated $416,000, and the 1936–45 cohort had $546,000.[17] For all cohorts, wealth from social security is roughly constant at about one-third of total wealth.

As a model, this group will in some sense not be that different from the current group of retirees. After all, it is quite usual for income to drop in retirement. But baby boomers, at all income levels, have been quite unlike their elders in their spending habits: the prospect of their senior years lived more frugally is unlikely to be an appealing one. And the disparities within the boomer population that already exist will only get wider as people leave the workforce. It will all add up to a strange world, one where some are happily a part of the luxury-leisure sector, hopping from spa vacation to spa vacation, while others are eking out an existence at a much more basic level. They'll be more like Brenda, the woman facing retirement with debt on her house and no real income outside of social security. "We're both relatively healthy and hope to stay that way," she says, "but if things don't change soon, I won't be growing old gracefully."

---

17. Calculations of wealth net of social security wealth are by the author using Butrica and Uccello's data. (See note 12.)

CONFRONTING LEISURE ENVY

In a world where some have leisure and some are pressed to the glass wishing they did, there are bound to be conflicts and envy. In the leisure economy, the divisions will be between young and old, as well as between generations.

Inter-generational envy over leisure time is set to be one of the themes of the coming decades. For those in Generations X and Y who are working flat out to pay off their debts and take care of their families, watching boomers—even if some of them are their parents—with time on their hands may become pretty grating. The retirees will have time to get involved in community activities, shop in off hours, hang out at the parks during the day and generally enjoy the benefits that retirement offers. Of course, that has always been the case between retirees and non-retirees, but up to now the distribution between the two has never been that noticeable. As the boomers move into the leisure economy, their presence will be increasingly noted, and undoubtedly resented.

That baby boomers are going to be getting price breaks to enjoy their leisure activities is not going to be popular either. Think about the senior discounts that are common across North America. They were put in at a time when seniors typically were less affluent than they are today. They have been palatable to companies because seniors have for years been a relatively small demographic cohort, as well as a thrifty one. Without the discounts, getting seniors to eat out or go to the movies at all would have been uphill work in many areas. There is already some resentment about those getting the discounts: it was in the mid-1990s that the term "greedy geezers" was first coined. Now think about the well-off baby boomers entering their senior years and wanting to use those same discounts. It will be a double insult for younger workers. Here are the boomers enjoying leisure, and pursuing their leisure pursuits—at a reduced rate to boot! That some of the boomers will not be particularly well-off is unlikely to make the envious feel much better.

It will be a challenge for business, and perhaps one that requires some creative marketing. During downturns, companies have always offered more discounts and special offers, reducing movie prices on certain weeknights, or offering special prices on haircuts with a salon's junior stylist for example. In the leisure economy, companies courting the lower income leisurites will need to think of offering those kinds of incentives on a continuing basis. Often those with lower incomes will have plenty of time, so strictly money low cost (buy a book of tickets at a substantially discounted rate) offers will work to get them into the theaters of wherever. In other cases, such as with younger workers, it will be a matter of time *and* money. In that case, the lower-cost, less time-intensive offerings, such as an "express" manicure for 20 percent less than the regular price, will be better ploys. But in a world where both incomes and time are polarized and there are all kinds of splits within the generations, businesses would be wise to think in terms of a "permanent" recession that may hit some component of their markets.

Boomer leisure will also be a source of inter-generational conflict for those having to pay for it—namely the younger workers. Much has been made of the social security system and what it will take to keep public pensions operational in both the United States and Canada when the boomers retire. Whatever the solution, it is inevitably going to mean some form of higher contributions from those generations still in the workforce. That will be an easy sell to voters, given that so many will already be in their retirement years and happy to support whatever measures make it possible for them to continue receiving their benefits. However, the measures are likely to be extremely unpopular with Generations X and Y, many of whom will be working flat out and not eager to support paying more to support the leisured boomers. The political clashes over these issues will intensify, with lobby groups and politicians pushing for—but not likely having passed—bills that adjust more of the benefits to income, or even assets.

Inter-generational conflicts aside, leisure envy might be the most pronounced of all within the baby-boomer population. After all, boomers have always envied each other their good fortune. In the late 1990s, some of it centered around who was into the stock market boom earliest and who was late to the party. By the end of that decade, neighbors at the same cocktail parties often had completely different portfolio experiences, depending on when their stock in Cisco Systems was bought or sold. Next, the bragging or shame was over housing: when you bought and where meant the dividing line between living in a bargain-rate palace or a hovel mortgaged to the hilt.

Now the buzz will be over who has the highest quality leisure time, the time to travel and to pursue whatever pastimes strike their fancy. There could well be neighbors in upscale communities facing very different leisure economy profiles. For one set, with their houses paid off and plenty of money socked away, travel, high-cost hobbies and meaningful community work could be their choice; many will choose to pursue those things well before they hit 65 or even 60. For the other set, retirement, even past age 60, may not bring poverty, but it may bring with it the need to continue to work part-time in a job they do not particularly like simply to continue to feed a mortgage that they did not pay off during their working years.

Envious glances are also likely to come from Generation X towards Generation Y. Generation X, after all, was the segment of the population who knew, unlike the boomers, that they did not want to make work their lives. Unlike Generation Y, however, they got few breaks from the economy that let them develop flexible jobs or hours. While they may have made some progress in crafting the work and home lives that they want, they are still likely to be aghast when they see what some in Generation Y are able to achieve in terms of work–life balance. Then again, at least Gen Xers may still be in a position to benefit from such things as parental leaves, and will perhaps be somewhat grateful. Boomers are likely to be simply aghast as they look at the restructured labor market, feeling that they put in the long hours without asking for much in the way of accommodation, only to watch Generation Y waltz in and be catered to in terms of how they want their work life to be organized.

Finally, within Generation Y there resides the biggest mystery of all: who among them will get the leisure they crave and, indeed, will they really want the leisure a decade or so from now? If Gen Y stays true to their principles and does want to have time away from the workforce—either to spend time with family or to pursue their own interests—then there is indeed likely to be some intra-generational envy at work if they actually get it. Some mothers—or fathers—will manage to be stay-at-homes and some will not, a situation not very different from today. The difference is that now, in many ways, the prestige is still with having a career, whether you are a man or a woman. But already the pendulum is shifting towards leisure—an awkward term for staying home with children to be sure—as the more coveted choice. As the leisure economy frees and empowers some and not others, envy is likely to shift from who is taking an expensive ski vacation to who has time to be home after school to take the kids to ski lessons—or maybe just to watch them play.

WELCOME BACK, FIDO

6

Work and play are two words used to describe the same things under different conditions.

—*Mark Twain*

Remember Kerry, the management consultant featured in the introduction? She quit work in search of a "European Life" and liked it so much that she never wanted to go back to "real" work. "Well, maybe if my family was starving or something," was how she put it.

Kerry's experience neatly sums up the way that the leisure economy is about to collide with the world of work as we know it. She has fashioned a life for herself that includes work as well as time for a variety of interests outside of work. Short of her facing starvation, the corporate world could not get her back at any price. She is simply out of the market. Very soon, many of her baby-boomer friends will join her on the outside, perhaps following her into self-employment or just entering retirement. The corporate world will not be able to get them back either.

At the same time that the boomers are reconfiguring their work lives, Generation Y will be hitting their 30s, reaching decent salary levels and forming families. Unlike Kerry and her friends, they are not embarrassed to admit they want "European Lives." Assuming they can swing it financially, many—either male or female—may not wait until they have teenagers before deciding to find an alternative to the time-crunch economy. And Generation X? They may still be in the work force, but they will be moving into the higher level jobs from which they've been blocked for so long by the baby boomers. As they take the helm, they will impose their own values on the workplace.

These changes may lead to a better quality of life all around—and a nightmare for the companies that have not experienced anything but a world where labor, baby boomer or otherwise, is abundant and willing to accept the terms of employment offered. In the old regime, the world of work effectively expanded, creating the time-crunch economy. In the new regime, the leisure economy will be created separate from the labor market—and then will have a profound impact on the workplace.

The big picture shows a labor force that will be tighter, where firms will need to hold on to their workers who have been so expensive to recruit and train. It will be very different from the story in the 1970s through the 1990s when scores of boomers (and later Generation Xers) were coming through the doors as retirements for the pre-boomers were a fairly insignificant offset. In fact, if there is a parallel, it might be the dot-com years, when labor in some sectors was so tight that workers negotiated bringing their dogs, cats or birds to the office. And yes, the days may be coming when such concessions are back in vogue. That might mean holding on to the boomers, and it might mean indulging the Yers by letting them sneak a Lab or two into the office. What it means most of all, however, is acknowledging that what workers want most is time, and the workplace is going to have to be configured to give it to them.

THE BOOMERS: EASING INTO THE LEISURE ECONOMY

The leisure economy, and by extension making concessions to workers, is really all about the boomers. Their sheer numbers and attitudes were responsible for the creation of the time-crunch economy. Now, as they leave work, they will create the labor shortages that will transform the workplace. The concept of a "labor shortage," though, is a tricky one. The idea has almost achieved the status of an urban legend: everyone knows someone who knows the facts and the government is sure there will be a "shortage" of millions of workers. In truth, it will depend on how quickly the boomers retire, and how employers handle the situation.

The Labor Shortage: Myth or Reality?

The upcoming labor shortage has been a hot topic for many years, with good reason. The potential bonanza for workers could be a disaster for business. U.S. economic growth has advanced at an average clip of over 3 percent annually over the past two decades.[1] That's been achieved through some impressive increases in productivity, but also through having more people in the workforce: the U.S. labor force has increased by an average of 1.4 percent annually over the same period.[2] By and large, companies have been able to find the right people, or at least people they could train for the jobs.

As has been the pattern through their working lives, the decisions that the baby boomers make about labor force participation have the power to influence not just their own leisure and work lives, but the leisure–work trade-offs for other generations too. The vast majority of baby boomers probably will head for retirement sometime in their late 50s or early 60s, as has been the pattern for many years. If the labor force participation rate edged up even a little bit—that is, if the percentage of boomers deciding to work in their mature years was higher than it has been in the past—it would go a long way towards erasing any future labor shortage And, of course, that is what we are already seeing. The labor force participation rate for those aged over 55 *has* been edging up in recent years. And as we saw in Chapter 5, many have-not boomers are going to have little choice but to keep working well into their senior years.

---

1. U.S. Department of Commerce, Average change in U.S. gross domestic product for the years 1986–2005. Calculations are by the author.

2. U.S. Bureau of Labor Statistics.

Even with those considerations, the concept of the labor shortage and the leisure economy looks safe enough, if less simplistic than the legends suggest. The boomers *are* retiring, and there will be a huge number of replacement workers needed to fill their positions. As of 2005, approximately 66 percent of the U.S. population aged 15 and over were either employed or looking for work. According to the U.S. Bureau of Labor Statistics, that percentage could slip to about 62 percent by 2025 and decline to 60 percent by 2035.[3] In Canada, over the next five years alone, 1.48 million Canadians are expected to retire,[4] and as we approach 2020, the number of retirees will increase exponentially in both countries.

That could mean serious macroeconomic consequences. We know, for example, that the U.S. population, according to the U.S. Census Bureau, has been growing at about 1 percent over the past decade, and at least until 2010 growth is likely to stay at about that level. As the population ages, population growth (assuming there is not a huge influx of immigration) will fall to about 0.3 percent by 2030, and perhaps even lower by 2050, meaning that labor force growth too will slide. On the other side of the equation, forecasts from the U.S. Bureau of Labor Statistics show that employment will grow by 18.9 million, or 13 percent, between 2004 and 2014.[5] Using the most basic calculation methods—subtracting demand from supply—some estimates suggest that the United States will have a shortage of 3 million or more workers as early as 2012.[6]

Whether or not there is an all-out lack of labor, there is no question that there will be big problems in individual sectors and industries, and within specific companies. A lot of it will come down to which sectors and companies have workforces that are disproportionately made up of boomers. Any sector that hired aggressively in the 1970s or early

3. Szafran, Robert F. "Age-Adjusted Labor Force Participation Rates, 1960–2045." Monthly Labor Review, U.S. Bureau of Labor Statistics, September 2002.

4. Bergeron, Louis-Philippe et al. "Looking Ahead: A Ten-Year Outlook for the Canadian Labour Market, 2004–2013." Human Resources Development Canada, October 2004.

5. "Tomorrow's Jobs." *Occupational Outlook Handbook*. U.S. Department of Labor, 2003. www.bls.gov/oco/occo2003.htm.

6. For a further discussion of the concept of labor shortages, see "Employment Projections to 2012: Concepts and Context" by Michael W. Horrigan (Monthly Labor Review, U.S. Bureau of Labor Statistics, February 2004).

1980s, and then much less so when the economy cooled thereafter, is probably in trouble. For both the United States and Canada, the federal governments are in this category (in the United States almost 21 percent of federal workers were aged 55 or older as of 2004[7]), as are education and much of health care. Energy is another case in point: a frenzy of activity in the 1960s and early 1970s meant workers were added to this sector in earnest; then harsher economic times caused a freeze on hiring. Much of the manufacturing sector is in the same position.

Should I Stay or Should I Go?

Although almost all companies are well aware of the potential labor supply crisis ahead, few have concrete business plans in place aimed at holding onto vital workers, or at least retaining some of their knowledge when they do retire. Now is the time to make plans: companies that are ahead of the curve on thinking about how to keep boomer workers happy will be the ones who are not scrambling to fill the gaps as the last minute—either because their workers have retired, or because they have been lured away by companies that offer a more attractive work environment.

Keeping the baby boomers on the job sounds fairly easy to do, given that the surveys constantly tell us that baby boomers would like to keep working long after the traditional retirement age. But there is no way to know the extent of the disconnect between boomers' good intentions and what will actually happen. The boomers who want to work the longest, as we know, are frequently those who have made the least money over their working lives and do not feel that they have enough socked away for retirement. Given that they are disproportionately in blue-collar and lower-skilled jobs, they may not be a match for the jobs that are begging to be filled.

The workers that employers are anxious to hold onto will frequently be in higher skilled fields that require a long period of training—areas such as accounting or health care. They will need highly skilled professionals, but that group of boomers are much more likely to have

---

7. "Older Workers: Labor Can Help Employers and Employees Plan Better for the Future." U.S. Government Accountability Office. Report to Congressional Committees, December 2005.

enough money put away for their retirements. They may spend a few years dipping their toes into the leisure economy before they are willing to give up their jobs, but eventually the lure of life beyond work will likely pull them away. Even among those boomers who initially do not see themselves as having enough money to retire, many may find an out—perhaps by eventually selling their houses and moving to lower-cost areas where their money goes further. "It's a no-brainer," says Teresa Ghilarducci, Professor of Economics at the University of Notre Dame. "People who can afford to retire generally prefer to retire." A study by the The American Association of Retired Persons (AARP) shows that the numbers bear this out: of the 41 million Americans who were not in the labor force in 2005, only about 2 percent said they wanted a job, and only about 30 percent of those who said they wanted a job had even looked for one.[8] So in many ways, the deck is stacked against employers who would like to hold on to their baby boomer workers. What might entice a worker on the fence about retirement to stick around a little longer? According to a survey conducted by the American Association of Retired Persons (AARP), the following were cited as "very important" by working retirees and pre-retirees:

- working in an environment where employee opinions are valued
- working for a company that lets older workers remain employed for as long as they wish
- being able to take time off work to care for relatives
- being able to set their own hours
- working for a company that offers good health benefits
- working for a company that offers health benefits to retirees

Another list captured what the group sees as either "very important" or "somewhat important." These included:

- having new experiences
- learning new skills

---

8. Rix, Sara E. "Update on the Aged 50+ Worker: 2005." AARP Public Policy Institute, April 2006.

- being able to work a reduced schedule before completely retiring
- working for a company that offers a good pension plan
- being able to work from home[9]

Interestingly, the list can be split into two major categories: those solely about money, and those related to the leisure economy. To be fair, the first category is probably the more important one for most pre-retirees. With many boomers' finances in a fragile situation, companies that offer meaty pension plans and health plans—especially for the retirement years—will be the ones that have the most success in holding onto workers. In one sense that makes it easier for companies who want to know how to keep their boomer workers or attract new ones: say it with money.

As well as more money, pre-retirees want more time. Many baby boomers have aging parents in need of care and attention, so being able to take time off to care for them is and will continue to be a huge concern. Indeed, it already tops the list of what workers want. Setting their own hours, working from home and working their own schedule also loom large for boomers deciding whether to stay or go. If employers don't change their workplaces to accommodate their employees' needs, they will likely only be able to hold onto workers who are in such unstable financial situations that they have no choice but to keep working. To maintain the rest of their workers—or at least have the option—employers will have to offer an enticing menu of leisure economy options.

Some companies are ahead of the curve. AARP publishes a list every year: The Best Places to Work. On their most recent list, the companies that get their seal of approval are those that provide flexible work arrangements of all stripes. Number one on the list, Mercy Health System of Janesville, Wisconsin, was not only first for 2006 but has also been first for the past six consecutive years. Within the non-profit system (63 facilities, including three hospitals) workers aged 50+ can take advantage of numerous options, including weekend-only positions, "seasonal" work programs that allow for long leaves (while

---

9. *Staying Ahead of the Curve 2003: The AARP Working in Retirement Study.* AARP, 2003.

maintaining their benefits) and on-call assignments. Volkswagen of America Inc. (number six on the list in 2006) is also worth mentioning. The company offers alternative arrangements ranging from flex time and compressed work schedules to job-sharing and telecommuting, as well as the opportunity to ease into retirement through part-time work.

Most striking about the AARP list is its heavy concentration of companies within the public sector or the para-public sectors, such as health, education and non-profits. In fact, of the top 10 finishers, only Volkswagen, First Horizon National Corporation of Memphis (number nine) and Hoffman-La Roche Inc. of Nutley, New Jersey were squarely in the private sector. There are several conclusions one can draw from this, including the fact that up until now creating programs to keep older workers in the labor force was neither good business, nor necessary, given the continuous flow of younger workers. Given that this scenario is not likely to hold for much longer, the private sector clearly has some catching up to do.

But if the public sector is ahead of the curve in keeping its own boomer employees happy, public policy may be behind the curve. As it stands, North American laws regarding pensions were developed at a time when it made sense to move workers out of the labor force as they reached the age of 65. After all, for decades we had the baby-boomer cohort coming into the labor force and providing a more than adequate supply of workers. Now, mandatory retirement may be gone but there are still rigidities that make it simpler for workers to retire according to the traditional time frames.

Defined benefit plans—basically pension schemes that provide workers with annual incomes equal to a certain percentage of salary times years of service up to a maximum—are a particular problem. At the most basic level, if you are eligible to collect a pension at a specific age, say 65, then working one more year means getting a pension for one year less. As many as two-thirds of U.S. workers are likely covered by these plans, and nearly half of those workers will be eligible for retirement over the next decade; this creates a big potential outflow from the workforce.[10] Switching to part-time work, therefore, looks pretty unappealing given that the result means not getting full pension benefits. At present, companies can generally get around this only by letting workers retire and then hiring them back on a part-time or consulting basis.

The Health Factor

Holding on to boomer workers is also contingent on their health. Despite their best intentions to keep working, many boomers may find themselves chuted into the leisure economy simply because their years in the time-crunch economy have had a detrimental effect on their health. That runs counter to the usual arguments about better health meaning longer lives, and indeed there have been increases in life expectancy for many workers. At the same time, many baby boomers have lifestyle issues that put them at risk for everything from diabetes to hypertension. Remember that the rate of obesity among all age groups has been growing in North America for a decade. According to a Canadian study, one in three Canadian boomers aged 45 to 59 was obese as of 2006, compared to one in four a decade ago. The rate of obesity among Canadian seniors was only one in four. Similarly, the percentage of boomers who smoke was about twice the rate of senior smokers (21 percent compared to 11 percent).[11] That does not bode well for boomer health into retirement. Carl Eisdorfer, professor and chairperson in the Department of Psychiatry and Behavioural Sciences at the School of Medicine at the University of Miami, cites something called "Eisdorfer's Law": for every five years of life after age 65, baby boomers can expect to double their rate of developing medical problems and diseases.[12]

Disabilities will also increasingly plague boomer workers—and companies—in the years ahead. According to a 2001 report from the National Organization on Disability, for those aged from 45 through

10. Towers Perrin 2003 workforce data in "Workers Age 50 + : Planning for Tomorrow's Talent Needs in Today's Competitive Environment." Prepared for AARP by Towers Perrin, December 2005.

11. "Baby Boomer Obesity Surpasses Senior, New Study Shows." Queens News Centre, February 14, 2006.

12. Stuart, Victoria, "Boomers on the Brink." *Miami Magazine*, Spring 1998.

54, there is an 11.5 percent chance of developing a disability of some sort. For those aged from 55 through 64, that percentage jumps to a whopping 21.9 percent. The disabilities in question include problems with hearing, vision, or dexterity, all of which could affect things such as use of computers. And indeed, it is small disabilities of these types, such as those caused by arthritis, that frequently help workers make the decision to retire—or at least that has been the case with pre-boomers.

Fortunately for the boomers, they are hitting their high-disability years at what perhaps will be a fortunate time. For one thing, technologies are being rapidly developed that can help older workers. Second, companies who want to keep them on the job will be more apt to do the capital spending needed than would have been the case in the past. Everything from voice recognition systems that help arthritic workers avoid using their hands to computer interfaces that make it easier for those with diminished vision—there is a plethora of devices that can help aging workers. What would happen without these innovations? They may be expensive, but many companies may think of them as part of the price of the leisure economy.

One final thought for companies that are hoping to hold on to baby boomers: sell them on the idea that working will keep their minds sharp. As well as more money and free time, surveys show that pre-retirees want to be mentally stimulated at work. As boomer-brain deterioration—from forgetfulness to Alzheimer's—becomes a hot topic, many people may be convinced that staying on the job longer and putting off Florida for a bit is probably a good idea. Indeed, research shows that using one's brain, whether doing crosswords or learning a new language, tends to keep the brain fit and functioning. While this may not work for every job or sector, stressing the mental challenge of work may convince some boomers to keep working for a while longer.

No matter which of these measures employers take, it is unlikely they will be wholly successful in mitigating the weaker labor force growth that is likely ahead. According to the Urban Institute, to reverse the projected decline in labor force growth, the labor force participation rate among workers aged 55 to 64 would need to increase to a level only slightly lower than for workers aged 25 to 49.[13] As for workers older than 65, it is probably not realistic to think that many of them are going to stay on the job much beyond retirement age. Of all older workers who left work between 1992 and 2000, only about 13 percent said that the carrot of part-time work would have kept them there longer. So ultimately the boomers are headed for the leisure economy. And that may be a good thing in itself, anyway. For those blocked by the boomer ceiling, seeing costly innovations used to keep the boomers around longer—especially if they see it as happening at their expense—is likely to make them brush up their own resumes. It will be quite a tightrope to walk for companies trying to keep all generations happy.

COURTING THE POST-BOOM GENERATIONS

Forty hours a week, 50 or so weeks a year. There may be some variations by industry—office workers may officially put in 35 hours, truck drivers officially a bit more—but the model of how we work in North America has been pretty cut-and-dried for decades. Part-time work is available, but it is disproportionately in the service sector and often in categories dismissed as "McJobs." Alternative arrangements, flexible arrangements, four days a week—these are available here and there, but in professional jobs they frequently offer very little in the way of a career path. If you want benefits—and frequently if you want a job—the choice is to work full-time, and probably add a dollop on top of that. But as the leisure economy takes shape, alternatives to the old model will stop being a rarity. They will grow for a variety of reasons, the first being that the next wave of workers value their leisure time more than those they are replacing.

As with the concept of a labor shortage, the idea that employers are going to accommodate workers in any way is sometimes greeted as if it is a fairy-tale. After all, there have been very few concessions to workers over the past few decades. From the ever-lengthening workweek through to the ever-shorter vacation, workers have been encouraged to

---

13. Penner, Rudolph G., Perun, Pamela and Steuerle, Eugene. "Letting Older Workers Work." The Urban Institute, Brief Series. No. 16, July 2003.

spend more, not less, time at work. Working mothers have entered the labor market in large numbers since the 1970s, but in terms of changing the structure of the work day or week, they have made remarkably little progress. For every one who has negotiated a four-day workweek or the ability to work from home occasionally, there have been dozens of others who have accepted the need for 40-hour-and-then-some weeks—or else just walked away in frustration because the demands of working full time are just not compatible with the responsibilities of having a family. As we have seen, in recent years, there has been a large loss in highly educated women in professions; many have opted to drop out. But if the labor market has not adapted to keep these talented women, why should we suppose it will shift now to accommodate others?

The answer is this: we are about to see shifts on both the employer's and employee's side of the equation. From the 1970s through the 1990s we have seen a specific mix that has tipped the balance away from flexibility in the workplace. A deep talent pool, thanks to the boomers and a North American economy that has been battered by several recessions, are one part of the equation. The other is that workers have, by and large, not been willing to walk away from jobs, even though they considered them less than ideal. Dealing with ever larger mortgages and increasing consumer needs, most have simply not had the option to quit. Both sides have bought into the time-crunch economy.

For the lucky workers in the labor-crunched industries, the time is coming when they can probably bargain for more money or time, or possibly both. Gen Y in particular has made it clear that they want a more "leisured" existence than either the boomers or the Xers managed to get during their working lives. Will they really follow through and demand fewer working hours—whether through longer vacations or anything else? Inevitably, if they do, they will one way or another be "sacrificing" the money they might have gotten otherwise. The jury is still out as to whether Gen Yers will accept less in terms of consumption. For a generation used to getting Play Station 3 within weeks of its release, it is hard to make the case that they will be happy with a more frugal lifestyle. In one sense, the name brand clothes and tech gadgets are a bit of a red herring: the real question for Generation Y is the cost of housing. The biggest budget item for consumers has always been housing, and the housing boom of the past few decades has only made things more difficult for young households. Although housing eats up 32 percent of all consumer expenditures in the United States,[14] younger households typically find themselves spending much more.

There are reasons to believe that the real (inflation-adjusted) price of housing may be headed down in the future. The same demographic factors that are limiting labor force growth also suggest that (again, short of a protracted increase in immigration) the three-decade upward push on housing prices may dissipate over the next decade. Although that is bad news for boomers hoping to unload their houses at the highest price possible, it also means that Gen Y may find it easier to get into the housing market. As well, given that the runaway inflation that ratcheted up inflation in the 1980s and early 1990s also seems tamed, interest rates can also reasonably be assumed to stay low.[15] The net result could be a more manageable cost of housing for Generation Y. In turn, that more manageable housing situation will give Gen Y a little more leeway in saying "no" to the time-crunch economy. A household with less money earmarked for housing costs would find it easier to keep one partner out of the workforce if they want, for example. They might also be more apt to bargain harder for more time off, rather than for more income.

From the worker side of things, though, the leisure economy is going to force many employers to realize that they have no choice but to acquiesce to what will be loud demands for different kinds of work arrangements. There is already the demand for jobs that provide more time away from the workplace. According to a 2003 study by staffing and recruiting company Spherion Corporation, 86 percent of employees agreed that life–work balance and fulfillment was a career priority, and 96 percent thought a company was "more attractive when it helped them meet family obligations through options like flextime,

---

14. *Consumer Expenditures in 2004*, U.S. Bureau of Labor Statistics, April 2006.

15. Interest rates have two components: one part covers the "real" return on borrowed capital, while the other covers the lender's expectation of inflation.

telecommuting or job-sharing. A follow-up survey in 2005 found that less than one corporation in five was in a good position to recruit and retain the talent needed.

Of course, it all comes back down to the concept of the labor shortage. Economist Peter Cappelli, among others, has argued that there are several compelling arguments for not getting too excited about any real shortage of workers.[16] At the top of his list is the fact that the labor force is not really one unyielding size but rather expands or contracts, depending on how much money is on offer. Think of it this way: if companies do find that labor is scarce, then they will inevitably offer more money to fill whatever positions they have open. In turn, this will lure in many of those on the sidelines who are not looking for work. Young people, for example, might find it more enticing to take high-paying jobs than to stay in school for graduate work, or stay-at-home moms might figure it is worthwhile to pay for child care and enter the workforce. But attracting workers will likely take more than money.

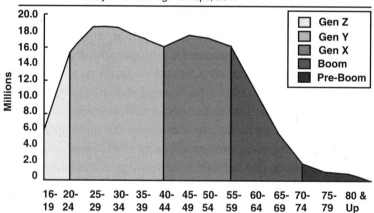

Generations in the Workplace, 2017
U.S. Labor Force by Five Year Age Groups, 2017

Source: U.S. Bureau of Labor Statistics projections, Author Divisions
Note: Because projections are in 5 year increments, divisions by generation are subject to rounding

16. Cappelli, Peter. "Will There Really be a Labor Shortage?" *Organizational Dynamics*, August 2003.

If working mothers have been the "canary in the coal mine" to test the flexibility of companies, many would say the experiment has been a dismal failure, especially for those at the highest professional levels. Many of the efforts made by companies seem to have been directed at helping workers handle the time crunch, rather than eliminate it. "Our company had a 'woman's committee'" says Jennifer, the lawyer who opted out of work. "It was supposed to help women cope with the pressures of being working mothers and being lawyers. But the emphasis was really on getting more help so you could do more at work. It would be like 'Okay, you need your nanny and you need your night nanny and you need your weekend nanny.' And the women who were doing the mentoring were the ones who had parented that way, which I didn't want to do." Similarly, a recent book by Carol Evans, writer for *Working Mother* magazine and author of *This is How We Do It: The Working Mother's Manifesto,* caught some criticism in reader reviews on amazon.com from readers who had issues with the proposed "solutions" to the problems of working and having a family. "This book does very little beyond re-articulating the theory, 'You, too, can do both—raise children and prosper at work, as long as you work 75 hours or more at your job,'" wrote one irate reviewer. "Rise at 4 a.m. to complete a task so that you can 'slip out early' by 45 minutes? Stay up after the kids go to bed, editing your work product? Have a Family Team Plan (I forget the exact word the author uses) that can shuttle YOUR kids places? … Come on, mothers. We deserve better." As it happens, the writer in question was in the minority in her condemnation of the book, and indeed, many would agree that the author's solutions are practical ones—or at least they have been up to now. For Gen X and Gen Y, though, the solutions may fall short, especially if they have a bit of bargaining power.

And remember, as the boomers retire it will frequently be Xers and Yers who will have to be lured, whether into the labor force or from company to company. After all, there are not enough workers to replace retiring boomers. True, some of the thinking came about because the generation that follows the baby boom, "the baby bust," is too small to replace the boomers when they exit their jobs. That might be true: we know that birth rates dropped off in the late 1960s through to the early 1970s and that in that particular chunk of Generation X, there may not be a huge number of workers to offset retiring boomers. However, we also know that Generation Y is quite a large cohort group, and they will continue to stream into the workforce over the next two decades or so. So there are workers—they are just a different kind of worker than we have seen in the past. That might certainly mean big adjustments for companies. If they are effectively using young and relatively inexperienced Gen Y workers to replace boomers, it might mean more training and glitches in production, but the work will get done. And, as Cappelli also points out, many of the younger workers have a high degree of education, thanks to an increasing percentage of college attendance. So there is an argument to be made that Gen Y workers newly entering the labor force will, in some respects, be a good substitute for retiring boomers.

But just because the Yers offer a potential labor supply does not make them a one-to-one match for the boomers. At the very least, it means that companies need to invest in serious training and lots of it, as well as well as in efforts to transfer the knowledge of outgoing employees to the younger workforce. More than that, however, companies that want to be successful in keeping Generation Y employees need to think carefully about the packages they are offering them.

What can employers do to bring in and keep the workers they need? Everybody knows the laundry list: telecommuting, flex-time, parental leaves, part-time work with pro-rated benefits, sabbaticals. Unfortunately, for many companies that list is white noise that comes from human resources departments and is ignored both by managers and employees. For example, as of 2006, only 23 percent of U.S. workers either worked from home or were given that option. A whopping 59 percent, however, apparently believe that telecommuting at least part-time is the ideal work solution.[17] "You still are dealing with the old mindset to some degree," says Pat Katepoo, founder of WorkOptions.com, a consulting

17. "Home and Office: Workers Want it All." Hudson Highland Group, July 19, 2006.
    http://www.prnewswire.com/cgi-bin/stories.pl?ACCT = 104&STORY = /www/story/07-19-2006/
    0004399403&EDATE.

company that specializes in helping workers create alternative work arrangements. "With things like telecommuting there is that stigma, that wanting to see face time. But the results of telecommuting are so well documented and so positive that you are seeing that change. A lot of work these days is about the deliverables, not actually seeing people physically in the office." Generation Y, in particular, shuns face time since they know perfectly well that technology will allow them to do many jobs from many different venues. As they hit their family for-mation years—and as their influence in the workplace grows—expect them to ratchet up the 23 percent of telecommuters.

The issues around part-time work are also extremely interesting. At the end of 2006, only about 23 percent of U.S. workers were part-time, and for managerial and professional workers the percentage was 18 percent.[18] It is one measure of the time-crunch economy: whatever workers want in terms of flexibility, they do not seem to want to work fewer hours. "I get twice as many enquiries about telecommuting as I do about part-time work," says Katepoo, whose company provides downloadable "boilerplate" proposals for workers lobbying for alterna-tive arrangements. "A lot of people want more control over their work but they are supporting lifestyles that require full-time work." Sharon Jordan-Evans, President of the Jordan Evans Group and the co-author of *Love 'Em or Lose 'Em: Getting Good People to Stay*[19] likens being a part-time worker in North America to being something of a second-class citizen. "There is a feeling that if you work part time, you must not really want to help this company. And you simply do not see part-timers at the higher levels." It remains to be seen what workers will ask for, but part-time work has a lot of potential to make the wish lists. For the aging boomers, part-time work may well be the best solution for workers, and like everything else the boomers have done, their demands will set a trend. For Gen X and Gen Y too, part-time work would provide the coveted time they want with their families. With

18. U.S. Bureau of Labor Statistics. Table A-28. "Persons at work by occupation, sex and usual full- or part-time status." 2006 (http://www.bls.gov/web/cpseea28.pdf). Calculations are by the author.

19. Kaye, Beverly and Sharon Jordan-Evans. *Love 'Em or Lose 'Em: Getting Good People to Stay*. San Francisco: Berrett-Koehler (2002).

a lot less to prove—and a self-assurance born of economic prosperity—the "second-class citizen" label is unlikely to bother them a bit. And for Gen Y in particular, part-time work might be something that both men and women will sample.

"I am very much interested in working part-time professionally," says 29-year-old Julian. "I have worked as an English teacher and an editor, and with both jobs, I have wished it was possible to split the job between two people and just take half the salary." If Julian eventually finds himself with several people to support and a huge mortgage, his part-time aspirations may come to seem like little more than a naive dream. If, however, he has a wife who earns a significant income plus a house with a manageable mortgage, the part-time option may look like a good one, and unlike a baby boomer he will not worry about the stigma that goes along with being a man without a full-time job.

The same is true for vacation times. John de Graaf of the "Take Back Your Time" movement sees 20-somethings as very ripe for the push for more time off. "They have seen what workaholism has done for their parents," he says. "They want freedom and balance. Even the young feminists I know really want balance in terms of their work and family lives." Claire Raines of Claire Raines Associates agrees that there is going to be a gap between employees who demand a life and the expectations of companies, particularly as it relates to Generation Y. "They are not going to give up their time all that easily. They are not going to say, 'Okay I'll take a job and give up all my leisure pursuits.' That's going to be a problem for companies that say, 'Yes, but there is work to be done.' So I think there will be a fundamental shift in the way that people work. They'll be more streamlined."

Still, if there are reasons to think that on the supply side there may be some mitigating factors to a labor shortage, it is also true that we really do not know what the "demand" side of the equation may be. If the economy is very hot for the next few decades, then workers may be in demand; if we are hit by a recession or two, the opposite might be the case. We also do not really know how things like the outsourcing phenomenon might develop in the future. Right now, we know that many North American jobs have been shifted overseas as employers find it cheaper and more efficient to do things like put a call center in India than to operate one in the United States. Gradually outsourcing is shifting to include professional positions in information technology and engineering, and the next wave may go even further. That could certainly put a damper on the demand for North American workers, as could a breakdown of barriers to bringing in skilled immigrants from abroad.

Then again, what employers may really be up against to attract workers is not just other companies or absolute leisure but self-employment. According to a study by outplacement firm Challenger, Gray and Christmas,[20] as of the second quarter of 2005, there had been a 3 percent increase in the number of Americans who are self-employed compared to five years earlier. Boomers and pre-boomers are forming businesses at a much faster rate. Over the same period, the number of self-employed workers aged 45 to 54 was up by 29 percent, while among those over 55 the growth rate was 25 percent.

Why the increase? To be fair, there is a negative side to it. Economic softness sometimes forces workers to form their own businesses out of desperation, and there is some evidence that older workers, finding it harder to replace lost jobs with equivalent ones, often take this route. On the plus side, for those who do decide, for whatever reasons, to form businesses, many more tend to be like Kerry and swoon over the freedom of not having to work for a single employer. "Working full time is a tether," says Pat Katepoo. "Once you are on your own you hate the idea of being tied to an employer, even if there is a degree of uncertainty to it."

As much as the boomers might be just about to fall in love with self-employment, it is also likely to be a huge draw for Generation Y. As detailed in Chapter 4, perhaps the only thing holding some back is the ability to cover health insurance costs, as well as the need to pay back student debt. Once they get into a more stable financial position, a decade or two into their working lives, they may strike out on their own, choking off another source of corporate labor.

The net result is likely to be a universe where many independent contractors, like Kerry, find clients among the large-scale companies

20. Challenger, Gray and Christmas. "Start-Up Explosion on the Horizon." August 24, 2005.

with whom they no longer wish to have an employment relationship—
or who no longer wish to keep them on their payrolls. For some who
start small businesses, leisure may well go by the wayside as they
find themselves working day and night. For others, though, given that
the nature of self-employment means working on contracts, going this
route means that they will see an increase in leisure—both voluntarily,
because they set their schedules to include it, or involuntarily, because
they cannot find enough work to fill all their working hours. One way
or another, they will be more a part of the leisure economy than when
they were conventionally employed.

How Generation X reacts when boomer retirements start to accel-
erate will be particularly interesting. When the boomers start to retire,
some Xers will probably find that the jobs they have long wanted will
be open to them. It will finally be their time to "shine" in the workforce, and it is possible that they will impose some of their own values.
In fact, barring a major economic downturn, they will find themselves
in the heady position of being in hot demand, something that they
were cheated out of at the start of their careers.

Recruiting Gen X workers means companies have to be able to
promise that they can take the offered jobs and still have a life. Sharon
Jordan-Evans has found in her surveys of Gen Xers that workers rank
"flexibility" as one of their top 10 goals in a job. "Historically, boomers
have been motivated by promotions," she says. "A boomer would say,
'Thank you for the promotion,' then make whatever sacrifices were
necessary. Gen Xers, in contrast, seem to be less willing to make what
boomers think of as 'sacrifices' and Gen Yers are right there along with
them. And the other thing that has happened is that boomers don't
want to embrace the 'whatever sacrifice is necessary' model anymore
either."

Gen X has already started to take the helm as managers, but
as boomer retirements really take hold they will make larger strides
towards imposing their values on the workplace. Boomer managers
are apt to impose the same rule-driven structure that was imposed
on them. A baby-boomer manager, for example, might be loth to give

too many employees time off at the same time in the summer, or during the Christmas holidays, worrying that the work will not get done. The Gen X manager would be more likely to grant the time: in his or her reality, the real risk is that unhappy workers will jump ship to an organization that acknowledges that their lives do not center on the labor market work. "The Xers are managing the way they want to be managed," says Jordan Evans. "They don't care about face time, and they tend to be more lenient in their style." Xers and Yers at the helm, therefore, means that the leisure economy can creep into the work force a bit at a time.

That X and Y managers are likely to be open to leisure-economy rewards is lucky, because offering more money to lure workers may lead to its own problems for companies. If real (inflation-adjusted) wages go up because of the labor shortages, then it may become viable for households to consider having only one partner in the labor force. For Generation Y workers, who have always been clear that they want plenty of family time, the timing may be just about right. By 2015 say, the oldest Gen Yers will be in their mid-30s and forming families. If they find themselves in a position to keep their standard of living (made easier because the real price of housing may be stagnant), while increasing their household leisure time, the choice may be a no-brainer: one partner, possibly but not necessarily the female, will drop out of the labor force and decide to stay home. It's a variation of what economists refer to as the "backward bending labor supply curve." As wages rise, workers (or households) are more likely to choose to work additional hours because of what they can do with the money. As they reach a certain income level, however, the extra benefits of working more hours pale compared to the benefits of gaining more leisure.

THE ALBERTA PROBLEM

It is not that far-fetched a scenario. Indeed, there is a real life example of this going on right now in Alberta, Canada, where an oil boom has produced wealth not seen there since the early 1980s. As a result, 2006 growth was 6 percent, which was Alberta's best performance in 26 years.[21] Thousands of people flocked to Alberta to take the scores of jobs created both in and out of the oil patch. Not surprisingly, the labor force participation rate within the province—the number of people either looking for work or working as a percentage of the total working-age population—has soared too, going over 73 percent by the end of 2006, compared to a national average of 67.2 percent.[22] At the same time, a curious phenomenon has also been observed: contrary to the national trend, the participation rate of women with children under the age of six has declined, going from 67.9 percent in 1999 to 64.9 percent in 2005. That's a huge decrease at a time when the Canada-wide participation rate for that group climbed from 67.6 percent to 71.8 percent over the same period.[23]

There have been plenty of theories put forth as to why mothers of young children are more apt to drop out of the workforce in Alberta than they are anywhere else. Some point to the fact that Alberta, unlike some other provinces, does not provide much in the way of childcare assistance or a provincial daycare program or to the fact that the province has traditionally been socially conservative compared to some other regions of Canada. While those factors may play a part, the real answer probably has more to do with the fact that wages have risen so much that choosing to have one parent at home—the mother—has become an economically viable option for many households.

So think about this in terms of the leisure economy. If the baby boomers' entry into the world of leisure does create shortages of workers in some industries, then we are likely to see real wages for skilled workers rise. This might be best illustrated by thinking of an example of a government department 10 or 12 years from now. Top heavy with baby boomer managers or professionals now, it is likely to lose workers like clockwork as they turn 60 or 65: after all, whatever the drawbacks of working for government, the pension system is comparatively generous and well funded. Anxious to attract the next generation

21. Statistics Canada. *The Labour Force Survey*, December 2006.

22. Ibid.

23. Roy, Francine. "From She to She: Changing Patterns of Women in the Labour Force." *Canadian Economic Observer*. Statistics Canada, Catalogue no. IL010, June 2006.

The Labor Force Is Aging
% Change in U.S. Labor Force by Age, 2007 to 2017

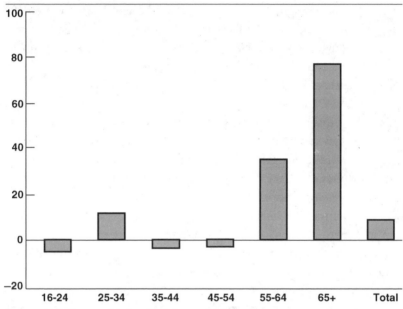

Source: U.S. Bureau of Labor Statistics projections

of professionals, the department is likely to raise wages, perhaps hoping to bring in workers from the private sector. They may also offer more rapid promotions to Gen X and Gen Y workers. Now think of this happening across all government departments and across much of the private sector too. Will it bring in more workers? It certainly might, since the payback from working is now higher in real terms. But it might also create the "Alberta Problem."

THE WORKPLACE OF THE FUTURE
Some companies are well ahead of the curve in recognizing that the leisure economy is coming. Michigan-based accounting company Plante & Moran (which perhaps not coincidentally ranked 12th in 2006 on *Fortune* magazine's list of Best Places to Work) gives employees a starting package of 20 or 25 days of paid time off (sick days and vacation combined) when starting—pretty hefty compared to the average of two

weeks in the United States as a whole. More than that, though, it actively works to help families balance their time between work and home. "We actually pair new mothers who have had children before, to give them informal coaching," says Leslie Murphy, a Group Managing Partner with the company. "And we have no set hours for anyone, except for the receptionists who have to be at work for specific hours. 'One size fits one'—we say that all the time." The "one size fits one" motto is a good one for Gen X and Y, who are looking for a different reality in the labor market than were the boomers. Up to now, however, this attitude has not been adopted by most corporations. "There is already a strain getting talent in the accounting field," says Murphy. "But so far, we have been fortunate that we do not seem to have an issue with attracting applicants. Our culture is attractive to new hires."

As much as it seems that the leisure economy may mean a more leisured workforce, the reality is likely to be somewhat different. Yes, more workers may find ways to telecommute or even to work part-time, and self-employment may give some the kind of blissful European existence that they never dreamed of during their days as wage slaves. As with everything else, however, the leisure-economy workplace is going to be as rife with haves and have-nots as everything else.

For one thing, the same technologies that will make it easier for Gen Y to make their case for working offsite will also increasingly blur the faint line between work and downtime. A 2006 study by Deloitte[24] suggests, "The division between work and private time will probably become yet more opaque ... By 2010 there may be few places to hide from either the phone call or email." While it is hardly news that technology has had a role in creating the time crunch, the Deloitte report also suggests that workers may get back more "at-work" leisure time: "At the same time, the growing range of web-based leisure applications may redress the balance for the workers, providing a growing opportunity for shopping and entertainment on company time." Depressingly, this sounds much like the "neo-leisure" that already exists. Indeed, it is well known that to a large extent, holiday shopping is happening

24. Deloitte Technology, Media & Telecommunication. "Eye to the Future: How TMT Advances Could Change the Way We Live in 2010." (2006).

more and more from work. In 2005, the National Retail Federation coined the term "Cyber Monday" to describe the phenomenon of consumers starting their online Christmas shopping on the Monday after U.S. Thanksgiving—using company computers and company time. As of 2006, a website called www.cybermonday.com had been set up to give shoppers online discounts—and attracted 300,000 visitors on the one day.[25] And another aspect of the leisure economy is that for many it will offer fairly low-quality leisure as they squeeze in what time off they can during the hours they already spend at work.

One last note: the leisure economy, with or without the boomers in the workforce, is not going to be without workaholics. After all, the generations before the boomers had their share of workaholics (before the word was officially coined), even when most workers were clocking in nine-to-five days. Similarly, even if many Gen X and Gen Y workers want lives that contain balance, there will still be some who are more than happy to keep their lives centered on work. As has always been the case, these are the workers who are likely to rise to the top of the organizations they inhabit. For those who want to choose a different path, however, the pressure to be a workaholic will start to lift. "The difference," says consultant Karen MacKay of Kerma Partners in discussing the situation for lawyers, "is that not everybody is going to be pushed to work all the time. Gen Y will impose their values and you might still have workaholic partners, but you could also end up with associates being able to have a life."

25. Source: National Retail Federation, www.nrf.com.

TIME TO CHANGE THE WORLD

You make a living by what you get. You make a life by what you give.

—*Winston Churchill*

"Smart, committed people with the right support and vision can have a huge impact. It's about using technology, not just for the privileged few, but for everyone." It was June 16, 2006 and William Gates Jr., founder and chairman of Microsoft, stood on a stage talking to a rapt audience, as he had so many times during his dazzling career. This time "Start It Up" by the Rolling Stones was not playing in the background as a prelude to the introduction of a new operating system, as when he unveiled Windows 95 a decade earlier. He was not standing next to Justin Timberlake either, as he did in 2005 as he enthused about a product called "Urge" that would compete against iTunes. In fact, the reporters were not gathered to hear about a new product at all.

Instead, Bill Gates was announcing that he was walking away from his company in order to concentrate on his philanthropic work. "The change we're announcing today is not a retirement; it's a reordering of my priorities," he enthused. With his wife Melinda at his side, Gates talked about putting his energies—and his fortune—to work in fighting poverty and AIDS, and providing education to the world's poor. The richest baby boomer of all was making the transition into the leisure economy, and he was taking his considerable resources with him.

Over the coming decades, throngs will follow Bill Gates into the leisure economy and use their personal resources—and time—to shape a new world. Some of them will be retiring baby boomers who will be able to simply shift their energies from the world of work to the causes that mean something to them; others will embrace volunteer work to fill what will seem like voluminous quantities of time.

The new surge in volunteer activity will not just be about the baby boomers either. Generation Y has already shown a penchant for volunteer work and has given notice that they would like to shape their lives to include more than labor market work. Giving time to causes they believe in will be high on their agendas even as they hit their power years in terms of their careers. All in all, there will be a new leisure class in force, and they will be shaping a new world, sometimes using their time, and sometimes using their money. Many, like Bill Gates, will do both. It is one of the reasons why the concept of a leisure economy is a somewhat fuzzy one. The term certainly applies to the place where the retired will be; volunteer work may be a major priority for them and their leisure time will drive this part of the economy. As well, the non-retired will also help to shape the new economy by spending increasing amounts of energy and resources on community service, making it an ongoing and important part of their lives.

The rise of volunteerism and philanthropy will be a powerful enough force to create a parallel world to the world of work. Many leisure economy participants will spend their time in this parallel universe and make a difference—indeed, a social and economic contribution to the world. This trend is one reason why although the time-crunch economy will become less prevalent in the years ahead, it will never completely fade. For the truly diligent, becoming part of this corner of the leisure economy will keep them as busy as ever.

Both non-profits and profit-making institutions will need to understand the coming changes. Organizations that use volunteer labor will need to plan for how to first attract the potential "workforce" that is coming their way. They need to get them in the door, and then they need to use them to their fullest economic potential. This could be bad news for companies that had hoped to keep these volunteers: their potential workforce could slip away as the non-profit sector perhaps offers non-monetary—and even monetary—rewards. As well, corporations will need to understand the pull that community service has for an increasing part of their workforce and that attracting and keeping the best employees may depend on just how well they are set up to participate in the volunteer world.

A MISHMASH OF VOLUNTEER ACTIVITY

The leisure economy may kick things up a big notch, but volunteerism is already a significant force in North America. In fact, a rise in volunteer activity has actually added to the time-crunch problem for many families.

According to the U.S. Corporation for National and Community Service, nearly 65 million people—close to 29 percent of the population—in the United States volunteered in 2005.[1] That represents an increase of 5.6 percent since 2002, perhaps reflecting a response to President Bush's November 2001 speech[2] in which he stated, "All of us can become a September 11th volunteer by making a commitment to service in our own communities." In Canada, Statistics Canada reports that 11.8 percent of Canadians, or 45 percent of the population aged 15 and older, volunteered their time in 2004.[3]

The idea of a "volunteer" sometimes brings to mind a middle-aged candy striper passing out magazines at a hospital, and indeed the figures confirm this image, in part. Women are more likely to volunteer than men, and about 8 percent of all volunteer activity in the United States is performed at hospitals or other health care facilities. After that,

1. "Volunteering in the United States." U.S. Department of Labor, December 9, 2005.

2. Address by President George W. Bush to firefighters, police and postal workers at the World Congress Center. Atlanta, November 8, 2001.

3. 2004 Survey of Giving, Volunteering and Participating. Statistics Canada Catalogue No. 71-542-XIE. The Canadian and U.S. figures are not directly comparable.

however, the stereotypes fade. The people most likely to volunteer are not those who have retired and have time on their hands: in fact, the most active volunteers are those who are already the most time-crunched. In the United States, Generation X and the Baby Boom were the most likely to give their time in 2005. People between the ages of 35 and 44 had the highest volunteer rate (volunteers as a percentage of source population) in the United States in 2005, at a rate of 34.5 percent. Close behind were those aged 45 to 54 (32.7 percent). Employed persons (31.3 percent) were more likely to volunteer than those who were either unemployed (26.4 percent) or out of the labor force altogether (24.4 percent).[4]

The more education you have, the more likely you are to volunteer, even though chances are you are in a high-stress job. College graduates had a volunteer rate of 46 percent in 2005, compared to 29 percent for the total population. Who are the most likely to volunteer? Parents. Thirty-seven percent of those who had children under the age of 18 were volunteers in 2005, compared to about 26 percent of those without children. In fact, parents are increasingly pressured to put time into their children's schools or activities, despite the fact that many hold full-time jobs. In contrast to their parents, who showed up at one open house a year and did not feel guilty to saying no to field trips, boomers have participated for their kids in droves. Still, on balance, those who are involved in family volunteering seem satisfied that they can integrate it into their lives. A 2003 study by the University of Indiana found that of those involved in family volunteerism asked to give their response to the statement, "Volunteerism makes my life more hectic," only 24 percent agreed or strongly agreed.[5] It's like the old adage that if you want something done, you should ask a busy person to do it: it is the busiest people who are the most likely to find the time to give their time.

After parents, the next most likely group to volunteer is youth. In the United States teenagers had a volunteer rate of 30.4 percent as of 2005, and in Canada they actually had the highest volunteer rate of any

4. "Volunteering in the United States." U.S. Department of Labor, December 9, 2005.

5. "Family Volunteering: An Exploratory Study of the Impact on Families." Center for Urban Poicy and the Environment. School of Public and Environmental Affairs. Indianapolis: Indiana University-Purdue University, 2003.

group at 55 percent. To be fair, in both countries the high participation rates may reflect a bit of "coerced" volunteerism in that since the 1990s many high schools have required a students to spend a certain number of hours in community service as a condition of graduation.

Whether we are talking about boomers or youth, it may be that volunteering is being used as a substitute for being involved in the political process. Baby boomers, in midlife, have become fairly apathetic about the electoral process. As a 2004 study by AARP puts it, "Boomers will be the last to appear at a political rally in which there is no discussion of issues that clearly affect them." Volunteering, however, seems to fill a different niche when it comes to making a contribution. The same can possibly be said for youth. "Young people are idealistic by nature," says Robert Goodwin, CEO of the Points of Light Foundation, a Washington-based group that has as its mission the twin goals of growing the quality and quantity of volunteering. "And these days many are disenchanted by the political process. So they volunteer instead ... they see greater potential for making a difference through volunteerism than they do from politics."

VOLUNTEERS IN THE LEISURE ECONOMY

So it should be a slam dunk for the non-profit sector: people with time on their hands will choose to volunteer, and that will provide a free labor force that will revitalize organizations throughout North America. After all, every baby boomer who leaves the labor force will have, at a modest estimate, 40 hours a week to spend doing *something*. Every household that chooses to have one earner rather than two will have another potential source of volunteer labor. Those Generation Y volunteers, trained by their high schools to head into soup kitchens, will surely go into volunteer high gear as they age. The leisure economy will be a world where those with leisure time will be spent boosting the not-for-profit economy—or will it?

Boomers: To Volunteer or Not

While there is certainly huge potential for a burst of volunteer activity through the next decade or so, it could well end up as an opportunity squandered. That's especially true when we talk about the baby-boomer generation, who are the most obvious candidates to take their talents to the non-profit sector. But the baby boomers will have many choices as to how to spend their time. From traveling to gardening, to simply remaining in the labor force, boomers will have a wide menu of choices when they decide what to do with the rest of their lives. If the non-profit sector is welcoming to them, it is likely they will head there in droves. Boomers could put so much time into the volunteer sector that they create an alternative labor market, where people do hours and hours of work without compensation. Although it would create a time crunch of a sort, it would be a different from the one we now have: one voluntarily entered into and with different rewards. Which way the pendulum will swing is by no means certain.

If boomers move from work to volunteering en masse, the amount of person-hours directed to the volunteer sector could be massive. Consider that in the United States alone about 7,918 baby boomers turned 60 each day in the year 2006.[6] Assume that half of them decide to devote five hours a week—about an hour each workday—to volunteer causes: it would add up to a total of 19,795 hours, or the equivalent of about 494 people working 40 hours a week. Now assume that they decide to work more than five hours a day, or that a similar number of retirees make the same commitment in 2007 and in 2008 and so on. That comes to a massive number of person-hours that could add up to a very potent economic force.

But it is not clear that boomers will actually choose volunteerism. True, boomers do have a high rate of volunteerism among the U.S. population, but they still only average 51 hours a year of volunteer activity. That's higher than any group except for those over the age of 65, but it still represents only about an hour a week, a fairly casual level of involvement.

In addition, although there is no hard data on it, many of the boomers' volunteer hours (and those of Generation X) are likely for causes that involve their (mostly Gen Y) children. This is suggested

---

6. U.S. Census Bureau.

by the fact that those aged 35 to 44 (the group most likely to have children in school, and by our definition predominantly Gen Xers) are more likely to volunteer than those aged 45 to 54 (a group that is predominantly boomers). For a large chunk of both Gen X and Gen Y, then, the causes they volunteer for tend to be related to their families, and are consequently causes they are likely to outgrow as their families mature.

"I put in a couple of afternoons a month in my kids' schools," says Karen, a 44-year old mother of three children aged between four and 12. "I've been doing it since my oldest was in preschool. I don't really have time to do anything else." Allie, 40, the mother of three boys aged from five through 10, says her household also focuses their volunteering on things that involve their children. "My husband coaches soccer," she says. "And I've gotten really involved in the school's fundraisers. It's a lot of work, but it's concentrated on certain times of the year. And I'm involved in their Sunday School too. We really don't have time—or don't make time—to do more than that."

Some think it is enough that boomers are volunteering at anything, and that the taste will be enough to keep them involved in their communities even as they outgrow their current causes. "They might not be involved in causes that they will stick with," says Robert Goodwin, "but they are getting exposed to what volunteerism is all about. They're learning about how organizations work, how to run fundraisers or whatever. So it's a real start for when they make the transition into their retirement years." Like many, he figures that the retirement of the baby-boomer generation could potentially result in a huge windfall of volunteer labor to organizations that need it, simply because there is a large pool of people who have been exposed to the activity. "But," he adds, "If the question is whether the organizations who can use boomers are set up to handle them properly, then the answer is 'no.' Unfortunately most non-profits do not do a good job of managing volunteers, let alone boomers. So that will be a challenge."

Indeed, the challenge may not be in getting the boomers interested in volunteer activity; it may be in channeling that interest properly. It is a challenge that is already being met, or not met, by many organizations. With boomers leaving the workforce every day, volunteer organizations are already being offered their help, with differing degrees of success claimed on each side. Today's senior volunteers (generations prior to the baby boomers mostly do not blanch at the term) have not demanded as much from the volunteer sector as the boomers will. If the profile of a "traditional" older volunteer is that of a woman who has raised her family, never spent much time in the workforce, and is happy to hand out magazines as a hospital auxiliary worker, the newly leisured boomers are a different breed altogether. Many, male and female alike, have held responsible positions within large organizations and are eager to use their skills in the volunteer sector. Unfortunately, many are already becoming disappointed at the opportunities offered them.

Nancy, 55, is a good example. Formerly a senior executive with a large financial organization, she found herself in the midst of a company restructuring at the age of 51 with, as she puts it, "just not that many projects I wanted to work on." Childless and with a working spouse, she was financially stable enough to take a generous retirement package, even though she had always worked and figured she would always continue to work. Part of her package included time spent with a management consulting firm that specialized in getting people like herself back into executive positions. "But I'd had such a full career. I'd been with my company for literally 30 years, my full working life, and I didn't see how I could replicate the experience anywhere else," she says. "So I asked them to spend their time setting me up in the volunteer world instead." It turned out to be an eye-opening experience.

"They set me up to talk to several organizations whose interests and values matched mine," she says. "For example, I met with the Executive Director of the ballet in my city. And what I found with the larger organizations is that they wanted people who could basically bring in money. If you could promise $100,000 a year in donations or whatever, then they wanted you on the board. And that's not really my circle—the gala crowd—so I decided not to go that route. Then I looked at other kinds of volunteering; for example, I was interested in driving cancer patients to their treatments. And again and again I found that what the organizations wanted were people who could make long-term commitments—every Tuesday for a' year, say. And I knew I wanted to be away for a few months traveling or whatever, so that didn't work. I was willing to work full time for a couple of months at a time on projects, but nobody seemed set up for that either. It was very frustrating."

Eventually Nancy did join the boards of several small non-profit groups, and she enjoys the work and the satisfaction she gets from it. Four years into retirement, however, she finds that she does not do a lot of volunteering. "I wanted to," she says, "but I ended up pursuing other interests instead." What other interests? "I travel quite a bit ... I go to the gym, sometimes work out with a personal trainer, play golf, bike. I see more family and friends, play bridge, joined a women's club, and even do more cooking then I used to. I do more sleeping too—eight hours a night. It's a very full life ... in some ways I'm still time-crunched but in a different way."

And so an opportunity was lost for the non-profit sector; every Nancy that is lost to other activities represents valuable labor that got away. "It is a glib leap to say that lots of boomers will start volunteering," says Linda Graff, a volunteer consultant. "Most surveys show that volunteer participation drops off at the age of 55 and the decline sharpens at about age 65. There is no reason to think it will be different with the boomers. For the boomers to like what they find in the non-profit sector, you'd need to change a lot of things, and it just isn't happening. We know that boomers are interested in short-term involvement but most agencies continue to ask volunteers to do long-term undefinite work. We know that there is an absence of short-term jobs. But I could count on the fingers of one hand the number of agencies who are rethinking their positions in significant ways in order to bring in boomers."

And indeed, first-wave baby boomers are unlikely to be pleased with what they see when they knock on the doors of non-profits. Bit by bit, however, things will change, in large part because there are movements afoot to make them change. In the United States, the Harvard

School of Public Health has teamed with the Met Life foundation to "reinvent" aging partly by drumming up baby-boomer interest in volunteering. "What we do is run media campaigns as a way to promote health and healthy behaviors," says Susan Moses, Deputy Director of the Center for Health Communications at the Harvard School of Public Health. "For example, we introduced the term 'designated driver' in the late 1980s by working with the mass media, in particular with the Hollywood creative community to have the term written into scripts. Like having a designated driver, she puts volunteering on the list of behaviors that that are good for people, and in particular will be good for aging baby boomers. "We want to get the message out that people still have a lot to contribute when (and if) they retire from their primary job. Volunteering is one activity that will help boomers and older adults stay involved in their communities while at the same time provide them with the opportunity to give back. But the organizations that use volunteers will have to retool to create new and interesting opportunities for the boomer volunteer. The media have an important role to play in creating a new, positive image of what it means to grow older and remain a contributing member of society."

The Corporation for National and Community Service launched its own campaign called "Get Involved" in 2005, aiming to increase the number of baby boomers involved in volunteer service, as well as to stimulate a public dialogue about the meaning and purpose of life after retirement. The national radio and television spots associated with these campaigns will make a difference, partly because they will put some pressure on non-profits to build organizations where boomers *can* make a difference. The biggest stimulus to volunteer activity, however, will likely simply come from example: there will be a kind of snowball effect as boomers test the waters of post–labor market community service, and more likely than not find that they like it. Not every baby boomer may be won, and it may take a while before volunteering becomes a preferred way for baby boomers to spend their time, but eventually the profile of being a volunteer is going to be perceived as hip, as has been the case with so many pastimes that the boomers have embraced.

Gen X: To Volunteer or Not

Whether the boomer volunteer craze will rub off on Generation X as the leisure economy takes shape remains to be seen. With the oldest Gen Xers now in their early 40s, most will still be in their "time-crunched" years for the next decade or so. Their volunteer participation rate is already the highest of all demographic groups, mostly because of activities involving their children. Very likely, that is where they will continue to channel their energies over the medium term. Any make-over of non-profits, though, will have the potential to make them more appealing to Generation X. As volunteers, Gen Xers tend to want to know a lot about the causes and the organizations they are supporting. The retooling that will make the non-profit sector more appetizing to the boomers is likely to make it more palatable to Gen X too. But do not look for this generation to revitalize community service just yet. As much as they want balance in their lives, Gen X is set to profit from the wave of boomer retirements ahead. For many, that will mean finally being able to get the promotions that they've craved for years, and putting in a last blast of hard work before their own retirements.

Gen Y: To Volunteer or Not

The interesting generation to watch will be Generation Y. As they head into their own time-crunched years, there seems to be a good probability that they will keep up their penchant for volunteering. Given their values, Gen Y is likely to continue the trend of volunteering for activities that involve their children, whenever they get around to having them. After all, their parents were heavily involved in their activities as they were growing up. "Both my parents volunteered with my activities when I was younger," says Christine, 21. "My mom volunteered in the library at my public school, helped out on field trips, and helped with reading and math exercises at school. My dad coached girls' basketball and often coached my soccer team when other parents wouldn't step up." Like many others in her generation, she has every intention of being involved in her children's activities. "Being involved in my children's activities would just seem normal," she says. Amy, 29, the working mother of an eight-month-old son, is already planning to get involved in her son's activities. "Right now we do a little volunteering through our church, but I see myself doing a lot more as Michael gets older. I'd want to be part of committees around his activities. My parents did that."

But Generation Y may well do double volunteering too: putting in time with their kids, but also involving themselves in broader causes. Baby boomers and Gen Xers may have the highest rate of volunteerism, but when they were in their teens and 20s they were far less likely than Gen Yers to be involved in the volunteer sector. "Will they keep volunteering? Well, some will and some won't," says Robert Goodwin. "Gen Y volunteers are like all other volunteers; there are several stages of progression that are applicable to volunteer enterprise: it starts as a trial, then a commitment, then becomes habit. And for some of Gen Y it has become a habit."

The question is perhaps whether they will have the time and energy to be involved as they grow older. Christine, now in college, continues to be a volunteer, helping out with a seniors' day program a couple afternoons a week when she does not have classes. But voracious volunteer that she is, she admits that she will probably cut back on that kind of volunteering when she has a full-time job and eventually a family. "I'd like to continue to do this kind of thing, but I'm being honest when I say that there will likely be a time when I can't fit it in."

Whether or not she can fit in extra volunteering, the main point may still be that we are about to see a surge of volunteers who are in their 20s and 30s, up to now a period of life when volunteering has tended to drop off. This might be especially true if Generation Y gets their wish and structures their lives differently from previous generations. Some of them want—and might get—part-time work or the chance to leave the work force altogether for periods of time, particularly when they have young families. If they succeed in that, then the mid-life volunteer rate may be much higher than it is for the baby boomers or Gen Xers.

What this all means for the years ahead is a bit blurry. Certainly, if we continue to see an increase in volunteerism, even while working hours and time spent driving to kids to activities keeps climbing, the time crunch will only get worse; indeed, the leisure economy may not look very leisurely at all. But whether we are talking about boomers,

Xers or Yers, the point may simply be that in the leisure economy, activities that have a personal meaning will have a place. If the yuppie kvetch of the 1990s was that there was not enough time to do every privileged thing on the agenda, the time crunch of the new millennium may look quite different: how to choose among so many meaningful things to fill the excess time available to all generations?

THE PHILANTHROPY BOOM

From volunteering, the next step is philanthropy. After all, arguably the most successful baby boomer of all has thrown down the gauntlet. Bill Gates, founder of Microsoft, announced in 2006 that in 2008, at the age of 53, he will leave his day job to concentrate on his charitable foundation. Although this may be the extreme version of this trend, in lesser ways many other baby boomers will follow him. Already there are signs that relatively young people, having racked up significant amounts of money from their careers or investments—or from inheritances—are thinking about giving back more than their time. As they age, they will realize even more wealth from sales of their assets, particularly real estate. It will be a powerful force in the leisure economy: people with money in hand and the time to decide where best to direct that money.

The term being bandied about now is "a new golden age of philanthropy," evoking the years between 1895 and 1915, when Andrew Carnegie and his ilk made significant fortunes and followed through with significant philanthropic works. You can already see it in the statistics. According to the U.S. National Center for Charitable Statistics, between 1996 and 2004 there was a 36 percent increase in the number of non-profit organizations in the United States. Although non-profit organizations such as chambers of commerce or civic leagues declined by 5.3 percent, public charities were up by 69 percent over the period—and private foundations grew by 87 percent. The last category totaled about 109,852, although that number can now reliably be characterized as too small, and certainly as much smaller than the number of private foundations that will exist in a decade or two.[7] According to the Center for Wealth and Philanthropy at

---

7. National Center for Charitable Statistics, http://nccsdataweb.urban.org/PubApps/profile1. php?state = US

Boston College, as much as $6 trillion could flow into the U.S. economy over the next five decades as gifts from boomers.[8]

"There are so many reasons that we are seeing a rise in philanthropy," says Liz Bremner, the former President of the Foundation Incubator, a Palo Alto, California–based organization that provides services to early-stage foundations. "The explosion of wealth during the dot-com years is part of it—we saw a significant increase in young philanthropists during the late 1990s. Then 9/11 and other disasters have spurred an interest in volunteerism and philanthropy. And of course you have lots of new activist billionaires—the Oprahs—setting an example. Now it is socially acceptable to say, okay I'm quitting work and I'm going off to run my foundation."

As a group, baby boomers in the United States are already the largest donor-generation. A 2005 study[9] by national direct response fundraising firm Craver, Mathews, Smith and Company found that boomers gave an average of $1,361 per year, compared to $1,138 for older Americans. Their causes tended to be a little different too. In order of importance, the pre-boomers are most interested in gun owners' rights, the environment, human rights and tax reduction. Boomers have a slightly different list. The environment and human rights are tied for number one, followed by advocacy for the needy and civil liberties. Although the boomers were as a group cited as being loyal to their charities, the report also warns that the best donors are the toughest to please and to retain. "The prime donors are much more likely to abandon an organization or cause because of perceived under-performance, because they have discovered a more effective organization or because they simply disagree with something the group did."[10] That's an interesting observation, given that in the leisure economy, boomers will have far more time to scrutinize the organizations they are supporting.

Baby-boomer (and later Generation X) women will also have control of much of the money, and will be making some of the decisions on

8. Havens, John J. and Paul G. Schervish, "Why the $41 Trillion Wealth Transfer Estimate is Still Valid: A Review of Challenges and Questions." Boston College Social Welfare Research Institute, January 6, 2003

9. "Boomers! Navigating the Generational Divide in Fundraising and Advocacy." Craver, Mathews, Smith & Company, 2005.

10. Ibid, p. 2.

how it gets spent. As time goes on, even more will be in their hands—and within their own decision making. After all, women typically live seven years longer than men, meaning that even now a significant amount of decision-making power is in the hands of women. But as the leisure economy takes shape, that power will shift to boomer women, who will be quite a different breed than the female philanthropists who have come before them. Between 2010 and 2015, as much as $12.5 billion is expected to be transferred into the hands of American baby-boomer women as the result of inheritances.[11]

Baby-boomer women philanthropists will form a special category of leisure haves. It is reasonable to think that as a group, they will be younger, better educated, and have more work experience and fewer children than the philanthropists before them. Some of their money will have come from their own efforts, perhaps even from entrepreneurial endeavors. When they start to give money to their causes, they will do so in ways that reflect their styles. "I'm not sure that it's correct to say, 'It's different with women and philanthropy,'" says Mary Ellen Capek, principal with Capek and Associates and author of *Effective Philanthropy: Organizational Success through Deep Diversity and Gender Equality*.[12] "What I've found is that people give when they are asked especially for causes they feel connected to ... and it depends on who is doing the asking. Up to now, women have not been asked as often as men are asked, although that seems to have changed significantly in the last decade."

As with volunteering, dealing with baby-boomer philanthropists—whether male or female—will present certain demands for organizations on the receiving end. "The boomers are focused on accountability," says Clint Mabie, Director of Donor Services for the Chicago Community Trust. "If they are involved in a project they want specific measurements of its success. Some organizations—big and small—are set up to give them those measures and some are not." Janice Schoos, Senior Managing Director with Archimede Philanthropy Partners, a consulting

---

11. The Cadillac Foundation, http://www.cadillacfoundation.org/adv_women.html

12. Capek, Mary Ellen and Molly Mead. *Effective Philanthropy: Organizational Success through Deep Diversity and Gender Equality*. Boston: MIT Press, 2006.

partnership that works with philanthropists, agrees that boomers want to know just how their money is making a difference. "If they give to an organization that puts computers in schools for kids, they want to know how that is changing the kids' lives and their academic performance. And some community-based organizations do not have the capacity to give them the numbers they want."

The philanthropy sector, as with every sector touched by the leisure economy, will get a make-over in the next decade or so. Time might be a little cheaper than it was for the new philanthropists, but they are not likely to see their money as any less valuable than it ever was. "There is an unprecedented amount of discretionary wealth now available," says Clint Mabie. "But it is coming from people who have made their money through hard work and good investments. Giving it to somebody else to spend is not going to be enough for them."

HOT AND NOT FOR PHILANTHROPY

Hot	Not
Accountability	Top-heavy organizations
Giving—targeted at specific projects	Lack of follow-through
Giving—followed by a volunteer role	"Blanket" donations
Women's issues	
Education	

THE ECONOMIC IMPLICATIONS OF "FREE" TIME

The leisure economy is a place where community service flourishes; from a social point of view that will bring with it many positives. At the same time, it will also introduce its own challenges, both to the economy and to business. After all, unleashing a large amount of labor power in any sector, whether profit-making or non-profit, means unleashing a potent economic force. Put another way, and using the Independent Sector's estimate of US$18.04 an hour,[13] the value of

---

13. The Independent Sector is a leadership forum for charities, foundations, and corporate giving programs in the United States and around the world. Each year they publish an estimate of the dollar value of volunteer time, based on the average wage of non-management, non-agricultural workers.

volunteer time in the United States equaled about $147.6 billion as of 2005. That's more than the value of the economic output of California, New York and Massachusetts combined.[14] Assuming that there continues to be a further increase in hours directed at the volunteer sector, a powerful economic force could be ready to unfold, and if it is well directed, it could make a huge difference.

Off the top is the question of whether the volunteer labor will displace paid labor. Americans currently volunteer 8.2 billion hours of labor annually. Assuming a workweek of 40 hours per week, a very crude calculation puts the hours of volunteer work a year at equivalent to about 205 million jobs—a number actually greater than the approximately 150 million people who were employed in the United States in 2006. So by some measures, one could make the argument that volunteer labor is already displacing paid labor. That might not be accurate, given that many of the volunteer jobs being done—from door-to-door canvassing to delivering meals to seniors—would undoubtedly just not get done if volunteers did not do them. Others, however, would probably be replaced by paying jobs. The issue may come to the fore as baby boomers take their skills to the non-profit sector. After all, many boomers will be retired professionals, from fields as diverse as health care, education, public relations or finance. They will be able to fill administrative and other positions that in the past have been staffed by paid workers.

ISSUES FOR VOLUNTEER ORGANIZATIONS TO PLAN FOR

- The labor is there—but if you don't fight for it, you'll lose it.
- Some boomers will want 'power' roles in your organization—can you create them?
- Be flexible—on hours, on months of work, on everything. One size will have to fit one.
- Gen Yers will volunteer—but only if the work is meaningful and they can have input.
- Have-not volunteers have lots of time—but they may need basic stipends to cover their costs.

---

14. Gross State Products (GSP), 2005.

"It's fair to ask the question about how the two things, volunteer labor and paid labor, interact," says John Gomperts, CEO of Experience Corps, an organization that matches volunteers with children from lower income urban areas in order to provide tutoring and mentoring services. "But I don't think it will really be an issue. In our case, for example, we are matching people to where there is an unfilled need." And if indeed North America does, as many believe it will, head for a labor shortage situation, there is likely to be little reason to worry about professional jobs being lost across the economy as non-profits choose to fill up with free resources. "If anything, there is going to be a shortage of non-profit labor," says Gomperts. "We know that we are going to need all kinds of resources that will be in short supply."

A stickier question, though, is how volunteers should and will be compensated for their time. Up to now, we have had the notion that volunteerism must always be work for free, a notion that might have to be reassessed in the leisure economy. The aging baby boomers in particular will be a group of haves and have-nots. The haves may not mind driving their aging SUVs to the non-profit organizations and helping out, but there will be others who will be wary of spending money in order to volunteer. Of course, there has always been a subset of potential volunteers for whom this has been true, but they were not boomers.

As with everything else, the baby boomers have the sheer weight to do what other generations have not: make volunteer work pay. "Non-profits in particular are starting to rethink the volunteer role, and part of that is learning that volunteers are not 'free,'" says Dr. Greg O'Neill, Director of the National Academy on an Aging Society. "Whether that means investment in volunteer managers or even paying them with a stipend or some other kind of compensation like health care benefits, you are likely to see it happen. The idea of a paid volunteer may no longer remain an oxymoron for the generation of baby-boomer volunteers."

That stipend, however small, may be crucial in getting the have-nots among baby boomers into the volunteer arena. "Experience Corps members are most often from the immediate communities we are trying to help," says John Gomperts. "We don't have people coming in from Virginia neighborhoods to help in D.C.; we have the people who live there. So they tend to be people of lesser means, but with a profound understanding of what is going on in these communities. We do pay a very small stipend, just to cover the costs of volunteering. Because if people are buying meals out or buying coffee or whatever when they usually would not be doing that, it probably covers that." Experience Corps has been in existence since 1996, and to date has mostly had participants from the pre-boomer age groups. They are perhaps wisely ahead of the curve, though, on dealing with the cost issue. Have-not boomers, as described in Chapter 5, will be the ones with time but without money. If volunteering is not at least cost-neutral to them, they may very well decide they cannot afford to do it. Just who pays the stipends will also be a source of debate. Government may pick up some costs, as they have always done with a select group of programs such as Foster Grandparents. But corporations could also perhaps play a bigger role in the future, sponsoring specific volunteer programs and picking up the costs for volunteer reimbursements and stipends.

But while the idea of stipends for volunteers—whoever picks up the bill—might seem like a good one, it will also come with its own baggage. For the lower income boomers who wish to take advantage of the stipends, it's fair to ask whether they are actually being exploited. Indeed, some view stipended programs as basically programs that pay labor less than the minimum wage. And that is one of the issues that might come to the fore in the years ahead: if a significant number of lower income boomers do end up taking on volunteer work for the money, then the question of whether the work they are doing should really be in the volunteer sector at all may become an issue.

The real problem for business will be what will happen to the labor supply if volunteering really does become hip. In surveys, baby boomers say they want to stay in the labor market, but many do not want to do it solely because of the money. After all, in the time-crunch economy, paid work has become synonymous with stature, prestige and self-fulfillment for many baby boomers. As of now, some volunteers are able to get some of those same rewards from the volunteer sector. "It took me a while to get a good match in terms of volunteering," says Maureen, a retired first-wave boomer. "But now I'm very happy with what I do. I'm an ex-journalist and I've worked in PR and I'm now using those skills for a really worthwhile organization." Others, like Nancy, were not able to find that match.

As baby-boomer volunteering gets more organized and better at publicizing what is available, however, the number of good matches is very likely to grow. The prestige of being a volunteer—even if the word eventually gets changed to better reflect baby-boomer sensibilities—is also likely to increase. After all, everything that baby boomers have ever done has been packaged as "cool" in one way or another. That is eventually going to include volunteering. All in all, it could eventually be a trend that is negative for those employers that had hoped to keep their PR specialists or whatever working for them—for money—rather than for non-profits—for free.

For companies that want to attract the right Gen Y candidates, integrating volunteerism into the workplace may be an effective strategy. "Yers will look for employers who are not merely socially conscious, but also socially responsible; that means organizations who respect the environment, care about their employees, create meaningful products or services and give back to the local community," says Carolyn Martin. Indeed, already some companies are seeing that as a draw for Gen Y employees. "It's almost a given to me that when we hire college graduates, they are involved in volunteer activities," says Catharine Jennings, a College Relations Specialist at office-supply retailer Staples. "They want to know what we do as a company . . . and more than that, they will ask me what I specifically do in terms of volunteerism. So they want to get involved in things we have going, and they also want to know that they can bring in their own causes and we are very open to that."

Both for those who want to bring a bit of the leisure economy into their lives by volunteering and for those who find themselves in the leisure economy and are looking for something meaningful to do, the volunteer sector is likely to become a larger societal focus for many years to come. "I didn't volunteer much when I was working," says

Nancy, whose words will perhaps ring true for many baby boomers, although they have yet to realize it. "Maybe I'd be part of Run for the Cure or the United Way every so often, but more often than not I gave my money rather than my time. I regret that—now that I think about it, there would have been time for it, and I would have had more to offer in terms of my network and all that. Anyway, what's important to me now is giving back and sharing. I want to contribute, and when I think about it I don't think I contributed much by working."

MAPPING THE LEISURE ECONOMY

We want the sophistication and joy of culture and music that comes with city dwelling—and doesn't come with sitting in the big home in the burbs watching the day go by while puttering, painting, reading, writing, making flies for fishing, customizing your own golf clubs, stringing your own tennis racket, tending your tropical fish."

—Real estate developer Robert Toll, co-founder of
  Toll Brothers Inc. and a baby boomer himself,
  explaining to The Wall Street Journal why his
  company is building luxury condominiums in
  cities for retiring boomers

Bruce R. Partain ticks off the advantages of the area he represents. "We have chamber orchestras," he says. "We have filmmakers; we have fine arts. We are a university town...we've got people here who are proficient in five languages. And we're making changes to the town to make it better too. We have a system of walking trails that have never been completely connected to the sidewalks. Well, now we're

183

connecting them ... that will be attractive to people deciding whether they want to live here." As President and CEO of the Nacogdoches County Chamber of Commerce, Partain might be expected to spend his time attracting business to the area he represents in east Texas. He does that too, but Nacogdoches, a picturesque area that prides itself on being "The Oldest Town in Texas," is setting its sights on bringing in more than companies looking for an affordable place to do business. Nacogdoches has an articulated plan to bring in households with time and resources, and part of Partain's job is to sell them on the advantages of living there.

He knows he has some competition in his sales pitch. The newly minted leisure economy participants—whether baby boomers or entrepreneurs or anyone else—will have some heady decisions to make as to where they will live. For the most part, the work world will be behind them, so living close to their jobs will not be an issue. Even for those who keep a toe in the workplace, telecommuting on a part-time basis will suit them just fine. And, plenty of them will have plenty of money—money that is going to stream into their communities and their own leisure economies. That means towns across North America—and internationally—are already competing hard for what will primarily be gray gold. As the pool of affluent households considering retirement rises over the next couple of decades, the competition is only going to get fiercer.

During the years the time-crunch economy has been in full swing, people have chosen where to live based on a few well-defined criteria. They could live close to where they worked, perhaps choosing very small accommodations, such as apartments; or they could choose somewhere larger but endure a longer commute. In the leisure economy, work is less of a consideration, at least for a significant chunk of the population. After all, the biggest group of leisurites will be retirees, who have left work behind. Their incomes may vary, but they will all have a plentitude of time. Younger leisurites may choose non-traditional places to live too. For any one who telecommutes or for households that have chosen not to have both partners in the labor force, the pull of living in areas close to a mass of jobs will be weakened. For both segments, the whole of North America—if not the world—is their oyster. Nacogdoches may be a winner in the competition, but then again, it may not. As the leisure economy takes shape, the town may look like a place where the needs of those who do not have to trek to work but still want to fill their leisure hours with meaningful pastimes can be met. But not everyone will want a small town: some will choose city condominiums, and others may opt for more rural retreats. Some will even stay where they are and maybe pick up a vacation property on the side. However you look at it, the leisure economy is going to change the map.

THE TIME-CRUNCH ECONOMY MAP

"It's not that bad," says Deena, an executive at a bank who recently bought a palatial home deep in horse country north of Toronto. "I drive about a half an hour and then I can get the express train into the city. On good days it takes me less than an hour." What about the bad days? "They're compensated for by the fact that I'm coming home to such a nice home," she laughs. Deena is a resident of an "exurb," a far-flung suburb where people who work in the city can live. Once upon a time, the exurb was a town whose residents made their living close to home, mostly through agriculture. Since the late 1990s, however, the town has undergone a growth bonanza; what was recently farmland now houses a mix of mini-mansions and much more modest homes. Those who live in such areas spend a lot of time in their cars but are compensated by the fact that they get to live in homes they simply could not afford in more populated areas. And that's the crux of it: a major part of the time crunch has been caused by people's decisions as to where to live. In one way, given the killer working hours of the 1990s plus the extra demands placed on families, it might have made sense for people to look for housing, however humble, near their place of business. Instead, the exact opposite has happened. In both the United States and Canada, workers have been choosing homes farther away from their jobs and accepting longer commuting times as part of the work package. Although the average commute to work was just 24.3 minutes each way in 2000, the U.S. census reports that one in six U.S. commuters—19 million people—took 45 minutes or more to get to work, up from one in eight in 1990. A subgroup of extreme commuters traveled even farther, putting in a mind-boggling 90 minutes or more each way to work—and they are the fastest growing segment of commuters. In Canada, as of 2005, commuters were logging an average of 63 minutes a day commuting, up from 59 minutes in 1998 and 54 minutes in 1992.

But although living close to work might be nice, for many workers it is a luxury that is priced firmly outside of their reach. The housing boom of the 1990s sent the median price of an existing U.S. home up from $169,000 in 2000 to $241,000 in 2005—a gain of 43 percent over five years. For many households, homes in or near urban areas were luxuries that they could not even consider. To be fair, though, it is not just a rise in land prices that has contributed to the cost of housing. Over the past few decades, the characteristics that constitute an "average" home have soared dramatically. Between 1975 and 2005, the average floor area in a new U.S. home rose from 1,645 to an all-time high of 2,434 square feet. Over the same period, the portion of new homes built with central air conditioning rose by 43 percent, while the portion built with fewer than two bathrooms fell from 41 percent to just 4 percent.[1] In the impossible equation of wanting more space, more time, and an affordable home, something had to be sacrificed. Many North Americans gave up their free time. Just as they have forgone vacation time and accepted that work is not something that is done in 40 hours, many have also accepted the constraints of commuting.

And so the time-crunch economy map has taken shape. Between 2000 and 2005, the U.S. population as a whole grew by 5 percent. Some of the fastest growing areas were exurbs. Among the fastest growing communities in the United States between 2000 and 2005 were Flagler, Florida (which grew by 11 percent and is 25 miles from Daytona Beach); Lyon, Nevada (which grew by 10 percent and is 80 miles from Reno) and Kendall, Illinois (which grew by 9 percent and is 50 miles from Chicago).[2]

---

1. National Association of Home Builders, "New Home Size Reaches All-Time High in 2005." June 26, 2006.

2. El Nasser, Haya and Paul Overberg, "Metro Area 'Fringes' Are Booming." *USAToday*, March 15, 2006.

In contrast, some of the traditional suburbs—particularly those around Boston, New York and San Francisco—declined in population over the same period.

In Canada, the 2001 census showed that between 1996 and 2001 the population grew most sharply in three broad urban areas: the extended Golden Horseshoe in Southern Ontario; the Lower Mainland of British Columbia and southern Vancouver Island, and the Calgary-Edmonton corridor.[3] As in the United States, some of the most marked hikes in population were in areas with a hefty commute to the core cities. In the Golden Horseshoe, for example, one of the sharpest growth rates was for the town of Barrie, a good 70 miles away from the Toronto city center. Once considered a picturesque waterfront community with charming summer festivals, over the past two decades the town has come to be considered a viable place to live while working in the city.

And so you can see them every morning at 6:00 or 5:30 or as early as 5:00 a.m.: the commuters burning up the highways in an attempt to beat the traffic. They buy the drive-through coffees and the books on tape, and gamely pick up their home lives at 7:00 p.m. (if the traffic's light) when they make it home and through their own front doors. They made their choice of where to live based on a specific set of criteria, and they have helped to create the time-crunch economy and the time-crunch economy map. Next to unfold will be the leisure economy, and with it a different geographic configuration for North America.

THE BIG QUESTION—THE BOOMERS

Boomers will have to make some choices as to where they want to spend their time once work becomes less of a priority. The first question will be whether they want to move at all. In fact, retired boomers may be less likely to pull up stakes than younger households. Traditionally, moving tends to happen when households are in their working years, rather than after retirement. A 2003 study by the U.S. Census Bureau found that only 4 percent of the population aged over 65 moved that

---

3. "A Profile of the Canadian Population." Statistics Canada, 2001 Census Analysis, Catalogue 96F0030XIE2001001.

year, compared to 14 percent of the population aged 64 and younger.[4] The Canadian statistics show a similar split between the mobility of seniors and that of the rest of the population. Between the census years of 1996 and 2001, about half the Canadian population changed addresses, compared to 18 percent of those aged over 65.[5]

But the baby boomers, as we have already seen, are not like other generations. Their leisure economy experience is going to be different from that of their parents, and they will decide where to live very carefully. That *might* mean choosing a new locale, although some are skeptical that the boomers will be any more mobile than previous generations when they hit their retirement years. "There are a lot more baby boomers, so it will look like people are moving more," says Chuck Longino, a professor of sociology at Wake Forest University in Winston-Salem, North Carolina. "But the proportion is not likely to change." Longino cites his own research, which shows that for decades, the percentage of households headed by someone over the age of 60 that has decided to uproot themselves has stayed constant at about 4.5 percent. "In the 1980 census, we did see that there was an elevation in migration levels that seemed to be due to veterans, who had more mobility status, were more likely to move. So we looked for that in the 1990 census and it just was not there."

Longino admits that the baby boom has a large and well-educated middle class which tends to encourage mobility. However, his research also shows that personal ties to friends and families are extremely influential in determining migration decisions, both in terms of keeping people at home, and in encouraging mobility—the "moving back to your roots" phenomenon. "It's more important than education or mobility experience," he says. For boomers the question is whether there are more who are tied to their communities, or more who have ties to other communities that they abandoned in their younger years but may return to later. Angela O'Rand, a professor of sociology at

---

4. Schachter, Jason P. "Geographic Mobility: 2002 to 2003." U.S. Cenus Bureau Current Population Reports, P20-549, Washington, D.C., Government Printing Office.

5. Statistics Canada, "Canada: A Nation on the Move." 2001 Census Analysis, http://www12.stat-can.ca/english/census01/products/analytic/companion/mob/canada.cfm.

Duke University, thinks boomers will not be inclined to pull up roots. "The boomers are going to want to be close to their grandchildren," she says. "For a lot of them, they don't have a lot of grandchildren." And it is certainly true that many boomers have so far been "helicopter parents" and are probably going to want to turn their attention to their grandchildren as the opportunity presents itself.

Others are betting that boomer leisurites will move in droves. "Boomers are much more likely than the Silent Generation to move," says Gene Warren, President of Thomas, Warren and Associates. "Fifty percent of the Silent Generation still lives within 50 miles of where they were born. Only about 10 percent has moved past retirement. With boomers, the figure may be closer to 20 percent. That's huge. With the Silent Generation it adds up to about 3.5 to 4 million households that have relocated. With the boomers, we may be looking at 15 to 16 million."

And indeed, perhaps what needs to be taken into account when talking about the boomers is that moving may be a savvy financial move for many households. Boomers are notoriously bad savers, and as Chapter 5 detailed, many are careening towards being leisure economy have-nots. In contrast, many boomers have struck gold in terms of the equity in their houses. According to the National Association of Realtors, eight out of 10 baby boomers own their own homes, and for middle-income homeowners the equity in their home accounts for half of their net worth.

Those who will think the hardest about where to go are likely to be in the mid-group between the haves and have-nots. Facing a retirement without enough put away in their retirement accounts or investment portfolios, the best solution might be to liquidate some of what they have in their suburban or exurban homes and find a location where homes are significantly cheaper. That's why the predictions of boomers staying put like their parents did in retirement may turn out to be incorrect. Those in the pre-boomer generations were much more likely to have saved prudently and to have very measured expectations for retirement. For baby boomers who have managed to achieve a certain standard of living during their working lives, the prospect of a big downgrade in retirement is not likely to be appealing. As a result, selling the house may look like a pretty viable choice.

Fifteen or 16 million households that are willing to sell their houses and choose somewhere else to live can exert a gigantic economic impact. They will be looking for a place to live out their post-work lives, and in essence their choices will define where the leisure economy thrives—and where it does not. That's why businesses that want to serve the leisure economy market, whether to sell skis or take care of banking needs, need to carefully calculate the areas that will see the biggest influx of boomer households, as well as of course the biggest exodus of householders who do not want the large homes they bought in exurbs when their families were younger.

Many cities and towns in North America are already actively launching programs designed to attract these migratory households. While the most desirable will be affluent households with money to spend and minimal demands to make on their communities, any leisure economy household can mean a boon to the areas they move into. Anyone who is part of the "mailbox economy"—those who may not have a job in their community but head to their mailboxes to pick up their pension checks (or paychecks from a company located far away) is likely to be a net asset to their community. After all, any incoming household will spend money on goods and services in their new community and pay property taxes to boot.

It has long been known that bringing in senior households tends to be a net win. In Florida, a veteran retiree state, a 2003 study found that elder residents represented a net benefit of $2.8 billion to the state and local governments.[6] In North Carolina, meanwhile, another survey concluded that older residents comprised 42 percent of spending in 2000, exactly double their share of population. It is not hard to see why. Any new entrants to a community will create jobs: more customers mean you need more people to tally up groceries or serve restaurant meals. But although many of the new jobs created will be in the service sector, not all will necessarily be "McJobs." Health care personnel are needed, as are staff in any of the leisure industries

---

6. Thomas, Warren & Associates, "The Impacts of Mature Residents of Florida." Phoenix, Arizona, 2002.

that the new households may patronize. That means ticket takers in the movie theaters, but it also means people to perform in and run community orchestras. Although it is hard to be precise as to how many jobs are created when a retiree household moves into a community, it may well be as high as 1.5 to 2.5 a household.[7] The new entrants can also provide a stabilizing force to their new communities. Since they tend not to be employed, businesses can open or close and it will have little impact on their spending patterns.

Where Will Boomers Retire?

So how will boomers choose where to live? There will be no one-size-fits-all leisure economy destination, but some specific characteristics will figure in people's choices. The best places to live will be where leisure time can be best spent, whether that means a city with a thriving arts scene or a country hamlet with the best opportunities for fly fishing. Of course, money and how to make the best use of it, will of course be part of the equation.

The Lure of Smaller Communities

It is no surprise, then, that smaller communities may look attractive to many baby boomers. According to a study by the U.S. National Association of Realtors, half of boomers who live in urban areas would like to retire in a small town, if not a rural area. Their list of what they want from their retirement towns includes lower cost of living, quality health care, better climate and being near a body of water.[8] "A lot will go to small towns," says Warren. "They're looking for that 'Mayberry' feeling." But a smaller town is relative. "If you come from Chicago, moving to Columbia, South Carolina (population 130,000) is like moving to a small town." Some communities will definitely have the edge in bringing in new leisurites, particularly those in the golden category. "Some people want to be where they can get *The New York Times* delivered," says Longino. "That rules out a lot of places."

---

7. Source: Thomas Warren & Associates, conversation with Gene Warren, August 1, 2006.

8. Bishop, Paul C., Harika Bickicioglu and Shonda D. Hightower, "Baby Boomers and Real Estate: Today and Tomorrow." National Association of Realtors, October 2006.

Indeed, a generation of pre-boomers has already found that making the move from city to country is sometimes not all it is cracked up to be. Some first-wave boomers got the back-to-the-land thing out of their systems decades ago when they flirted with baking whole grain bread and making macramé on communes. Others perhaps never went that route—but have romantic notions of how it might be to adopt a simpler life. Stories abound of former suburban dwellers picking the idyllic retirement community of their dreams, then finding community resentment, poor services—and a dearth of lattes in the local coffee bar. For some who have been accustomed to the small comforts of life in a big city, striking out into an "undiscovered" area is not worth it, even if housing prices seem to be unbelievably low. One has to wonder how happy the boomers—a generation not known for self-sacrifice—will be with the limitations of smaller communities. The smartest communities are the ones that realize that the boomers are coming and are already taking steps to make them more comfortable.

As with everything else, the baby-boomer experience may prove to be somewhat different than has been true for earlier generations. Towns across North America realize the potential of boomers to bring in wealth, and like Nacogdoches, many have well-articulated plans to make relocation glitch-free. Some states have even made the process more formal. In Mississippi, for example, towns can apply to become "Certified Retirement Cities." Those that qualify go through a rigorous screening process by Hometown Mississippi Retirement, the state's official retiree attraction program, and have been evaluated on such things as an affordable cost of living, taxes, crime rate, medical care, recreation, educational and cultural opportunities and what they term as the "most important" on their website—a welcoming community. So far, 21 communities have passed muster to receive the designation. Other states, including Louisiana and Texas, have similar programs.

For other areas, the efforts to integrate boomers are being made not so much because the boomers have been deemed desirable, but simply because it is realized that they are coming, like it or not. In Wyoming, an influx of ahead-of-the-curve retirees and U.S. census predictions made it clear to planners that by the year 2020, the state would have the highest proportion of residents over the age of 65 in the United States. Realizing that the in-migration could be a bumpy process, especially for small towns, the state launched the "Wyoming Boomers and Business Initiative" in 2002, and commissioned a series of workshops and reports designed to ensure that the inflow was beneficial for both the newcomers and those who already lived in the state.

WHAT BOOMERS WANT:
THAT "MAYBERRY FEELING" WITHOUT BEING IN MAYBERRY

- Low cost of housing
- Proximity to larger centers
- Good health care facilities
- Entertainment and cultural diversions
- Low crime rate

College Towns for Culture and Learning

College towns hold a lot of promise as potential homes for leisurites. Typically, they have vibrant social and intellectual scenes close at hand, both of which are going to be high on the requirements list of many baby-boomer retirees. In addition, given that college towns have previously been residential centers for the young, most have had years to build up an infrastructure of rental accommodation and a transit system to match. Continuing education is going to be a hot trend for baby boomers, and for some there will be no better place to pursue it than at their alma maters.

For those who want to take the whole thing one step further, there is the possibility of living right on campus or very close to it. Developers, realizing the draw of college towns, have already started breaking ground on dozens of condominium and housing projects across North America. One company, Campus Continuum, focuses solely on developing, marketing and operating university-branded 55+ Active Adult Communities that are tightly integrated with their academic hosts. "We're marketing a lifestyle, not marble countertops," says Gerard

Badler, managing director of the company. "We ask the colleges to provide the land, then to make programs and services available to the residents—things like the library and the fitness center, and invite residents to campus events. We estimate that about 30–50% of our residents will be alumni or retired faculty and staff, and the rest will be attracted by the lifestyle." Mary Ellen DeFrias is the Senior Outreach Coordinator at the University of Massachusetts at Dartmouth, which is currently looking at the feasibility of becoming involved in a similar project. "We know we have a significant segment of the population who are interested in lifelong learning. We already have a group of learners—from their 50s through to their 90s—who want to be in a classroom even though they have worked all their lives. So what we are looking at is whether people will actually want to live on campus while they do that. If they did, they'd have the ability to use all our facilities—the dining halls, the athletic complexes, the theater, the recital halls." Thomas Kepple, President of Juniata College in Huntingdon, Pennsylvania, agrees. "Colleges like ours have enormous numbers of opportunities for participation in classes and lectures. We have experts here maybe four nights a week. It's attractive for those retirees who don't see themselves as going to Arizona or California."

From Vacation Property to Home

But while some leisurites will want to head for lecture halls, others will want to spend their retirement years in their vacation homes. The NAR survey shows that of the 7 percent or more boomers who own vacation homes, about four out of 10 plan to convert them into their primary residences when they retire. This means that areas of North America that have had a boom in vacation home building may find they also have a boom in retirees sooner rather than later. "For the wealthiest boomers, the vacation homes will be where they want to be for part of the year at least," says David Foot, Professor of Economics at the University of Toronto and the author of *Boom, Bust & Echo: Profiting from the Demographic Shift in the 21st Century*.[9] "They will be able to sell

---

9. Foot, David K. with Daniel Stoffman, *Boom Bust & Echo: Profiting from the Demographic Shift in the 21st Century*. Toronto: Stoddart, 1996

their suburban homes and buy a condo in the city if they want, plus have the grandkids come visit at the vacation home if they want."

Bright Lights, Big City

The leisure economy map may also mean a flow of wealth into North American cities as retiring boomers decide that urban life is for them. It could well be a reversal of what we saw from the 1950s through the 1970s, when there was a decline in cities, with a resulting increase in suburban, especially exurban, development. Cities, after all, have every kind of arts, athletic and cultural experience within their midst, as well as transportation systems to suit every leisure economy have or have-not. They also have large numbers of community organizations that can provide volunteer opportunities. And with time being the most precious commodity of the new millennium, they provide an opportunity for those with a toe in the work world to live close to where they work, whether full time or part time.

Of course, cities also have some major downsides, notably the fact that they tend to be more expensive than the suburbs and exurbs. Indeed, the relatively high cost of living is one of the main reasons people have flocked to the suburbs over the past decades and why city growth is likely to be focused on the haves of the leisure economy. Luxury home builder Toll Brothers certainly thinks so. The company that has since the 1960s been known for high-end suburban homes has started to develop housing in Manhattan, Queens, Brooklyn and Hoboken, New Jersey—all distinctly urban. Quoted in *The Wall Street Journal*, founder Robert Toll likened the switch to realizing that today's retirees—the baby boomers—want different kinds of "resorts" than the retirees that came before them. "We are following the people," he was quoted as saying. "We have been a builder to the baby boom since we began. First that took us into the move-up luxury home business, then into golf course resort communities. It has also taken us into the active-adult communities. The city is a combination resort community, but the resort is New York City or Chicago or L.A. or Miami." Like everyone, though, he can only guess as to how many suburbanites will actually pick up stakes and move to these cities. "I don't think you will see more than 10 percent or 15 percent shift gears and decide to move to the city. ... Suburban patterns still remain in place."[10]

According to a report by Professors William Lucy and David Phillips of the University of Virginia, the suburb-to-city shift may already be well underway. After studying 22 U.S. central cities in large metropolitan areas relative to their suburbs, they found that between 2000 and 2004 per capita income in the cities went from being equal to about 86 percent of their metropolitan areas to about 89 percent. Conclusion? The cities must be attracting an inflow of higher income households. However, when they looked at family incomes rather than per capita incomes, they found that the numbers told the opposite story, implying that the high-income households being attracted into the cities were non-family households.[11] "We are seeing it in all kinds of cities," says William Lucy. "From Buffalo through to Houston to Chicago—the biggest change was in St. Louis. Why? Well, the cities physically include many more condominiums that are near downtown now, and they are attracting baby boomers. Baby boomers now include childless couples and they are an important part of the story."

Going Global

Of course, there is no guarantee that the dividend from the leisure economy will be spent anywhere in North America, city or country. Boomers, after all, have traveled internationally and will cast an eye on areas around the world when choosing their retirement havens. The phenomenon of "snowbirds"—from Canada or the colder states—migrating to Florida for several months a year is a pre-boomer phenomenon that can cause that state's population to fluctuate by as much as 20 percent over the course of a year. Canadian boomer retirees may choose to keep going to Florida, or they may find Costa Rica, the site of many of their trekking holidays in their younger days, is just as cost-effective a destination. Similarly, American boomers may choose Costa Rica or Panama or any of dozens of other retirement

---

10. Corkery, Michael, "Mr. Toll Turns to Towers." *The Wall Street Journal*, December 13, 2006, p. B1.

11. Lucy, William and David Phillips, "Cities Performance Improves Since 2000 Census", University of Virginia, April 5, 2006.

destinations around the world. Although foreign places may not feel like home yet, by the time the first wave of boomers settle there, the second wave may find the conveniences they offer very competitive with, say, a condo in Fort Myers. Businesses that want to attract boomer dollars in retirement might be wise to note that they are accessible, even if they are no longer residing on North American soil.

Likely Losers

As well as figuring out which areas are likely to be winners in the leisure economy, it is also important to know which will be losers. Warren notes that many of the rust belt states may be in danger of losing a slice of their tax bases. "If you look at Arizona versus Massachusetts, they are about the same size. Well, Massachusetts has a much higher proportion of those 65-plus in their midst. If all these people from these rust belt states were to move, you would see a ton of lost revenues from the northern states."

Another potential leisure economy loser: the exurbs, which may be particularly vulnerable to a long-term decline in housing prices. After all, few exurbs have the leisure economy characteristics valued especially by the baby boomer leisurites. The have-nots that purchased monster homes may find they want smaller homes in retirement. "They [exburbs] boomed because of the big houses," says William Lucy. "But these places do not have added place value. And the houses themselves will decline in house value. As the houses age, they will be replaced be others that will be better."

THE YOUNG AND LEISURED, THE YOUNG AND TIME-CRUNCHED

The decision to move house will not be restricted to retirees. Anyone who has a bit of equity in their homes may be tempted to cash it in and find a part of the map where it will go further. Although primarily boomers fall into this category, many in the older part of Gen X could also be part of the trend. They may have bought in high-priced areas fairly early in their careers (perhaps with help from their pre-boomer parents) and even with a housing correction, they could see a fairly sharp increase in their equity. They'll be moving into their peak earning years through the next decade and may stick around in their corporate jobs to pick up the spoils when the baby boomers retire. But early retirement for them may look pretty good too, with some figuring they do not need to stick around until 60, or even 55 to take some leisure. True, their retirements may not be as well financed as if they had followed a more conventional path. But remember, for the post-boomer generations, leisure is a high priority. For those households that can figure out how to live well on less work time and income, the temptation to cash it all in may look pretty good.

But the post-boomer generations may shake up the map without quitting their jobs altogether. Generation Y—or "Generation Net" as they are sometimes called—know that they do not have to show up at an office and sit in front of a designated computer screen to do their job. They understand technology; most of them will probably be able to set up whatever they need without help from boomer or Gen X bosses. They also hate busywork and mandatory face time. All in all, the model of a long commute from a suburb, or worse yet an exurb, just for the sake of showing an employer they are present is a bad fit for this generation. If circumstances were different, they might be told to put up with it anyway. But these are extraordinary times.

With the upcoming talent shortage in North America, many companies are going to be increasingly open to employee proposals to telecommute from remote locations, well outside of regular commuting distance. Some companies are gingerly making tracks in that direction already. *The Washington Post* recently reported on a pilot project that will allow trademark lawyers employed by the U.S. Patent and Trademark Office to move anywhere in the continental United States and work from home. Although the program is the first that will actually allow the lawyers to move far afield, it is hardly the agency's first foray into telecommuting. At the start of the project in 2006, the agency already had 220 of its trademark lawyers—out of 265 who were eligible— telecommuting. "Telework is a fabulous retention tool," deputy commissioner for trademark operations Deborah Cohn was quoted as saying, adding that the new program was started because many employees wanted to move away from the Washington area for family or lifestyle reasons. "We want to keep them," she said. "They are good employees."[12]

Still, it is a bit early to know exactly what Gen Y will want in housing when they enter the market in a big way. The oldest of this generation is still in their mid-20s, a time when traditionally people may enter the market. But Gen Y is a Peter Pan generation, and has been putting off making the big life decisions such as marriage that other generations typically made when younger. Not surprisingly, their choices in housing so far have typically favored urban environments, as indeed a younger population tends to. That's partly why condominiums have sprouted at an astounding rate in most cities, and why so far they have tended to be populated with the young and, in particular, childless couples. The longer they wait to get married and form families, the longer the boom in city living may go on.

Ultimately though, Gen Y will age and form families, and when that happens, people tend to want to move to bigger houses. Will they sustain the traditional trend of moving to the suburbs? If this generation is truly less materialistic, they might pass up the 3,000-square-foot homes in favor of smaller spaces closer to where they work, avoiding the time crunch of a commute. Or, they might figure out how to make entrepreneurship or telecommuting work for them and head for small towns, avoiding a time crunch in that way. If either of these scenarios occurs, then Gen Y will have effectively made their own contributions to turning the time-crunch economy map into the leisure economy map. But look for a have-and-have-not aspect to this decision too. It will be the most educated and in-demand Xers and Yers who have options as to where they live and how much time they spend getting to work. For others down the food chain in terms of human capital, getting into the housing market at all may continue to mean a mix of exurb living and commuting.

NEW COMMUNITIES, NEW CHALLENGES

If the haves of the leisure economy are primarily the older generation, then the inflow of retirees will cause some interesting dynamics for the

---

12. Barr, Stephen, "Trademark Office to Experiment with Telecommuting." *Washington Post*, October 25, 2006.

towns they choose. They'll have clout with their new communities: no one will want them to move away and take their stable tax bases with them. That means that their priorities will be embraced by the community. Younger households may want more playground equipment in an existing park, for example; the older residents may rally for walking trails instead. In such a dust-up, it may well be the boomers who win the battle. "Miles of walking trails along landscaped grounds," after all, reads well on a website designed to attract more retirees. "State of the art monkey bars," does not, even if the grandkids will be visiting occasionally. Some do not think it is likely to be much of a problem. "True, we're making some changes for the boomers but they are changes that everyone can benefit from," says Bruce Partain. "If we put in walking trails, well that's great for all ages—it's something I'd like." Gene Warren agrees, noting that the boomers who are moving do not have an issue with paying taxes to support their new communities: "Paying taxes is not a big deal to them. If you're from say Pennsylvania, you're used to paying higher property taxes than you're going to in the Southeast anyway. And sure they're going to support schools. They get that an educated population is good for them."

Then, there is the question of what happens once the newly arrived boomers cross the line from young and active to old and frail. For the first few decades of retirement, a retiree will certainly contribute to the tax base, particularly one in the Golden Leisurite category. Once their health begins to deteriorate, however, the fun starts to dwindle. Nevada, currently the state with the fastest growing population of those aged over 65 (it went up by 16.8 percent between 1990 and 2004) is warily planning for what might be a spate of long-term expenses. "Right now they are not costing us much," *the Economist* magazine quoted the state's deputy director of the Department of Health and Human Services as saying. "But look at Arizona ... Twenty years ago it was great. But now they need lots of hospitals."[13]

If they boost health care costs in a community, a not unreasonable expectation for households that are predominantly older, the cost

13. "The Baby Boomers Retire: Of Gambling, Grannies and Good Sense." *The Economist*, June 20, 2006.

(in both Canada and the United States) is not borne by the local level of government. In the Canadian case, some health care costs are borne on the provincial level, which may make some provinces wary about giving their blessing to towns that want to attract older migrants. In the United States, however, health care is almost totally a federal government responsibility. That means for local governments and states, there is everything to gain by welcoming retired baby boomers. So even if there are costs to be borne down the line, the migration is going to be encouraged and probably will continue in a big way for many years.

And, if things work out well, the leisure economy map will feature a sense of community as a priority. Boomers will be looking for ways to be involved in their new communities, perhaps through fundraising or volunteer work. With proper planning from the non-profits and local planners, the boomers will represent a potential bonanza of labor and expertise for these areas. The same is likely to be true for those in Gen X and Gen Y who choose to be part of the leisure economy. Many will move to smaller towns because they are looking for a sense of community and will be open to the idea of doing volunteer work.

We will not see the end of the suburbs or the exurbs or the cities: many of the trends that created the time-crunch economy will remain intact as we head into the next two decades. But for many, pulling up stakes and finding a new place to live will mean the chance to be part of the leisure economy—and it is a chance that they will not pass up.

SPENDING TIME AND SPENDING MONEY

For everything there is a season
And a time for every matter under heaven
—Ecclesiastes 3:1–8

"You start with a gray-scale picture, then you just follow the instructions to put on the right colors. It's easy ... and the paint and brushes are included," says Betsy Edwards, as she demonstrates a Paint-Your-Own-Masterpiece kit to a bemused onlooker at the Craft and Hobby Association Summer 2006 trade show. The kit, which is basically a grown-up version of what used to be called a Paint by Numbers set, will let the budding artist create a lovely, 16- by 20-inch rendition of Vincent Van Gogh's "Terrace at Night." "It is a great product for baby boomers," continues Betsy, the Director of Education for manufacturer Royal and Langnickel. "They want instant gratification from their crafts and this will give it to them. It doesn't take too much effort, and then they have a painting."

As a manufacturers' representative, Betsy has a lot of competition for attracting retailers at the show. Over 1,000 exhibits crowd the Donald Steven auditorium in Chicago, with scrapbooking supplies jostling for space with kits that will let you make your own evening purse. Booths selling every kind of bead imaginable spill out their wares on some corners, while opposite exhibitors urge a passerby to see their felted wool. A rumor that representatives from one of the big craft store chains are passing through has everyone perked up and wanting to catch their attention. The mood is upbeat.

It is easy to understand the enthusiasm of the exhibitors. The U.S. craft and hobby industry is a $30 billion industry already, and many feel that the sky is the limit when it comes to the outlook. Hobbies take time, after all, and the nascent leisure economy means many more people will have a lot more of it. That thought has even started to get the attention of Wall Street. In 2006, Michael's stores, a chain of craft warehouses, merged with two private investment firms at a reported merger price of $6 billion, while EK Success, a company with a stronghold in the $3 billion scrapbooking segment, was acquired by GTCR Golder Rauner LLC, one of the biggest private equity firms in the United States. For investors, the hobby industries offer some golden opportunities for returns. After all, if the leisure economy starts to take hold, people will be rug hooking and beading in earnest—won't they?

Well, maybe. True, it will be a complete about-face: we will go from a society with too little time on our hands to one with a lot of it—and in some cases too much. That means it is not unreasonable to assume that many people will turn to hobbies and crafts to fill their time. Then again, the scrapbooks will have a lot of competition. From golf to reading, from gaming to travel, every leisure industry is citing "positive demographics" in their business plans. Even assuming that the new leisure time will be spent on leisure activities, the leisure industries will have a lot of tough competition—from each other, as well as from every possible pastime that can fill up a day. From the companies enticing boomers to work longer to the non-profits urging youth to volunteer, it is a competitive market when it comes to people's time, and it will soon get even more competitive.

Further complicating matters is the fact that the uncomfortable trade-off between time and money is not going away any time soon. If the leisure economy means fewer people are working and earning income, it also will mean that there is less money to spend, in aggregate, in North America. That means all facets of consumer spending will shift in the leisure economy. All in all, it means a tricky time ahead, whether you are a consumer, a business or an investor.

THE LEISURE ECONOMY AND CONSUMER SPENDING

"We're hoping to sell our house in the burbs, so that we can get an amazing condo in the city," reads one post on the "Feathering the Empty Nest" message board on ivillage.com. The writer, a woman named Wendy, is busy figuring out what she should salvage from her old life as she moves into her new one. "Assuming we can sell, we want to start fresh ... most of our furniture and appliances are very old. Now it's time to replace them ... We really need to upgrade ... We want to get a new home theater system and we have no idea what to buy ... What's the difference between a plasma and a DLP? What exactly is HDTV? What's the best TV to buy?" Wendy's post triggered a lively discussion from other happy empty-nesters, many of whom had done some serious research and comparison shopping.

If all the leisure economy participants were like Wendy, the world ahead would center on a vibrant North American economy. People might be selling some assets (like Wendy's suburban home) and buying new ones, whether condos or home theater systems or safari-treks to Africa. Better yet, it would be a world where prosperity would be spread among all leisure economy participants, even those in younger age groups. In this fantasy, young parents opting for four-day workweeks would still be able to buy their children Olily T-shirts at $50 a pop if they wanted.

Sad but true though it may be, something is going to have to give. Wealthy boomers will still be around in decent numbers, and they are not going to let consumer spending collapse, even in retirement. And there will still be plenty of working households that will be keeping the economy afloat. Still, make no mistake about it: a world with more people choosing leisure is one where the economic growth will be somewhat lower than it would be if everyone chose work. The smaller the number of people working, creating value and getting paid, the lower will be consumer spending overall and the lower the rate of overall expansion.

As of December 2006, about 66.4 percent[1] of the U.S. population and 67.2 percent[2] of the Canadian were "participating" in the labor market. Although it is impossible to know exactly what boomer retirements and the rest of the leisure economy trends will do to participation rates, we can assume that it will send them lower. We can also assume, with some degree of certainty, that a lower participation rate will take its toll on the economy and on consumer spending. The most complete projections on this come from the U.S. Federal Reserve, which in a 2006 survey came to some fairly dramatic conclusions.[3] Making the assumption that the U.S. labor force participation rate will drop 3 percentage points over the next 10 years, they projected that economic growth over the decade would average less than 3 percent, compared to 3.3 percent over the past decade. Although they did not make any specific forecasts as to what that would actually do to consumer spending, a slower increase in the number of people working,[4] by extension, means slower gains in consumer spending than we have seen in the recent past. In addition, although the Federal Reserve study takes into account baby-boomer retirements and the behavior of recent cohorts of men and women, it does not put in any other "leisure economy" assumptions about labor force participation. For example, if Gen X and Y were to reduce their labor force participation rates (because more Gen Y women opt out when they have children, for example) then their assumption of a 3 percentage point drop in participation is likely to be not conservative enough.

As well as the macroeconomic question of how quickly the market will grow, there is also the question of the growing income gap in North America. At the very least, the rich will get richer and the poor

1. *Current Population Survey.* U.S. Bureau of Labor Statistics, December 2006.

2. *Labour Force Survey.* Statistics Canada, December 2006.

3. Aaronson, Stephanie, Bruce Fallick, Andrew Figura, Jonathan Pingle and William Wascher. "The Recent Decline in Labor Force Participation and Its Implications for Potential Labor Supply." *Bookings Paper on Economic Activity,* vol. 1 (2006). pp. 69–154.

4. The projected drop in the labor force participation rate implies a much weaker *growth rate* of employment in the years ahead, but not a drop in employment. Given that the U.S. (and Canadian) population is forecast to grow over the next decade, partly as a result of immigration, employment will also grow, albeit at a much slower pace than we have been used to since the 1960s. Growth in monthly payroll employment in the United States averaged around 200,000 a month in the 1990s, and could be half of that over the next two decades.

will get richer at a much slower rate; more likely, the poor will get poorer while the rich get richer. Add to that the fact that there will be huge income disparities among the retiring boomers—and potentially among those younger households that want more leisured lives than they saw their older brothers and sisters get, and you have a very complicated situation when it comes to predicting the long-term health of the leisure industries, or indeed of any industries.

Leisure economy participants will have different economic priorities than those in the work economy. They will have more time, meaning they will not always choose products that for a higher cost will save them a few seconds, perhaps giving lower quality in return. In some cases they will also have less money, meaning that not only will they buy less, but that they will choose what they buy much more carefully. Then there are the golden leisurites: the ones with plenty of time and money. They will be an economic force, but perhaps not an easy one to harness. With lots of choice and lots of time to do research, they will be a coveted niche, chased by many and caught by few.

If there is a single consumer trend that characterizes the leisure economy, it is that every consumer spending experience can and will take more time to complete. Every leisure experience will in a sense compete to be a "hobby," or it could if retailers are savvy. That's true if we are talking about drug stores, for example. Baby boomers could pop in to pick up a prescription and go, or they could be enticed to stay longer and talk to the specialist in organic nutrition who has been brought in specially to talk to them about changing their diet to help improve their health. They could also be urged to hang around a bit longer and check through the new craft supplies. Will they be willing to stay longer still to talk to a guest herbalist or a personal trainer? If a leisure economy participant comes in to buy a lipstick, would she be willing to stay for a skin care seminar? "Spray ladies" selling perfume just won't cut it. An educated and selective population will be willing to use their newly acquired time, but only on things they consider enlightening, intelligent pastimes. This means there will be a need for bigger stores with different lines of products than have been seen in the past. Keep in mind that time is the newly available good in the leisure economy, and every single retailer and every single manufacturer should be thinking about how best to capture it.

The leisure economy is going to take hold at a time when consumers are already looking for more than just straight products. In the book *The Experience Economy*[5] authors Joseph Pine II and James H. Gilmore put forth the theory, "Work Is Theater and Every Business a Stage," to make the case that successful businesses have to offer their clients more than a product—essentially they have to offer them an experience, which is really what they're selling. The classic example of this is the Walt Disney Company, which was among the first to figure out how to offer an experience and incidentally move merchandise. They also cite companies like Nordstrom and Saturn as examples of the experience economy at work. Indeed, since the book was written, we have seen the concept in action in all kinds of businesses, from the Build-a-Bear workshops that let kids make their own teddy bears and give them their own "hearts," to Starbucks, which has managed to charge for the experience of sitting down in their pseudo–living rooms, as well as for their lattes.[6] As the population ages, the experience economy is only going to go into overdrive. After all, many households have spent a lifetime loading up on dining room suites and matching china and minivans. While they will still want some of these things, what they are likely to want most is new experiences.

To date, the upper income end of the population has been particularly focused on spending on new experiences. An American Express survey of its platinum card users found that among households with incomes of $100,000 or more, 59 percent said that they received the most personal buying satisfaction from experiences such as fine dining, travel, entertainment and cultural/arts events, sporting events, personal health and beauty services and home services. Only 21 percent said they got their greatest satisfaction from personal luxuries such as automobiles, fashion or jewelry.[7] As this segment of the population ages, they

5. Pine, B. Joseph and James H. Gilmore. *The Experience Economy: Work is Theatre & Every Business a Stage.* Boston: Harvard Business School Press, 1999.

6. Gulati, Ranjay, Sara Huffman and Gary Neilson. "The Barista Principle: Starbucks and the Rise of Relational Capital." *Strategy and Business.* Issue No. 28, Third Quarter 2002, pp. 1–12.

7. American Express Platinum Luxury Survey. Conducted by Pam Danziger, president of Unity Marketing, 2004.

will no doubt continue to want those services, but they will be able to spend even more time on them. Rather than a once-or-twice a season visit to the ballet or the ballgame, they will find themselves able to buy seasons tickets, and what's more, to make it to all the performances. It is why the leisure economy and the time-crunched economy will exist simultaneously for some consumers. They will indeed have many more leisure choices, and being able to indulge in them will take up more and more of their time. What exists now is the tip of the iceberg: the leisure economy will also be a place where the experience economy thrives.

But it will not just be upper income consumers who will trade goods for experiences. Many people will have time rather than money, and they will structure their spending in a way that takes the best advantage of that fact. That might mean spending time learning a new craft, and then spending some money on supplies for it, or it may mean spending time alone on volunteer activities that do not cost anything but provide much in the way of satisfaction. That's why the assumption that all leisure activities will grow with the leisure economy may not be a valid one.

Even for those products that are strictly goods, manufacturers might be best served by realizing that they can sell things that are more time-consuming than has been true in the past. In the health and beauty category, for example, products are frequently billed as "quick," promising to repair skin or smooth hair in 30 seconds. But a population that doesn't have to run out the door each morning might pick up on products that promise more for a larger investment of time—a conditioner that promises much silkier hair if you leave it in for an hour, for example. Such products already exist, but tend to be marketed to a very young demographic—teenagers—because the manufacturers believe they have time to preen. Retired boomers will have the time, too, and will no doubt have the motivation to make a little more effort to look better and more youthful. We already see the start of it—from facelifts to botox to laser surgery—but what is around us now is no doubt just the beginning of an industry explosion to come.

There will always be people who have money and no time, but they will soon be outnumbered by those who have both money and time, as well as by those with lots of time and limited money. Even the Sandy's of the world, with their disposable income and interest in plasma televisions, will increasingly bear the imprint of the leisure economy. Wendy, after all, was not rushing out to her nearest Best Buy to pick up the first television set she saw. She was using her leisure time, reaching out to a wide community to get as much information as she could about her purchase. If there was a time when she would have made a snap purchase, it is now gone.

PICKING THE LEISURE ECONOMY WINNERS AND LOSERS

So what categories of consumer spending, and of hobby spending, will be the winners in the leisure economy? There are two major categories to forecast. The first, and certainly the more difficult to project, are the future leisure spending patterns of Gen X, and in particular of Gen Y. Although we can certainly chart how they have spent their money to date, and although it has certainly included hefty amounts on entertainment, travel and recreation, it is difficult to predict how they will budget as they age, and in particular how they will budget when they have the opportunity to leverage their advantage in the labor market and buy some time off with it.

Easier to chart are the spending patterns of the baby boomers. They are the ones who will find themselves with the most leisure and who have never shied away from spending money on leisure activities. "Their spending habits have been tracked from the time they were in their teens," says Chuck Longino of Wake Forest University. "There were some boomers who got out of college and put off buying houses because they wanted really good stereo equipment." Generations X and Y like leisure spending too, maybe even more than the boomers. That should make it easy to predict a boom for the leisure industries, but of course it is not that simple.

Entertainment

Take the category of entertainment, for example. The aging boomers alone surely represent a huge potential audience for someone. Television viewing, for example, increases with age. According to the American

Time Use Survey in 2005, the average person aged 45 to 54 was spending two hours and six minutes a day watching television on a weekday, compared to two hours and 36 minutes for someone aged from 55 to 64 and three hours and 44 minutes for those aged 65 and up. All things being equal, as boomers move from their 50s to their 60s, they could potentially spend another hour or two a day watching the tube; multiplied by millions of boomers, it is a potential bonanza for the industry.

But it is a complicated world, with many diversions that could take away from television watching. The pre-boom generations may be more likely to watch TV as they age, but boomers are being bombarded with a ton of new media, any of which could claim a bite of their time. A report from Wall Street firm Piper Jaffray, for example, shows that among those with online video, TV viewing is on the decline.[8] That's most true for the youngest viewers: 60 percent of 25- to 34-year-olds use YouTube to watch video content online, compared to 22 percent of 45- to 54-year olds. Boomers may not be as agile with technology as their children, but their technical literacy rate is quite high, and they will have plenty of time to learn more. So forecasting a boom in any kind of media is almost impossible: not only is every kind of media competing with each other, any kind of entertainment is competing against every other diversion.

What we do know is that in terms of spending, people generally reduce their spending on entertainment as they age. According to the 2005 Consumer Expenditure Survey, household spending on entertainment peaks between the ages of 45 and 54, where people spend an average of $3,034 a year on entertainment, compared to $2,388 for the general public. Households in the 55 to 64 age group spend $2,429, while those aged 65 to 74 spend $2,143. But there are reasons to believe that the boomers may spend a bit more than previous generations. Ten years ago, the 55- to 64-year-old age group was spending an average of $1,578 a year, or about $2,022 in 2005 dollars. In fact, spending by the 55- to 64-year-old group has grown for every category of entertainment spending over the period, meaning that the boomers have been more

8. Green, Heather. "Piper Jaffray Report: Online Video Up While TV Viewing Declining." www.businessweek.com, "blogspotting." January 8, 2007.

People are Spending More on Entertainment

U.S. Spending on Entertainment, $2005 dollars

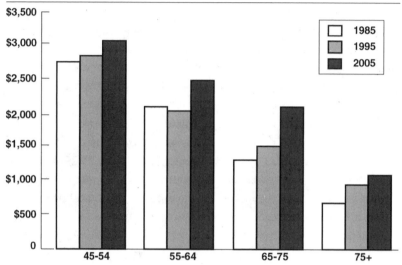

Source: U.S. Consumer Expenditure Survey, various year and author calculations

likely than previous generations to spend on entertainment as they draw closer to their retirement years.

The ways the entertainment industries will interact with the younger generations is even harder to call. Generation Y has an attention span of about a nanosecond. They like TV and iPods and texting—and amusement parks and experiences in general too. So figuring out how they will use their time in the future is tricky. No matter what entertainment, hobby or sport, the difficulties are the same.

What we *can* forecast, though, is how things will likely shake out on a strictly demographic basis. As the graph below shows, just accounting for the change in the demographic distribution of the population, we can say that there is likely to be a sharp increase in time spent reading and a smaller one in the amount of time spent participating in sports.

With that in mind, the following are some thoughts on how various categories of leisure spending may change as the leisure economy evolves. Which ones end up the ultimate winners in garnering the

Time Spent on Some Leisure Activities Will Rise
Projected Change in Number of Hours Spent on Selected Leisure Activities (%)

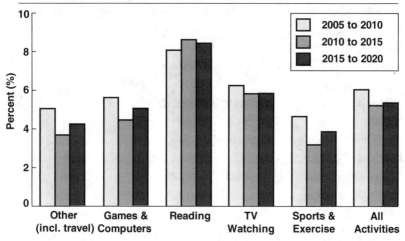

Calculations are by the author based on American Time Use data and census projections of population.

time, attention and money of the leisurites may ultimately depend on which industries lobby the hardest to attract them.

Reading, Libraries and the Written Word

Reading has become a smaller budget item for households for the past decade. As of 1995, the U.S. Consumer Expenditure Survey shows that the average household spent $162 on reading materials—equivalent to about $207.60 in 2005 dollars.[9] In contrast, in 2005, the average U.S. household was spending just $126 a year on reading materials—a dip of 65 percent over the 10-year period. Still, other data suggests that time spent on reading has not really declined, even if Americans are spending less on reading materials. The American Time Use Survey found that Americans over the age of 15 spend just over three hours a week reading as of 2005, almost exactly the amount of time they spent in 1985.[10]

9. All data have been converted to 2005 data by using the U.S. Bureau of Labor Statistics inflation calculator found on www.bls.gov.

10. American Time Use Survey 2005. U.S. Bureau of Labor Statistics. Historical data is from John P. Robinson and Geoffrey Godbey. *Time for Life: The Surprising Ways Americans Use Their Time.* Pennsylvania State University Press, 1997.

It seems reasonable to believe that the advent of the leisure economy will herald a huge increase in reading, especially among aging baby boomers. After all, expenditure on reading tends to rise with age. The Consumer Expenditure Survey data show that as of 2005, households headed by someone aged from 55 to 64 spent $167 a year on reading materials, compared to $143 for a household headed by someone between 45 and 54.

Still, there are reasons to be wary of whether the boomers will turn to reading in a big way during their retirements. In 1995, when the pre-boomer generation was in the 45- to 54-year-old age group, the average household in that age group was spending $199 a year on reading materials—or $255 in 2005 dollars. In contrast, as of 2005 those in the 45- to 54-age group were spending just $143 dollars on reading materials. One explanation for the huge gap is the time-crunch economy. After all, as the busiest and most workaholic generation ever, boomers have been the ones who have been most likely to fall asleep with the same book open on their nightstands for a year—hence eliminating the need to buy another one. Once the leisure economy frees up time for them, perhaps they will turn to reading in a big way. However, the other explanation is that boomers are simply not readers the way earlier generations were, and even in retirement they will look for other activities to fill their time.

Assuming that at least for some part of the population the lack of time explains the drop in reading, the coming decades are likely to see a boom in various kinds of reading. Reading groups and book clubs, for example, which meet a need for boomer (and Gen X and Y) experiences, are well poised to catapult on their success since the 1990s. Another thing that might lead to a surge in the popularity of reading is the realization that reading is a good way to keep our minds active and potentially ward off memory loss and dementia. This concern will also boost all kinds of intellectually stimulating pastimes that have not been big with boomers up till now—things like doing crosswords or jigsaw puzzles. We already see it in the popularity of games like sudoku—and the growing popularity of games like bridge and chess. There is also likely to be a surge in writing—not books necessarily, but blogs. For anyone with a bit of time on their hands, writing a daily or weekly blog and posting it on the Internet will be an easy (and time-filling) thing to do.

Together the potential shifts pose a big challenge—and opportunity—for libraries. There is certainly the opportunity for libraries to meet a big need for socialization, book clubs, reading materials and more as the leisure economy opens up. At the same time, aging boomers will not want services designed specially for seniors. Used as they are to high-tech workplaces, they will demand more: technological tools and a Starbucks-type atmosphere where they can relax and hang out for extended lengths of time. Whether that means actually serving coffee is not clear, but what is apparent is that a potential surge of use could bring libraries new clients, donors and volunteers for decades to come.

TRENDS FOR LIBRARIES TO CONSIDER

- Start a "Now's the Time to Read" campaign for retired boomers.
- Draw in your audience and make them stay a while with boomer-friendly seminars—but don't make them feel old!
- The Starbucks formula is worth considering—perhaps charge a membership to be part of a "library club" that serves premium coffee and offers comfy chairs.
- Book clubs—for all ages—have the potential to explode. The trick is to target tiny niches—by age, by sex, by interest, by book format.

Cooking, Eating Out and Everything in Between

For years, the time-crunch economy has seen a move towards eating out rather than cooking. In 1995, about 38 cents of every dollar American spent on food went to food eaten outside of the home. By 2005, that percentage had climbed to 44 percent.[11] The increase would probably have been even more pronounced had not so much of the food eaten at home been prepared elsewhere, whether it was take-out pizza or prepared rotisserie chicken from a supermarket. Between 1993 and 2001, the number of U.S. households who reported cooking "two or more times a day" dipped from 35.9 percent to 32.1 percent.[12]

---

11. *U.S. Consumer Expenditure Surveys*. U.S. Bureau of Labor Statistics, various years.

12. "Cooking Trends in the U.S.: Are We Really Becoming a Fast Food Country?" U.S. Energy Information Administration, 2002.

The trends may be about to reverse: one of the great surges of the leisure economy is likely to be a return to cooking in rather than eating out. All things being equal, households tend to eat at home more as they age. Consider that in 2005, those aged 45 to 54 spent 46 percent of their food dollars outside of the home, compared to 44 percent for those aged 55 to 64 and 40 percent for those aged 65 to 74.

The shift has always been related to income, and the baby boomers are not going to be an exception to other generations. Many of those in the middle-income quintiles during their working lives have spent years being somewhat income-squeezed and very time-squeezed. That has meant that convenience products, take-out meals and eating in restaurants were all rational food choices for them. In retirement their real squeeze is going to be money, plain and simple. For this group and those in the lower quintiles, that portends a big shift towards food preparation at home rather than restaurant meals and take-out.

Of course, boomers may not yet have the skills to cook: not only have many relied on a combination of prepared foods and restaurant meals for years, but they have also found that the time crunch has precluded them from setting the regular shopping-preparing-serving schedules that so marked their parents' lives both before and after retirement. Here is an opportunity for anyone who can teach them how to cook: formal cooking schools, supermarkets or adult education providers can step up and provide courses to teach them to make simple meals. As with everything, boomers are not going to want to be told, "Learn to cook for your senior years." The emphasis has to be on learning to cook simple, healthy and delicious food.

Generation X and Y also provide a huge opportunity for an increase in cooking rather than spending money on prepared food. Some, of course, will continue to be time-crunched and will rely on the Lunchable Pizza Snacks or packaged crackers and cheese that have been such a staple of the 1990s. But part of the trade-off between work and leisure that the post-boomer generations so want means a loss of income, and that means spending time rather than money. And Gen Y, in particular, has been raised with the Food Network making cooking sexy with chef superstars.

Does that mean restaurants are doomed? Of course not. Over the past couple of decades, eating outside of the home has gone from being an occasional treat to a regular occurrence for many households. If you look at the 55- to 64-year-old group, you can see that although that group, who were then comprised of pre-boomers, were only spending 38 percent of their food dollars outside of the home in 1995, by 2005 the boomers had moved into that age group and were spending 44 percent of their food dollars outside of the home.[13] All generations are in the habit of eating out, and those that can afford to do so will probably choose to do so even more—and spend their time on things other than cooking. So the restaurant industry is unlikely to disappear anytime soon, although they might be wise to cater to budget- and health-conscious boomers and Gen X and Y households, as well as to the upper-end boomers.

TRENDS FOR FOOD-RELATED BUSINESSES TO CONSIDER

- Cooking—from simple dinners on weeknights to gourmet meals on the weekends—will boom. The problem is that a lot of former take-out or go-out boomers will have to learn how to cook.
- Slow cooking will get a whole new meaning—meals will not have to be "30-Minute Express" anymore. Longer preparations (making bread, chopping vegetables) and longer cooking times (roasted instead of pan-fried) will be the norm. That means different products and different presentations.
- Gen Xers and Yers will use their new leisure for food preparation, partly for health reasons. That means less packaged food for kids' lunches and more veggies and fruit cut up by parents.
- Restaurants should think in terms of expanded roles: holding seminars and tastings, offering a series of cooking lessons, acting as meeting places for groups and being part of a community.

Education—However You Define It

The education system is likely to be one of the big winners in the leisure economy, but it will be a very loose definition of education. With

---

13. Survey of Consumer Expenditures (various years) and author calculations.

time on their hands, everyone from stay–at-home parents to retired baby boomers will be open to the idea of expanding their minds, but they will not necessarily look to the traditional means to make that happen. From learn-to-do-beadwork seminars given by craft stores to doctoral programs at universities, there are hundreds of potential opportunities for all kinds of education providers to teach those with time on their hands.

The number of adults pursuing some kind of education is already soaring. According to the National Center for Education Statistics, in the United States in 1991 about 33 percent of all adults participated in some kind of adult education program, be it a course at a college or a required program provided by their employer. By 2001, that percentage had risen to 46 percent. While those in the labor market are most likely to be studying, the statistics show that over the period all age groups were more apt to be learning. Although the percentage of those aged from 40 to 44 engaged in some kind of learning went from 49 percent to 54 percent over the period, that was a tiny increase compared to other age groups: for those aged between 55 and 59, the increase was

Education is More Popular at All Ages
U.S. Participation in Adult Education Over Previous 12 Months

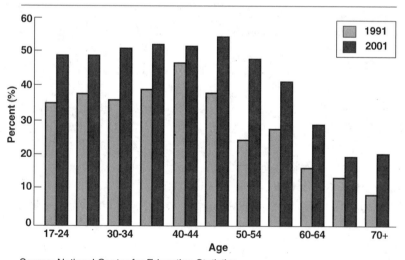

Source: National Center for Education Statistics

from 29 percent to 44 percent, and for those aged 60 to 64 it was from 17 percent to 31 percent.

The statistics show that those with the most education are most likely to acquire more. Only 20 percent of those with an eighth-grade education or less were enrolled in an adult education program, compared to a whopping 65 percent of those with a bachelor's degree.

Colleges and universities are already seeing an influx of retiring baby boomers. "Boomers are going back to school in their 40s, in their 50s, some in their 60s. These are people who are still working, but who may be looking for personal enrichment, or maybe for a career change," says Angela O'Rand, a professor of Sociology at Duke University. "In the Masters of Liberal Arts program in which I teach, the overwhelming number of adult students have had volatile careers and are either planning a career change or want to be ready for one if they need to be." Like others, she expects boomers to continue filling college halls well into retirement but wonders if the schools are prepared for the deluge. "The public schools are more prepared," she says. "They are used to a commuter population. And the business schools are used to older students. Some junior colleges are getting prepared too. But the majority of institutions—especially the public schools—are used to a younger, domiciled population." And the boomers will not be intimidated by the thought of entering any hallowed halls. After all, prior education is one of the main determinants of demand for education later in life, and compared to earlier generations, boomers are the best educated ever.

For some, heading to the local college or university will not be about leisure; it will be about training for a second career. That will especially be true of baby boomers who retire or are forced out of their original careers, but there will be many variations on the theme. For example, if one spouse in a boomer household gets into their highest earning years and continues to work, the other might drop out and pursue studies leading to a completely different career. The same is true for Generation X. As boomers retire and they hit their career peak, it may become financially viable for them to change jobs and head for a second career.

Education is going to be yet another way to divide the haves and the have-nots of the leisure economy. "Those who are in sufficiently

good health, are motivated by having enjoyed prior years of education ... and can afford to pay ... will reap the benefits of "successful
aging," according to Professor Ronald Manheimer of the University
of North Carolina. "Those who do not fare so well because of poor
health, limited incomes, lack of motivation because of more restrictive
prior education ... will find comparatively little from which to choose
in the way of intellectually challenging programs. In fact, those who
do not fit the image of successful aging will be chastised as somehow
'failed agers,' [yet] more castigation of those who seem not [to] have
seized the opportunity to age well. It doesn't require much reflection to
see that this scenario is an extension of current trends."[14]

So are those who have been have-nots for most of their lives destined to be have-nots in the leisure economy too? Clearly, if you have
not had much exposure to education early in your life, you are not
likely to pick it up in retirement. It does not have to be this way, however. Given that there is a real social benefit to lifelong learning—if
nothing else, it might serve to keep aging minds sharp and ward off a
wave of dementia—there is surely a motive to encourage those from
all kinds of educational backgrounds to head back to school. Perhaps
this needs to come from the haves who will have time on their hands
to set up programs where they volunteer; they can perhaps guide the
have-nots back into the educational system.

Education encompasses a much broader definition than the traditional channels, and the leisure economy will present a huge market
for many offerings. From the kind of do-it-yourself workshops already
offered by the likes of Home Depot to the beading seminars now offered
by places like Michaels, businesses have already stuck their toes into
the world of providing "educational" offerings to consumers. But the
field is wide open for more. Retired boomers, especially, will have time
on their hands for more than just 45-minute seminars and will be open
to the idea that retailers can offer them. For companies, taking advantage of the trend may mean teaming up with established education
providers, or it might mean offering their own courses.

---

14. Manheimer, Ronald J. "The Older Learner's Journey to an Ageless Society: Lifelong Learning on
   the Brink of a Crisis."(draft), 2005.

Association. "People retire, but they don't die. And even if you are just trying to ward off Alzheimer's, crafting is a good way to do it."

Crafts may also be a good fit for many baby boomers, given that they do not ask too much of participants in terms of physical activity and appeal to a wide range of income groups. For the retiring boomers, though, the main problem may be that they lack the skills to actually do any of the craft projects that appeal to them. "What we find is that if they don't have the skills by the time they are 20, they don't pick them up over the next three or four decades," says Betsy Edwards. That means that that the purveyors of the craft kits either have to make the products easy to learn or invest in teaching in a bigger way. But boomers are finding their way slowly through the craft maze on their own. "I went to sign up for a yoga course but it was full," says Liz, a 55-year-old retired teacher and first-wave baby boomer. "Rug hooking had some openings, so I figured, why not? I thought it would be a lark. Now I'm so into it I've been petitioning my local craft store to stock more supplies, and I've got a whole circle of friends who do this too. I'm even looking at developing a little niche business selling supplies on my own. And no, this is not something I would ever have imagined myself doing. When I was teaching high school, I did not have the energy or time left over to get involved in 'crafting' and I never thought it would be my thing either."

Among baby boomers, men may comprise the biggest potential market for crafts and hobbies. "Things like scrapbooking are evolving because of digital cameras," says Berger. "The technology aspect of it makes it more appealing to men." And men may be a growth market for the hobby side of things. Indeed, the CHA estimates that 60 years ago, male-oriented hobbies like model train building and the like accounted for the bulk of the industry, compared to maybe 10 percent now. Given that once men get their teeth into a hobby, they tend to like to buy every gadget they can get, drawing in the boomers could be extremely lucrative for the industry.

You can see that with the model train building industry. The industry has seen something of resurgence since the 1980s, in tandem with boomers hitting their higher earning years. (In the 1950s, when the boomers were young, toy trains were the most popular toys for boys in the United States.) According to "World's Greatest Hobby" (www. greatesthobby.com), a resource site for model train building, there are now 500,000 model railroaders and train hobbyists in the United States and Canada. In fact, boomer icon Neil Young has a "train barn" containing an extensive model train collection, and is a 20 percent stakeholder in Lionel, the largest U.S. maker of miniature trains. From building model airplanes to collecting Hot Wheels cars, the market for male-oriented hobbies probably has a big resurgence ahead.

But boomers aside, Gen X, and in particular Gen Y, are also prime candidates for growth in crafts. Spurred by celebrity involvement, crafts like knitting have surged in recent years. And scrapbooking is also hot among youth. Gen X and Gen Y both have in their midst keen scrapbookers—like Diana's babysitter, and some who are even younger. (Even Gen Z—those born since 2000—seem to be keen crafters. According to the CHA data, 9 percent of scrapbookers are under the age of 6.)[16] The chances of them bringing their involvement in crafting into their time-crunched years seem

---

TRENDS FOR CRAFT AND HOBBY BUSINESSES TO CONSIDER

- The new leisurites have time to turn their hobbies into "obsessions"—and if they do, they'll buy aggressively.
- The overlooked market so far? Men. If you can connect them to a passion (model trains, woodworking) they will be your best customers.
- Working boomers have been too time-crunched to think much about crafts and hobbies. If you want them to start, you'll have to get them interested, then teach them from scratch.
- Think craft clubs, craft meetings, craft seminars, craft conferences—time is available if you make them feel it is worth their while.
- Gen Y is looking for a "rich" life and that could include crafts and hobbies. Don't forget to target them too—and give them ways to do activities as a family—learn-to-knit classes for mom or dad, plus the kids.

---

16. "Scrapbooking, Needle Arts and Beading Attitude & Usage Study." Ipsos Insight Inc. for the Craft and Hobby Association, July 2006.

good too. Unlike the boomers, they are on record as wanting to keep up with a myriad of interests and many are getting involved in crafts at younger ages. That means that the overall demographics are great for the industry and for many niches within it.

Fitness and Sports

The leisure economy would seem to bode well for the sports and fitness industries, but the demographics for this sector are quite murky. Participation in sports and recreational activities tends to decline as the population ages, and the sports that an older population chooses tend to require less equipment. The most popular sports for those aged 18 to 24 is billiards, with a whopping 31 percent of the population participating. No wonder Gen Y has caused the sport to have something of a resurgence in the past few years. By contrast, only 15 percent of those aged from 35 to 44 play billiards—and only 2 percent of those over 65. Next on the list for youth is walking, followed by bowling and camping.[17]

What are the hot sports for leisurites? For ages 55 to 64 and 65 onwards, the top three are the same: exercise walking, exercising with equipment, and fishing. But even here you have to be careful: although fishing, for example, is one of the most popular sports among those aged over 55, it is also true that people are less likely to be involved in fishing past 55 than before. The net conclusion is that, with the exception of walking, where participation is pretty constant across all age groups, involvement in all sports activities declines as the population ages. That means that the population over age 55 is in some sense an untapped market. They have more time, but they are participating less.

Nor do older people necessarily spend more time than the young participating in their sports of choice. According to the 2005 ATUS data, the average person spent about 16 minutes a day participating in sports, exercise and recreational activities during the week, and about 20 minutes each day on the weekend, for a total of just over 2 hours a week. Older people have more time to spend exercising during the

17. U.S. Census Bureau. "The 2007 Statistical Abstract," Table 1233. www.census.gov/compendia/statab/tables/07s11233.xls.

week, and hence do not feel the need to be weekend warriors, but the total time spent on exercise is not that much different. The population aged between 55 and 64 for example, spends a total of 1 hour 36 minutes a week exercising, compared to 1 hour and 38 minutes for those aged 65 plus.[18]

Even with these realities, the leisure economy is still likely to herald a boom in leisure participants—or at least it has the potential. For companies that come up with products or offerings that will keep the baby boomers in the game longer, the spoils could be very marked. For those who are hard-core exercisers, participation after the age of 55 does not drop off, and indeed could boom. The golf industry provides an excellent example. As mentioned in Chapter 1, the sport was meant to be a big winner in the 1990s, and by some measures it was. But, like so many other leisure activities, it was a victim of the time-crunch economy. Let's do some very basic calculations. True, people are more apt to golf when they are young than when they are old. According to the U.S. census data, the highest participation rate for golfers was among the group aged 25 to 34 where 17 percent participated, compared to about 11 percent for the 55 to 64 group and 6.8 percent for those 65 plus. However, according to the U.S. National Golf Federation, as of 2005 about 7 percent of those aged 60 to 69 were what they called "core" golfers, compared to 5.8 percent of the general population.[19] Core golfers in this specific age group visited a driving range an average of 25 times that year, compared to 18 times for the general population. Given that according to the census bureau there is expected to be an increase of over 11 million Americans in this age group between 2005 and 2015, that translates into an increase of over about 786,990 core golfers in this age group—and an extra 1.97 million rounds of golf over the decade.[20]

Then too, there is the possibility that the baby boomers will handle aging and sports participation differently than did earlier generations. Although it is impossible to be sure that will be the case, we do know

---

18. Author calculations based on the American Time Use Survey for 2005. Bureau of Labor Statistics.

19. "Golf Industry Report." National Golf Federation. Volume 6, Second Quarter, 2006, p. 9.

20. Author calculations based on U.S. Census Bureau data. Calculations do not take into account the drop in core golfers in the 50- to 59-year-old age group over the same time period.

that gym memberships among baby boomers are the highest among any age group, and that having been core gym members during their working years, many boomers are likely to keep working out as they age. That should bode well for increased participation rates for those 55 plus, compared to what we have seen in the past.

The have-and-have-not phenomenon is also going to be very visible in the way that the sports—or more specifically hobby-type sports—grow. The haves, especially those at the top of the income distribution, will be able to choose among activities that require both time and money. That includes the most expensive, capital-intensive pastimes such as yachting. Indeed, private clubs have an excellent chance to recoup some of the losses of the time-crunched economy. Offering as they will the chance to pursue a sport as well as to enjoy the whole experience of enjoying the dining room and a host of other activities, clubs that target their markets carefully could see a burst of membership during the next two decades. Clubs do not have to be exclusive to see their memberships grow, however. Any kind of gym or club that serves the leisure population should be thinking of how to keep their participants in longer once they cross the threshold. Those who used to sprint in and out to play a game of squash during their working years will suddenly have more time. If offered a variety of activities to complement the squash game—a juice bar or a walking group or a book club—they just might be induced to pay a higher fee and stay longer.

The real question about the leisure economy concerns the post-boom generations. The boomers will be older and will have more time on their hands. Generations X and Y may have less of a time crunch, or some portion of them will, but it is not clear how much time they will want to devote to athletics. It could be a higher percentage than for previous generations; a subset of Gen Y, after all, grew up with swimming lessons as almost a necessity, and with soccer and gymnastics and skating lessons too. Already they are saying they want balanced lives, and presumably that means more participation in those activities as they move into their time-crunched years. Creating opportunities for them to keep activities they enjoy in their lives could be successful for companies that attempt it.

Gambling and Other Addictions

Walk into any casino in North America, and if you have not yet reached retirement age, chances are you will feel youthful. Gambling—spurred by new casino developments in particular—is already proving to be a draw for many of the pre-boomer elderly, with about 11 percent saying they gamble on vacations compared to 7 percent of the boomers and 6 percent of Generations X and Y.[21] An aging population will only increase the size of the potential audience for this pastime, as well as the problems associated with it. According to a study by Professor David Oslin of the University of Pennsylvania, as many as 11 percent of seniors who gamble say they spend "more than they should" at casinos or on other forms of gaming.[22] Just assuming that the percentage stays constant, the aging of the boomers could mean a surge in the number of problem gamblers in North America.

The baby boomers may be especially susceptible to the lure of gaming. They are a large group and have a lot of accumulated wealth—both reasons that there will be intensified efforts to draw them into casinos (rather than into gardening clubs or libraries). For many, especially the have-not leisurites, the gaming experience will offer the kind of time-consuming social interaction they can't get elsewhere—complete with free buffets and perhaps free rides from local community centers, courtesy of the casinos. Although gambling might be a benign pastime for the bulk of leisurites, if there is a potential problem, it is with the have-not boomers who don't have money to spend on travel or expensive hobbies, and harbor a perhaps not-so-secret desire to top up their retirement savings.

It is perhaps also worth noting that baby boomers have already had various issues with addictions that could come to the fore again once they have more time on their hands. There are already reports that boomer addicts are seeking help for drug addictions that they have toyed with since the 1960s, which have not been major issues through most of their lives. In retirement, some may be looking for ways to deal

21. "Travel across the Generations." Travel Industry of America 2006 Research Report, p. 29.

22. Levens, Suzi et al. "Gambling Among Older, Primary-Care Patients." American Journal of Geriatric Psychiatry, January 2005. 13:69–76.

with declining health—or simply a way to relieve boredom. Inevitably, some small percentage will end up as substance abusers, as indeed has always been the case for alcohol or other addictive substances. But given that many older adults have traditionally sought help for alcoholism, not drug addiction, the advent of the boomers into their leisure years perhaps heralds the need for drug addiction programs targeted especially to older adults.

Travel—Short and Long Term

It is a bit of a dichotomy: the time crunch means that people have only tiny slivers of time off, yet are leaving plenty of vacation days on the table, untouched. At the same time, the travel and tourism industries are among the fastest growing in North America, and not just because of an influx of international visitors. In fact, there are a multitude of reasons why the two trends exist concurrently. Income growth across the economy may be stagnant, but for some aging boomers it has been on the rise, and they have been happy to spend it on the experience of travel in preference to everything else. Others, in all income groups, have been able to carve out holidays of durations as short as a day or a few days and spend whatever money they can on them. And, in general, the boomer-dominant population has considered travel something that they cannot do without, no matter what their income level. So if at the margin some super-workaholics have been happy not to take time off, others have been taking their holidays for them—or at least spending enough to compensate the industry for those who don't believe in vacations.

In the leisure economy, people of all age levels will value time off and that will be positive for travel, albeit in all kinds of different niches. Not surprisingly, everyone wants a piece of the affluent baby-boomer market, comprised of people like Nancy, 55, who have relative youth, good health, and enough money to work their way through a wish list of places they want to see. "I'm retired now, and my husband will retire in a few years," she says. "We made a list of places we wanted to go, and there were places that were on my list, but not on his. So I'm getting through those now by myself, and then when he retires we'll do the rest of the list together." In general, baby boomers, especially those with hefty budgets, will have a long list of things they want to see. From luxury spa vacations to travel to pursue volunteer interests, they will shape leisure travel in the way that best fits their sensibilities.

And it cannot be said often enough: the big change coming is that many people (particularly baby boomers) will be able to spend more time on travel than they ever could before. That's potentially even more important than the fact that many will have more money than they did when they were busy paying for groceries for a family and chipping away at their mortgages. For the two-weeks-off-if-you-really-need-them workers, the ability to take a month or two months or more to travel will be a novelty that may take last for years. Like Nancy, baby-boomer women will also be an important component of the travel market. Many of them will be single, whether through widowhood (as has tended to be the case for their parents' generation of senior travelers) but also through divorce or never having married. They will have been traveling for many years already, but doing so in much smaller doses. With their leisure years, they will be willing to spend on the packages and opportunities that best meet their needs. Whether women or men, the boomer leisure travelers will not want to be singled out as seniors, even if someone comes up with a clever substitute for the term. They will be enticed to spend their newly acquired time on projects or seeing places that are advertised as entertaining or life enhancing for everyone. They're likely to say "yes" to the two-week gourmet holiday to learn Provençal cooking outside Nice and "no" to any holiday marketed as suitable for seniors or those fifty plus.

And they will say yes to the spa holidays that take longer than a couple of days. Once upon a time going to a spa was an exclusive, expensive and time-consuming experience. In the 1990s, however, the industry realized there was a niche for those who had neither the income nor the time to visit a full-fledged spa. Hence the development of day spas. According to the spa reservation service Spa Finders, as of 1989 there were about 30 day spas in the United States. Now, there are around 1,600 and they generate between $700 million and $850 million in revenue per year. Day spas are certainly not disappearing, but in the leisure economy there will be room for packages and holidays that take longer than 90 minutes. At the extreme, one could go from visiting a spa occasionally to living at one: already developers are offering "condominium spas" with luxury services available where people live.

But spas and gourmet holidays are always going to be directed at the upper end of the market. As well as the high-income, high-wealth boomers, there will be another key segment interested in traveling, albeit at a much more modest level. They will have lots of time but a limited income stream. That could be a boon to the Recreational Vehicle (RV) market, for example. As of 2005, nearly 8 million households owned a recreational vehicle—about a 58 percent increase from the 1980 level.[23] The data (culled from a study done by the University of Michigan Survey Research Center) also showed that the typical RV owner was a 35- to 54-year-old home owner with an annual income of $68,000 a year and traveled an average of 4,500 miles a year. Getting an RV to see North America may not be for everyone, but it is relatively cheap and could fill copious amounts of time—both important markers of what a large segment of the newly leisured will want.

What will the post-boom generations want in terms of leisure economy travel? There are far more variables to consider. As a group, Generation Y has been more catered to and pampered in terms of vacations than any generation before them. A popular travel guide (sold in some toy stores as well as bookstores), *Frommer's 500 Places to Take Your Kids Before They Grow Up*,[24] contains a list spanning museums in Chicago and the beaches of Normandy. For the younger wave of Gen Y, every long car trip has been made easier by having a DVD player in the car. Not only do many hotels offer kid packages or special kids' camp programs, but for those at the top of the household income range there have been things like the "Summer at the Spa for Keiki and Teens" at the Hilton Hotels in Hawaii, which offers goodies like Ti-Leaf Cooling Wrap and Island Aromatherapy for those barely old enough to drive.

---

23. Quoted in Kennedy, Kelli. "Baby Boomers Push RV Ownership to Record." *The Associated Press*, May 22, 2006.

24. Hughes, Holly. *Frommer's 500 Places to Take Your Kids Before They Grow Up*. New York: Wiley, 2006.

Disneyworld, which for years has specialized in making dreams come true, now makes little girls' dreams real by letting them spend time at the "Bibbidi Boppidi Boo" salon, where for around $75 late Gen Ys and Gen Zs can get a fantasy hairstyle, make-up job and perhaps press-on nails to match.

Anyone in Gen Y who can afford it will be eager to continue their high-end travel experiences and will perhaps extend them to their children. The affluent among the post-boom generations will also increasingly treat travel as a necessity, and indeed as an experience they want to give their children. The children part might take a while, for now Gen Y is generally in their early 20s and a chunk of them are still negotiating leaves from their employers to take longer trips and sabbaticals, not parental leave. Others are in the early years of their careers and are going the traditional route of less expensive, perhaps packaged, holidays. The more interesting question regarding Generation Y is what they will do over the long term.

The biggest question mark is whether Gen Y as a generation will be able to negotiate more time off work and whether they will get around to using that time. If so, and it requires some optimism to think they will be successful in both tasks, the average length of a holiday could creep up over the coming decades. The caveat is that for every day not worked, there is an income cost. Although Gen Y travelers may desire to take themselves or their families far afield, the reality may be that their lifestyle choices—valuing time over money—may not give them the cash to take high-end holidays. So there may be a resurgence in close-to-home day trips and holidays, which do not require a lot of money. Whatever they do, however, once they have families they are likely to make their traveling very child-focused, perhaps even more so than their parents.

PROFITING OR LOSING FROM THE LEISURE ECONOMY

So we are headed into a world where there is plenty of leisure time and at the very least the will—and maybe even the income—to spend on leisure experiences. Does that mean you should liquidate your portfolio and put all your holdings into resort stocks? If you run a business, should you forget serving time-crunched consumers and instead put all your efforts into retirees—or whatever out-of-the-workforce boomers decide is an acceptable handle? The answer to both questions is of course no: as important as it will be, the leisure economy is not going to totally eclipse every other economic force. Still, profiting from the leisure boom will mean some re-jigging of portfolios, business strategies and attitudes. To make the most of the shift ahead, you need to understand some crucial truths about the leisure economy. Whether you are an investor, a consumer, a business owner or just an interested observer, here are some crucial truths to keep you ahead of the curve.

REALIZE THE LEISURE ECONOMY IS ABOUT HAVING MORE TIME

It is not a new story: the median age of the population in North America is headed up. Most of the focus until now has centered on how older people consume different products and services than younger ones, and how that is likely to shift consumer demand. And while it is true that the demand for progressive lenses and hearing aids is going to grow, that realization captures only part of the story. Older people have more discretionary time on their hands than younger ones. That means you can sell them on things that take longer to do, and it means they have the opportunity to take more time to research any buying decision.

Whatever you are selling or whatever service you are providing, ask yourself if someone with the luxury of time might want to use your product. Would they buy a four-day pass to your amusement park instead of a day pass? Would they watch a longer movie? Would they stay longer in your store or restaurant or health club? Would they choose a craft project that takes months, not hours, to do? Ultimately you might decide that the answer is "no" and make your business plans accordingly. But you have to consider the time question in every single scenario.

REALIZE THE LEISURE ECONOMY IS NOT JUST ABOUT THE BOOMERS

The biggest push may come from the aging baby boom, but alone that would not be enough to create the leisure economy. There's more to the story: there is a real desire on the part of the post-boom generations to build lives with a significant component of leisure in them. What that means exactly is complicated. It might mean leisure, as in time spent away from work. In turn, that could mean they will take more cost-effective holidays, eat at home more, and so on. It may mean more stay-at-home parents of both sexes because neither feels they have anything to prove by being in the workplace.

Alternatively, for some families, it may mean high-cost leisure experiences (memberships at ski clubs or vacations abroad) paid for by lots of labor force work. But remember that Gen Y, or at least a portion of them, will find themselves in an advantageous labor market position once the boomers retire. If their real (inflation-adjusted) incomes rise to reflect that, then some families will find themselves in the have-their-cake-and-eat-it-too position of having more leisure time as well as more money to spend on leisure activities.

IF YOU'RE IN RETAIL, MAKE PEOPLE WANT TO STAY AWHILE

That may seem counterintuitive when almost every business has concentrated on how to move people through quickly, but successful businesses need to think about how to give people the option of staying awhile. That does not mean that people want to line up at the counter for longer periods; indeed, with so many high-quality leisure experiences in competition, the pressure to get clients and customers through low-quality experiences quickly will continue. But the Starbucks model of cushy chairs, newspapers and a "stay awhile" atmosphere might soon be the model for all businesses. Not every McDonald's will want to invest in couches, but for neighborhoods rife with baby boomers, even fast food outlets need to think about retaining their visitors.

COURT THE HIGH-END LEISURE ECONOMY

Yes, there will be a group with much more time than they ever had before and sufficient money to try new things. They will be able to buy high-end holidays and spend weeks, not days, exploring new places. They'll be heady with their new luxury item—time—and open to trying new things. If you can get just a tiny piece of this market by selling them gourmet holidays or fancy walking shoes or just the right engine for their newly acquired model train hobby, then you will be on your way to significant profits.

For those who succeed in hitting the right niche, success will be there for the taking. The trouble is, it *is* a niche market; by no means will all aging baby boomers be rich in income or for that matter even in time. In addition, competition for the affluent boomers' wealth will be fierce. And even if you do succeed in at attracting some of their dollars, remember that the needs of the newly retired boomers will change over time. Sixty-somethings may want hiking holidays through the Pyrenees and perhaps will go back year after year—for a while. But sooner or later, they will reach an age where they will hit health problems and so will try something else: you will need to find a new market for your offering or change your offering. All in all, the high-end leisure economy is a great get—but it will be hard to attain and even harder to keep.

COURT THE LOW-END LEISURE ECONOMY

The leisure economy is all about diversity and inequalities. In addition to the golden leisurites who will have time as well as money, consider those who will have nothing but time. They will not want the convenience products or time-saving devices they wanted when they were working. Think about what they *will* want: things that offer cachet with a less-than-premium price tag. These are the baby boomers who did not save as much as they had hoped for retirement, but they do not think that should subtract from their personal style in any way. They will be looking for cheap thrills. Can you make DIY projects look cool—and then show them how? Can you make embroidery, which they probably associate with their great-grandmothers, seem cool—and then sell them lessons? There may be a market in baby boomers who finally have the time to learn to cook. Consider both the high end—those who want to learn how to make risotto with porcini mushrooms from scratch (before, the half-hour of stirring would have been out of the question) and the low end—those who are on a budget but have the time to make pizza dough from scratch (instead of ordering in every Friday).

As well as the boomers, also think about courting those in the post-boom generations who have actually sacrificed money for time. This group will be looking to spend less money, not more. When they do open their wallets, it will be for things that offer significant experiences or value. Unlike the boomers, they might bring DIY projects into their time-crunched years; indeed, there is already evidence that they are spending time on things like crafts. Low-cost, time-consuming leisure experiences (making a model from a kit, or sewing) might be a big hit with this group. They might also find themselves somewhat reluctant supporters of the environmental movement too, which provides opportunities in itself. From organizing car pools (to save gas costs) through to growing their own vegetables, many environmentally friendly choices may make good budget sense to them.

THE LEISURE ECONOMY IN YOUR PORTFOLIO

This is a tough one: knowing that the leisure economy is unfolding does not mean knowing which companies are best positioned to take advantage of it. There are well-managed sports equipment suppliers and bookstore chains and there are poorly-managed ones. Pick the wrong one, and knowing that people will want to play golf or read won't help you at all.

Even so, your portfolio should include industries that will be well positioned to profit from the leisure economy. That might mean bookstore chains, or it might mean a manufacturing company that has worked out a strategy to provide flexible schedules and not lose all their engineering talent to retirement. Or, it might mean including in your holdings a share of a real estate property in a college town that will be set to bring in baby boomers. Configuring your portfolio properly might also mean knowing what to divest yourself of in the leisure economy. If you are heavily invested in products that match the time-crunch economy, you have your back to the future—and your returns might show it.

MAXIMIZE VOLUNTEER LABOR

As people move into the leisure economy, their time will be there for the taking, but only if you approach them in the right way. Organizations that use volunteers can benefit from them, or they can squander the opportunity to tap into their talent. The new leisure class will have skills and experience (and possibly money to donate too), but they will only share these assets with organizations they figure are in sync with their values and offer them the chance to create meaningful experiences.

Everyone who runs a non-profit group should be thinking how best to use volunteer labor, and so should a variety of other organizations. If you operate a tourism bureau or are trying to attract labor into your town, boomer bloggers could attract a bonanza of PR to your area. Do you know how to motivate them or even how to contact them? Making the best of leisure economy labor means thinking creatively and making the best use possible of the available volunteers—even if they have not formally announced they are available.

REBRAND YOUR COMMUNITY FOR THE LEISURE ECONOMY

Whether to attract retiring boomers or young families, leisure experiences are the hallmark that will bring new people to your community and retain those you want to keep. Do you offer theater, festivals, fireworks or outdoor recreation activities? Do you package those experiences and sell them to local people and potential visitors? Do you work with local developers to make these offerings a part of the selling points for living in your town or city? If you are a real estate developer, do you work with municipal planners and local municipalities to create strong community amenities? These are crucial questions for those who want their town or city to have a prominent place on the leisure economy map.

You do not want to live in the exurb that everyone deserts when they head for that picturesque college town that gives them better value and more experiences in retirement. If you see your community becoming a bleak place, now is the time to rebrand and turn it into an appealing community that offers meaningful leisure experiences. You cannot change the weather—a town in Minnesota will never compete with one in Arizona on the basis of sunshine—but you can change almost everything else.

TIME IS AS GOOD—OR BETTER—THAN MONEY

Baby boomers thinking about whether to keep working will not want an all-or-nothing scenario: they'll prefer a menu of options from which they can create a work–leisure balance that works for them. Maybe that means working the rest of the year and taking summers off; maybe it means working the rest of the year and taking winters off. Maybe it means working on contracts, or part-time, or some combination of all of these. If this flexibility sounds complicated and expensive to offer, think about just how complicated and expensive it might be to replace every baby-boomer employee you might lose if you don't offer it.

The boomers are not the only ones who will want these options. From Gen Yers who want a chance to trek through Asia to working parents who want to keep their careers while spending more than slivers of time with their kids, an increasing number of people may say "yes" to something less than the full-time, five-day week, 50-work-week year. Part-time work still has a certain stigma, particularly among professionals. In the leisure economy, the part-timer will be envied and admired. Smart companies will recognize this and create opportunities for the best and brightest among them to pick a work package that exactly matches the mix of income and leisure they desire.

The switch from the time crunch economy to the leisure economy will not be instantaneous. After all, it took a long time to work ourselves up into the economy-wide frenzy. We're starting the 21st century in North America as a society that not only has little "free" time, but also takes pride in that fact. Undoing that situation will take a while. We see hints of the leisure economy now, from the first-wave boomers leaving their jobs and thinking about spending more time at their vacation homes to the new Gen Y graduates telling their bemused employers that they "want a life." The full-blown leisure economy may take a while to reveal itself, but it is coming.

Will the leisure economy make us happier or healthier or better as a society? That is a tough one to answer. Generally speaking, working more has made us more prosperous and that, in itself, has allowed us to enjoy not only more consumer goods but higher quality leisure too. Wealth, after all, has bought us the skis and the beach holidays and the home entertainment systems. But we may still be able to have our cake and eat it too. If as an economy we manage to boost our productivity so that the work we do is worth more, than we might manage the time off and the income progress too. That is, after all, what has happened several times through history, including in the early years of the 20th century, when economic progress allowed workers to negotiate shorter work weeks. This time around the time-and-money split will likely be less balanced, and more centered on the

Chapter 10

economic haves. Others may get the time, but have to learn to live on less in the way of material goods.

But haves or have-nots in terms of money, those who choose to give themselves the gift of time will gain other intangible benefits. The time-crunch economy has certainly cost us in terms of health, both physical and mental. The leisure economy may be a complicated thing, but its real upside may be found in the tranquility it offers to a society that hasn't had much use for it. Maybe we'll like it when we try it.

INDEX

Index